S0-AWA-300

Collecting Printed Ephemera

Bought of Barclay & Co
WAX CHANDLERS
At the Crown & Beehive, opposite the Little Theatre,
HAY MARKET,
Bought of Sam. Carver
MERCER, WOOLLEN DRAPER &c.
A Variety of fashionable Waistcoat Pieces.
MARKET STREET
HAVERFORDWEST
WHOLESALE
WAREHOUSE
COMMERCE HOUSE
CARPET
WAREHOUSE
W. WILLIAMS & Co.
VICTORIA NEEDLE WORKS.
BOUGHT OF JOHN JAMES,
Manufacturer of Needles, Fish Hooks, & Fishing Tackle.
SAIL & PACKING NEEDLES, SAILORS' PALMS, SAIL MAKERS' TOOLS &c.
BOUGHT OF JOHN BLANCH & SON,
GUN MAKERS.
No. 29 Gracechurch Street
ESTABLISHED 1809.
Worcester.
BOUGHT OF A. DEIGHTON AND SON,
Booksellers, Stationers, Bookbinders, Printsellers.
BY APPOINTMENT TO HER LATE MAJESTY THE QUEEN DOWAGER.
ENGRAVERS, LETTER PRESS, LITHOGRAPHIC AND Copper Plate Printers.
GENERAL CIRCULATING LIBRARY
PATENT MEDICINE WAREHOUSE
STAMPS.
J. B. MARTIN.
Dr. TO
JOB MASTER
OMNIBUS
FLY
AND GENERAL FUNERAL CARRIAGE PROPRIETOR
LIVERY STABLES
AT MITRE HOTEL & SUN HOTEL
CHATHAM.
FIRST CLASS FOUR HORSE DRAGS, BREAKS FOR PICNICS, BROUGHAMS, LANDAUS AND WAGGONETTES.
YOUR FAVOURS AND RECOMMENDATIONS ARE MOST RESPECTFULLY SOLICITED.
OMNIBUSES LEAVE BOOKING OFFICE CHATHAM, TO MEET ALL TRAINS.
RIDING HACKS FOR LADIES.
SPECIAL ATTENTION PAID TO WEDDING PARTIES
British, French and American
DRY GOODS.
Baltimore,
Bought of HENRY W. COOKE,
S. E. Corner of Hanover and Lombard-sts.
Boston
Bought of Callender & Learnard,
IMPORTERS AND DEALERS IN FOREIGN AND DOMESTIC HARDWARE, CUTLERY, GUNS, &c.
CORSETS AND SKIRTS
WHOLESALE AND RETAIL.
BOSTON,
Bought of MRS. C. M. ADAMS,
300—WASHINGTON STREET—300.
SPINAL CORSETS,
LADIES' FURNISHING GOODS.
Rockland,
Bought of G. A. Safford,
WHOLESALE AND RETAIL DEALER IN
Flour, Corn, Meal, Fine Feed, Middlings, Fish, Pork, Lard, Choice
FAMILY GROCERIES, BUTTER AND CHEESE.
TERMS CASH.
MAIN STREET, AT THE BROOK.
L. B. Bishop's Sons,
DEALERS IN
MULES,
Corner of Grand and Bishop Streets, Jersey City, N. J.
3921 Market Street, Philadelphia, Pa.
New York
To John Gibson, Dr.
83 BEEKMAN STREET
NEWBURYPORT,
Bought of IRELAND & TREFETHEN.
SOFAS, SOFA BEDS, DINING, CARD & CENTRE TABLES,
BUREAUS, LOOKING-GLASSES, COUCHES,
NOS. 24 AND 26 MARKET SQUARE.
ALL CLAIMS MUST BE MADE WITHIN 3 DAYS AFTER RECEIPT OF GOODS
176 Washington St. BOSTON,
BOUGHT OF
WEEKS & POTTER
IMPORTERS & JOBBERS OF DRUGS AND DRUGGISTS' SUNDRIES.
RESURGAM
Bought of THE WORLD TYPE WRITER AGENCY,
THE "WORLD" TYPE-WRITER AGENCY, No. 80 STATE STREET, HARTFORD, CONN.
Devonshire Street, Boston.

Collecting Printed Ephemera

Maurice Rickards

Abbeville Press · Publishers · New York

Most of the specimens appearing in this book are from the Maurice Rickards Collection, now in the ownership of the Foundation for Ephemera Studies, London.

Library of Congress Cataloging-in-Publication Data

Rickards, Maurice, 1919–
Collecting printed ephemera.

Bibliography: p.
Includes index.
1. Printed ephemera – Collectors and collecting.
I. Title.
NC1280.R5 1988 769.5 88–18252

ISBN 0–89659–893–4

First published in the UK by Phaidon · Christie's Ltd., Oxford, 1988

Design and arrangement by Maurice Rickards

Printed in Spain by Heraclio Fournier S. A., Vitoria

Frontispiece: *British and American billheads 1776–1888*

Contents

Take a straw and throw it up into the air;
you shall see by that
which way the wind is . . .

JOHN SELDEN

Preface

Interest in printed ephemera, the 'minor transient documents of everyday life', dates back to John Selden. But it has grown greatly in the last few decades. It owes much of its present momentum to two twentieth-century pioneers, John Johnson, founder of the Oxford collection that bears his name, and John Lewis, whose book *Printed Ephemera* rekindled interest in the early 1960s.

Twenty-five years on, the present book is an attempt to provide something of a sequel to the work of these two trail-blazers, to reflect the growing importance of the field, and to introduce the subject to a widening circle of collectors, curators and researchers.

It is customary among anthologists (and in a very real sense this book is an anthology) to quote Montaigne: 'I have gathered here an offering of other people's flowers, bringing to them of my own only a thread to bind them with.' Never was the sentiment more apt than in the present case. This offering is indeed a gathering of other people's fragments, the ephemera of other lives and other times.

But the quotation is apt in another, more pointed, sense. Most of the items illustrated here have survived through the care and initiative of others, ephemerists of every degree, known and unknown. Many of them, we do know, are members of the Ephemera Society. These particularly are the people to whom acknowledgement and thanks are mainly due—those without whom neither the Society nor this volume could have been brought into being. And it is to them, as well as to future ephemerists, that the book is dedicated.

A full roll-call of thanks would run, literally, to hundreds—a minimal list appears on page 224—but there are some names for special mention. Certainly the founding Council Members of the Society: Patrick Robertson, Peter Jackson, Amoret Tanner, John Hall, Graham Hudson, Calvin Otto and John Lewis—over the years all have contributed their knowledge, advice and expertise. As have pioneer members Honor Godfrey (now President of the Australian Society), Sally de Beaumont, Bill Wright, and many others. So too the leading members of the offshoot societies, in America William Mobley, Jack Golden, William Helfand, Sam Murray, Rockwell Gardiner and Alfred Malpa; in Australia Murray Walker, Mimmo Cozzolino and Andy McGuigan, and in Canada Barbara Rusch, Peter Sindell, Morris Norman and Arthur Alder.

With the inauguration of the Foundation for Ephemera Studies in 1984 the subject of ephemera received yet further stimulus. The Foundation, a registered educational charity, in 1986 took into its keeping the collection from which most of the specimens shown here are selected. As these lines appear the Foundation is appealing for support for a permanent study and exhibition centre.

All of these elements—John Johnson, John Lewis, the various societies and their members, the Collection, the Foundation, this book—all are part of a general pattern. The role of ephemera as a collecting interest and as a research medium is increasing. It is the author's hope that the present reader, whether old hand or newcomer, will share the general pleasure in an exciting and significant trend.

As for the book itself, it is offered as a general survey of present-day ephemera collecting, not as an exhaustive study. Much has had to be left out, and it is to be noted that the sections on categories and themes are selected merely as examples from an almost infinite range of possibilities.

However selective, it is hoped the gathering will please the reader as much as it has beguiled the gatherer.

MAURICE RICKARDS

Fitzroy Square
London W1
April 1988

Foreword

Ephemerists come in as many shapes and sizes as ephemera. This is a book, therefore, for a wide variety of readers on both sides of the Atlantic. There will doubtless be some readers who have never heard the word ephemera before. Few such readers, however, will fail to grasp its rich human interest: few will reach its last pages without having a few surprises on the way.

For historians 'ephemera' is a key word. In the reconstruction of the past everything is grist to the historian's mill, and what was thrown away is at least as useful as what was deliberately preserved. As our sense of past time changes, we try to strip away the intervening layers and discover the immediate witnesses. If there were no Ephemera Society—and it was founded as recently as 1975—social and cultural historians, in particular, would have to create one. Of course, their necessary task is to consider ephemera along with other types of evidence. Quantitative evidence is of very special importance.

It should be added that the printed ephemera which are the concern of the Ephemera Society and which make up the fascinating subject matter of this book, are not the only kind of ephemera. Pottery has a longer history than paper, and in the late 20th century the most ephemeral of our own products are the first drafts on a word processor, which are subsequently erased and may never see the surface of a desk. Television programmes, too, are still inadequately archived, and they can disappear into the air as quickly as most of the words on sound radio or, in earlier centuries, the music of a popular song sung in the streets. One of the most interesting sections of this book deals with ephemera before the age of paper. It is here, perhaps, that there are most surprises.

Maurice Rickards is particularly well qualified to write this volume. He has been the moving spirit behind the creation of the Ephemera Society, and he is a friend of everyone inside and outside the Society, who either collects ephemera or who wants to know more about one piece of it. He has also organized many exhibitions, and appreciates from personal experience just how revealing an exhibition of ephemera, public or private, can be. A book is in a sense a permanent exhibition, and such a book has hitherto been lacking. As President of the Ephemera Society, an office which captures my interest and gives me great pleasure in the process, I commend this book with unqualified enthusiasm.

ASA BRIGGS

Worcester College
Oxford
March 1988

U.S. SENATE
Impeachment of the President
ADMIT THE BEARER
MAY 5th 1868.
GALLERY.
Geo. T. Brown
Sergeant-at-Arms.

Part One

AN INTRODUCTION TO PRINTED EPHEMERA

EASTWOOD & PERRETT,
Silversmiths & Jewellers,
111, Thames Street,
Windsor.
Jewellery & Plate repaired.
PLATE LET ON HIRE.
Mourning Orders expeditiously
EXECUTED.
DROIT

What <u>*is*</u> *ephemera?*

Some would prefer to say 'What *are* ephemera?' Right at the outset, before we even begin to define the word, we need to sort out its grammatical status. Is it singular or plural? Like many other of our imports—*graffiti* for example, or *data*—the word has come into the language without due process of scrutiny. Once arrived, it was let out on free range. The matter of grammar was left to look after itself.

There is another difficulty: pronunciation. Should it be eph*emm*era or eph*eem*era? Some say one, some the other. Between the two problems, of number on one hand and pronunciation on the other, it might be thought there is enough difficulty to put the word out of the running altogether. Why not try something else? And with the problem of definition unresolved (as indeed it still is) the temptation to find a substitute is overwhelming.

But it is too late in the day. There *is* no substitute. Like the founders of the Ephemera Society, who decided at their inauguration in 1975 to settle for the word, and to let it take its evolutionary course, we must bow to usage. So far, in the matter of pronunciation, general usage seems to favour eph*emm*era (in America it is quite settled). In the matter of singular or plural, general usage admits both: ephemera *is*, or ephemera *are*—you takes your choice.

As to derivation, we are on slightly firmer ground. Essentially, the word refers to something short-lived (Greek *epi* about, around + *hemera* a day). It has thus served as the specialist's term for the mayfly—said to live only for a day—and by astronomers and astrologers and navigators the word *ephemeris* is used for a calendar or table of days.

The word has a battered history. With its numerous neighbours and near relations (ephemeridae, ephemerae, ephemeron, ephemerides etc.), it was never a word for the man in the street. It lurked for centuries in the half-light of semi-learned talk, to be trotted out in one guise or another for want of anything better, then to be put away for a generation or two till it had been almost forgotten. It first appears in our present sense in Dr Johnson's *The Rambler* (No. 145, 1751): 'These papers of a day, the ephemerae of learning'. (Johnson himself was not too sure of his plurals. His use of 'ephemerae' ran neck and neck with other writers' 'ephemeraes', 'ephemera', 'ephemeras' and 'ephemerides'.)

Johnson's papers of a day were in fact the minor journals and gazettes of his time. Their unsung editors he commended for their contribution to history, albeit that 'their productions are seldom intended to remain in the world longer than a week'.

But for the ephemerist of modern times, the collector of what the Ephemera Society's literature describes as 'the transient minor documents of everyday life', the term ephemera takes in a far larger swathe. It has come to be applied to virtually any 'non-book' printed matter, principally of paper, designed in the main for short-term use—often implicitly for disposal.

The term thus applies to a huge corpus of miscellaneous papers, some of them more transient than others, most of them destined at some stage for the waste-bin. It includes anything from admission tickets to reward notices, tax forms to summonses, stationery to advertising. The range is so wide it is often easier to list what it does not cover than what it does.

Dr John Johnson (unrelated, we believe, to Samuel) was the founder of what has become the world's largest and most celebrated collection of ephemera, now housed at the Bodleian Library, Oxford. Even he found difficulty in defining the term ephemera. The John Johnson Collection of Printed Ephemera, he said, was of 'common printed things . . . what is commonly thrown away—all the printed paraphernalia of our day-to-day lives, in size from the largest broadside to the humble calling card, and varying in splendour from magnificent invitations to coronations of kings to the humblest of street literature sold for a penny or less'. On another occasion he wrote, 'It is difficult to define it except by saying that it is everything which would normally go into the wastepaper basket after use, everything printed which is not actually a book. Another way of describing it is to say that we gather everything which a museum or library would not ordinarily accept if it were offered as a gift . . .'. (In the last particular, we may note, Johnson is now happily proved wrong: to-day's libraries and museums are catching on.)

Some 40 years later, in the first issue of the journal *The Ephemerist* in November 1975, the Ephemera Society ventured another not-too specific guideline: 'The word ephemera presents some difficulty—as well for its meaning as for its pronunciation. To the uninitiated the word is faintly suspect. To the initiate it may or may not cover a multitude of items, from cigarette cards to uniform buttons. To the Ephemera Society it has fairly precisely defined limits: it covers "printed or handwritten items produced specifically for short-term use and, generally, for disposal".'

The journal went on to refer to 'a vast range of transient oddments—tickets, leaflets, stationery, labels and other trifles', but rigidly excluding 'such substantial items as uniform buttons which are neither printed, nor handwritten, nor paper, nor normally designed for short-term use and disposal'.

In the same issue *The Ephemerist* conceded that there are borderline areas. One such category is packaging which, though three-dimensional, is certainly transient, and another is souvenir material which, by definition, is designed to be kept for ever.

Still, in the 1980s and 90s the task of clearly defining ephemera remains too much for anyone. The best we can manage is a generalized description of its qualities: on the whole it is made of paper, generally printed, but sometimes handwritten; generally two-dimensional (though it may be a package or a pillbox); generally transient (though it may also be a marriage certificate or a royal proclamation); generally an incidental, unself-conscious fragment, like a school attendance card (though it may also be a multi-coloured prize certificate).

And there are yet other problems. For example, the distinction between a handful of unrelated ephemera and an archive. Which items belong in a collection, which in a Record Office? When should a single waif and stray be returned to the bosom of an archive? How right or wrong would it be to take, for example, a children's puzzle card, found in a box of family papers, for inclusion in a Museum of Childhood? Is it a single item of ephemera, or part of a family record? The point, warmly contested, remains to be resolved.

Another little matter is the distinction between a pamphlet, a minor publication, ephemera, and a book. A formal distinction is made in the library world between an unbound work of 32 pages or less and a bound volume of anything more than that

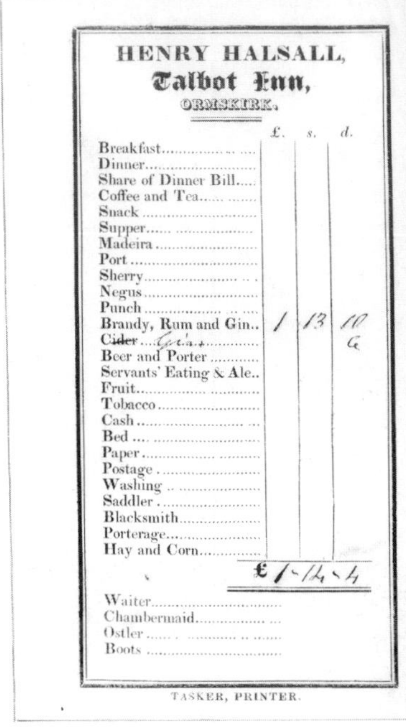

HENRY HALSALL,
Talbot Inn,
ORMSKIRK.

	£.	s.	d.
Breakfast			
Dinner			
Share of Dinner Bill			
Coffee and Tea			
Snack			
Supper			
Madeira			
Port			
Sherry			
Negus			
Punch			
Brandy, Rum and Gin	1	13	10
~~Cider~~ [illegible]			6
Beer and Porter			
Servants' Eating & Ale			
Fruit			
Tobacco			
Cash			
Bed			
Paper			
Postage			
Washing			
Saddler			
Blacksmith			
Porterage			
Hay and Corn			
	£1-14-4		

Waiter
Chambermaid
Ostler
Boots

TASKER, PRINTER.

With evocative mentions of servant eating, porterage, chambermaid, ostler and boots, this 1820s inn tally is typical of John Johnson's 'common printed things', the throwaway evidence of everyday life.

number. To the librarian the larger work is a book. The smaller, which may consist of anything from eight to 32 pages (with or without paper cover), may be classed either as a pamphlet, a 'minor publication' or 'ephemera'. This use of the word ephemera, hallowed in library tradition, today makes for confusion, and the ephemerist does well to beware. So does the librarian.

In these and many other grey areas the answer must be left to the individual. There is no hard and fast list of officially sanctioned categories. As more than one philosopher has pointed out 'all is ephemeral'. The essential appeal of most forms of ephemera lies in their fragility, their vulnerability—the very *improbability* of their survival.

Indeed, for many ephemerists, the drive to collect is the drive of chivalry—to rescue, to protect, honour and admire. The intending collector will weigh these responses when assessing the claims of one against the other. How ephemeral, how vulnerable, are garment labels and biscuit tins? How much do they seem to stand in need of our care and protection? Perhaps it was not for nothing that the John Johnson collection came to be called a 'Sanctuary of Printing'.

At John Johnson's 'magnificent' end f the ephemera scale is this ticket to the coronation of George IV—an ercise in extravagance and printing rtuosity. The embossing work is by Dobbs, London's leading exponent the art, and the two-colour printed image features William Congreve's anti-counterfeit compound-plate method, later developed by Charles Whiting (page 206). The method had one of its earliest airings at this royal occasion.

The appeal of ephemera

Just as the ancients conceived of the *genius loci*, the soul and spirit of a place, we may perceive a *genius papyri*. In every fragment of ephemera resides the spirit of the paper—the abiding essence of its message, origin and content.

It is easy to scoff at this idea, and many who do so will dismiss the whole notion until they light upon some unexpected personal memento—a forgotten school report, perhaps, or a youthful love-note. Suddenly a piece of paper takes on a new existence. It is imbued with a special quality that differentiates it from every other similar piece of paper. It is the same quality that distinguishes an actual signature from a facsimile, a 'genuine' painting from a fake. It is present in ephemera as pointedly—sometimes as poignantly—as elsewhere.

Who can deny the sudden sense of reality, the sharpened empathy, that some of these items generate? Here (on page 183) is the actual slip of pasteboard, inscribed with the name of Mr Cuthbert himself, that instructed him in January 1861 to 'Supply the bearer with a bag of coals'. That charity card, with its small but vital promise of winter warmth, still holds something of the magic of its moment. We are brought across the years, within a breath of the persons of the drama—Mr H. S. Thompson, who issued the ticket, Mr Cuthbert the coalman and, most important of all, the Bearer. The *genius papyri* operates not only in the personal memento but in the wider world.

It is of course not part of the proposition that the item should necessarily bear a manuscript addition—nor indeed that it should refer to a specific person or persons unknown. The mere fact of its existence, even devoid of clues to time or place, is evocative enough.

And evocation lies not only in the trace and shape of the images and characters it bears, but in the substance of the paper itself. The whole item, legend, image and substance considered together, encapsulates its spirit. As we examine the paper, its tint and texture (listening, even, to the slight sounds of its handling) we are transported in all but fact to the moment of its first appearance.

In the matter of earlier eyes—those who have scanned these documents before us—it is not too fanciful to propose that they too are a component in this experience. The point is explored in an unpublished essay (M. Rickards, *The Study of Ephemera*, 1977):

> An implicit component of every item of ephemera is the reader over our shoulder—the eyes for which the item first appeared; the living glance that scanned the paper even as we ourselves now scan it . . . Not only can you 'hear their voices', as Trevelyan put it, you can merge your glance with theirs as your eye scans the very words that met theirs. You become, as you read, an intimate part of the detail of their experience—not just overhearing them, but being momentarily *within* them . . .
> . . . Thus it is that we find our way into L. P. Hartley's 'foreign country'—the past—by

Green & Archer's
NORFOLK and SUFFOLK
VANS & WAGGONS,
No. 26. SUN STREET,
BISHOPSGATE STREET WITHOUT,
Every Tuesday, Wednesday, Thursday & Saturday, at 11 o'Clock precisely.
£ s. d.
Carriage *Article*
Paid out
Warehouse
Porterage
JOHN LEONARD, Porter.
Goods fetched in from any part of Town, by addressing a line as above.
W. R. Newman, Printer, Widegate-street, Bishopsgate.

> means not only of the news we get of it through books, or the touch and feel of its artefacts, but of the unobliterated paths that former eyes have traced in print and manuscript . . . you may in some measure appreciate that other country, those other people, by sharing some part of their direct experience. But from the instant sight of the *actual word on the actual paper of the past*, your mind is touched as sharply as theirs was, raw and clear, unveiled.
>
> . . . As we survey a battered public notice or a dog-eared printed paper, we are aware not only of the sum total of duration (implicit in its wear and tear), not only the buffetings and bruisings that its condition proclaims, but the countless scannings it has undergone—the multitude of readings and re-readings. It is, as you might say, 'eye-worn' . . .
>
> . . . It is this host of past readings that we also seem to conserve in these rescued fragments, and which, when we throw them away, we somehow irretrievably destroy . . .

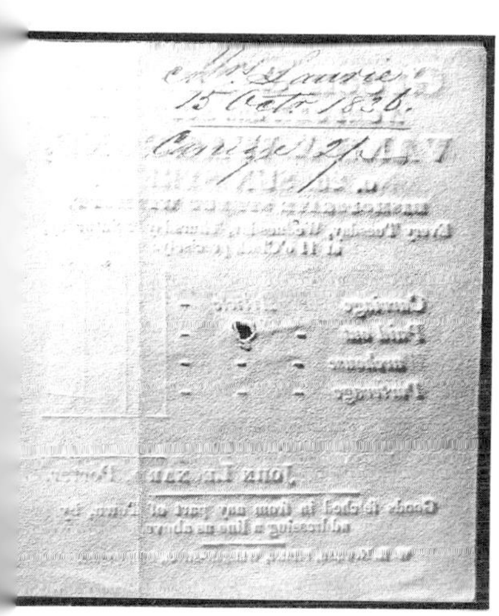

inter's type appears in some cases t only as a printed image (left) t, from the back, as a three-mensional impression of the actual etal (above). A common fault in rly printing, the effect is vertheless prized by some collectors an added element of authenticity. The centre hole, also a common ature of the period—and another uch of authenticity—comes from e use of a filing spike.)

Not all ephemerists would go this far, but the concept cannot be altogether set aside. Few would deny at least a fleeting thought for those whose glance has come before them. They too are part of the heart of the matter.

There is yet another respect, more down-to-earth, and readily visible, in which the printed paper may evoke the moment of its inception. The character of the paper itself is of course a subject for special study (see pp. 218–19), but the impression of the printer's type upon it may sometimes bring to it a dramatic new dimension—to be specific, a third dimension.

Known variously as the 'punched', 'relief', 'embossed' or 'braille' effect, this is the physical indentation of the surface of the paper by the impact of the printer's type or printing block. The result is seen as a more or less heavily marked, raised impression on the reverse of the paper. The image is of course un-inked and the wrong way round, but in a good cross-light the text may be almost as legible from the back as from the front.

The modern printer sees the effect as a fault. Ideally, pressure should be only enough to transfer the ink from the printing surface to the paper—not to stamp it in. In today's technology, which does away with three-dimensional type and printing blocks, the fault no longer occurs, but the early round-the-corner printer often made an unmistakable impression, and at one time even the quality printer was inclined to 'punch'—indeed enhancing the effect by damping the paper for a better impression.

Intentional or otherwise, to the ephemerist the effect appears as an engaging bonus. Here, captured in the substance of the paper, is very much more than the conventional surface marking: here is the mould of the solid type itself.

In this extra dimension the image conveys not only the message but the method. As we touch the raised impressions on the back of the paper, it is as though the printer's metal still exists. To the eye, as we hold the paper to a raking light, the characters spring into three dimensions. And not only the type, but the printing press and all the other physical aspects of the operation, the chase in which the type was held, the bed and platen of the press, the paraphernalia of the workshop—even, we may say, the living presence of old Ebenezer himself—are all brought to reality.

The clarity of the embossed effect may range from the finest and most delicate *basso relievo* to the merest pattern of intermittent hummocks denoting separate words. The definition of the image depends on pressure and on the character, thickness and humidity of the paper. To the connoisseur, its presence in any degree is a source of curious satisfaction.

There is an analogy with the archaeologist's imprint studies, where the impression of a vanished object, set in a moulding medium, conveys as much as the object itself. In ephemera the 3D record has a special magic.

The historical record

Part printed, part handwritte court-room papers are ephemera o specially telling kind. T committal order, made by the Justi of Liverpool in 1836, orders Governor of Lancaster Gaol to h the felon William Spencer fo year's hard labour, during wh period he is to be twice whipp The document, duly endorse records the whippings, the first days before the end of the senten the second on the d before discharg

As Arthur Marwick has said (*The Nature of History*, 1970), there is inborn in every individual 'a curiosity and a sense of wonder about the past'. We share with Trevelyan a fascination with the transience of things, with 'the quasi-miraculous fact that once, on this earth ... walked other men and women, as actual as we are today, thinking their own thoughts, swayed by their own passions; but now all are gone, one generation vanishing after another, gone as utterly as we ourselves shall shortly be gone ...'

There is also, as the ephemerist knows, the quasi-miraculous fact of evidence, the trail that the generations leave, each calling forward to the next, each testifying to its own link in the chain.

Part of the evidence is consciously devised—books, poems, paintings; part is unwitting—the unconsidered throwaways of the day. This second part, the minor transient documents of everyday life, may offer evidence in one sense more telling, more valid, than the formal written record.

History, it has been said (*Ephemerist*, January 1980), may be divided more or less down the middle. Half of it is to be found on library shelves, the other half in the world's waste-bins. 'We are familiar, from the library, with the facts about nineteenth-century poverty; the record is fulsome. But how infinitely more telling, more potently compressed, is the actual workhouse admission form, the debtors' prison diet chart ...' But there is more to it than mere compression: 'Whereas the formal record is once removed from actuality, these—tickets, forms, notices, certificates or whatever they are—these are the instrument of the very moment, in some cases its embodiment ...'

Their value as evidence comes not only from their closeness to the matter they convey, but (as Marwick also points out) from their remoteness from historical intention: 'A primary source is most valuable when the purpose for which it was compiled is at the furthest remove from the purpose of the historian.' In fact, the more 'unwitting' the primary source, the more unself-consciously spontaneous the ephemera, the better. And much of it, we must concede is very unself-conscious.

Take for example the tradecard of Mrs D. U. Smith, of 256 East Second Street: 'BAKING. I am now ready to do all kind of Baking, such as Fruit, Angel-Food, Cream Cake, Etc.' If not wholly unself-conscious, Mrs Smith's card does suggest she did not consider herself part of the mainstream of American History. That she has become a part of it at all is due to the chance survival of a modest tradecard, her only monument, here on page 108.

Or take the announcement of the Sale of Scottish Street Manure (page 137). Again, a document not conceived as historical record. But it is through this piece of paper (and perhaps this alone) that posterity comes to know of this aspect of the internal economy of Coldstream in October 1865. The same may well be said of the sale notice from Cooper County, Massachusetts (page 136). A no-account matter at the time, a notice of a sale of slaves has become a poignant piece of socio-historical evidence.

Also unself-conscious in its time was the 'letter of accommodation' for out-patients at St George's Hospital, London, in the 1840s (page 172). Among its articles of admission are hints of the dire realities of the time. One such hint reminds the subscriber that no-one with an infectious disease, nor anyone suffering from tuberculosis, asthma or ulcerated legs, nor anyone pronounced incurable, will be admitted. An appeal is also made for the gift of lint or cloth for bandages, 'a valuable present to the charity'. Likewise a reflection of the times (page 173) are the Rules of the House of Recovery in London in 1810: 'Lime washing the walls and cielings (*sic*) of small crowded rooms and airing the bed linen, and scouring the floor, will generally prevent an infectious fever from spreading'.

Other spur-of-the-moment documents are the BEWARE handbill of the H. C. Rowell Company (page 131), in which trade malefactors are lashed ('They are frauds'), and the Turnhouse Aerodrome plea to careless passengers (page 166): 'Don't step on the wing'.

It is in items like these that we see the human story close and sometimes raw.

It was ever so. Even in the ephemeral fragments of papyri, the throwaways of the ancient world, the same qualities are present. In the introduction to *Select Papyri* (1932), A. S. Hunt and C. G. Edgar point out 'the intimate glimpses and amusing details' that the excavated material provides. The papyri have special qualities, say Hunt and Edgar: 'One such quality is their unconscious and ephemeral character. Herein they differ markedly from inscriptions, which were designed for public view and for posterity, and whose candour is not always above suspicion.' As a rule, those who wrote these fragments were off their guard: 'They are to be seen following their ordinary daily pursuits with a refreshing absence of pose . . . They neither make nor possess any claim to fame, and therein lies their interest. For such people are seldom to be met with in the pages of the ancient historians, where the limelight is commonly focused upon outstanding personalities, while the humbler folk . . . are left to lurk in obscurity.'

In spite of its tendency to candour, the ephemera record may not be wholly free of guile. In the field of advertising, whose history is jam-packed with ephemera, there may be guile to the point of naivety. But this too serves as a marker of its times. In the outrageous claims of the quack, for example, we see naivety not only on the part of the patient but of the pedlar; there is, as it were, a conspiracy of ignorance. Baldwin's Pills of Health; somebody's Blood Capsules; somebody else's Head and Stomach Pills; Steedman's Soothing Powders ('relieve feverish heat, prevent fits, convulsions etc. . .'), these (pages 170, 171) are among the more respec-

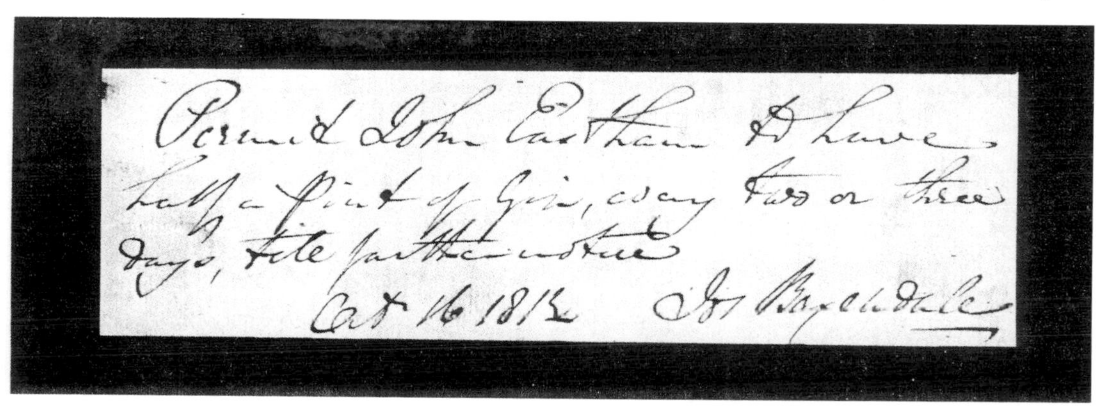

Permit John Eastham to have
half a Pint of Gin, every two or three
days, till farther notice
Oct 16 1812 Jos Baxendale

'Permit John Eastham to have half a pint of gin, every two or three days, till farther notice. Oct 16 1812.' Signed by Joseph Baxendale, presumably a physician, this note dates from the time when debtor-prisoners were allowed such outside comforts as they could muster.

table of the nineteenth century's lapses. And even that most irreproachable of products—Bovril—teeters on the brink of double-talk. Bovril's cravatted manager explains that all Bovril is excellent; Invalid Bovril is good for invalids: 'In case of sickness, doctors prefer it'.

Advertising ephemera provides evidence in profusion. It conveys not only guile and gullibility but, in the long run, a slow trend to sophistication. As the nineteenth century moves on it reflects a more literate and better informed public and an advertising industry constrained, if not by the needs of credibility, by legislation.

Among its many strands of evolution, advertising ephemera brings evidence of the rise of the copywriter. At the outset it was considered right and proper for the advertisers themselves to write the words. It was they, after all, who knew better than anyone else what they wanted to say. Thus it was that home-grown copy came up everywhere. It was as instantly recognizable as Mrs Smith's Angel-Food.

A typical example is the chatty piece by Mrs Hamlin, proprietress of the New Photograph and Ambrotype Rooms in Gardiner, Augusta, Georgia (page 133). Her studio is at street level, says the handbill, avoiding the necessity of climbing flights of stairs 'which as everyone knows makes the heart go pit-a-pat, and the brains go whirl-a-gig'. (We note in passing that she, like most of her photographic contemporaries specialises in TAKING PICTURES OF THE DEAD.)

Surgeon-dentist N. C. Hill, on the same page, addresses his customers in more measured terms. He 'respectfully informs the citizens of this place . . . he will be in readiness at all times to wait on those who may be in want of his professional services . . .'. His style is a half-way house between the do-it-yourself effusions of the 1850s and the copywriters' wiles of the 1900s.

In the matter of measured terms, the collector of advertising ephemera notes a number of standard nineteenth-century phrases. Someone, it seems, at some stage put together a literate form of words for a tradesman neighbour, and it got passed on to others. Certainly in Britain, every other innkeeper, chemist, draper, optician and chimney-sweep took pleasure in 'informing the nobility and gentry' that he had opened (or re-opened) an establishment in the neighbourhood, and that it was his single concern, by diligence and attention to the needs of his distinguished patrons, to merit (or to continue to merit) 'the privilege of their esteemed custom'. Even the all-American Mr Hill, far removed from the taint of the British class system, 'respectfully informs' citizens of what he will do for 'those who favor him with their patronage'. (We see that America had actually been infected long before. Aaron Oliver, letter carrier, in 1799 returns sincere thanks to his former customers 'and intends, by unabated diligence to merit a continuance of their favours'.)

The style is seen at full strength in the 1820 tradecard of James Stent, new incumbent at the Antelope Inn, Dorchester (page 165): Mr Stent 'respectfully announces to the Nobility, Gentry, Commercial Gentlemen, his Friends, and the public in general, he has taken possession of the above established inn . . . and he hopes that by an unremitting attention to their comforts, to merit a continuance of that patronage so liberally bestowed on his predecessor . . . It will be his constant care to keep Post Horses and Carriages of the best description . . . and no exertions will be spared to render the accommodation at the Antelope Inn worthy of the patronage of the public'. History is silent as to how Mr Stent made out in his new venture, but from this item of ephemera at least, we may conclude he was a man who knew a thing or two.

(A standardized form of words is seen, by the way, not only as between Britain and America but between Britain and Europe. The tradecard phrases 'all sorts' and 'makes and sells' are to be found in a number of languages: 'Thomas Wright makes and sells all sorts of mathematical instruments . . . (London, 1718); 'Dese en meer

UNION
PHOTOGRAPH
AND
AMBROTYPE GALLERY,
WOOD'S BLOCK,
Nearly opposite Irving House,
Main St., Cambridgeport.
Ambrotypes of sick or deceased persons taken at their residences.
Copying neatly and carefully executed.
HENRY NEWMAN,
HENRY W. TURNER.

The age of advertising brought not only tradecards and handbills but promotional product labelling. The metal-framed ambrotype, successor t the daguerreotype, carried a printed backing card, today collected for its social-history sidelights.

andere zoorte van . . . Tabak, is to koop by Willem Steyn . . .' (Amsterdam, *c.*1800); 'Diese und alle andere Sorten Toback werden fabricirt bey Johannes Oehrens . . .' (Hamburg, *c.*1760).)

The development of a generalized advertising vocabulary may or may not have been merely fortuitous; whatever it was, it reflects a growing awareness of the need for 'selling copy', the special language of the new and more sophisticated guile.

But it was not only in the matter of words that the selling element took precedence over strict accuracy. As time passed, the pictures too were not above suspicion.

As the nineteenth-century commercial engraver came to the fore, with his own special renderings of shops and factories for tradecards and billheads, there emerged a convention of candid misrepresentation. Partly in deference to the ego of the shopkeeper or mill-owner, and partly to overstate the matter to the customer, your local shops became taller and grander than they really were, factories became bigger, longer and more chimney-stacked. It became a universally accepted ploy—a tacit understanding between proprietor, engraver and customer. The flight of fancy on the grocer's paper bag, the long perspectives on the factory letterhead, these were to everyone's liking—a sort of national wink. If the practice was referred to at

TELEPHONE 35Y.

CALNE, 30th Sept 1912.

Mr. Walter Keevil Bowhills

BOT. OF C. T. HAWKINS,

FAMILY BUTCHER

HAWKINS

PRIME BEEF MUTTON, LAMB.

PICKLED TONGUES, CORNED BEEF &c.

LICENSED DEALER IN GAME. WENHAM LAKE ICE.

1912.				
July 4.	Breads.	8 . 6	4	–
6	Q^r Lamb	11½ 10	9	7
	Ribs Beef.	10^10 9	8	1
20.	Leg Lamb.	7^5 11	6	8½
Aug 3.	Bst Nk Veal	4^10 10	3	10½
	Hq^r Lamb.	9½ 11	8	8½

An invention of the trade engraver, lilliputian passers-by brought size and status to the high-street shopkeeper. The convention emerged in the early 1840s, and survived, with ever-diminishing stock figures, into the twentieth century. This example from Calne, Wiltshire, is from 1912.

all (which, most of the time, it was not) it was put down to 'artistic licence'.

One direct effect of artistic licence was a universal decision to reduce the size of human beings. This, a master stroke, had the effect desired. By contrast, everything else in the illustration appeared enormous.

The result was a sort of letterhead race of pygmies—minuscule horses and carriages, delivery wagons, workpeople and customers—stock inhabitants of the commercial and industrial scene. The example on page 89 (Hadden's) is not untypical. Specimens survive in which the disparity of scale is even greater. Some collectors take a fascinated interest in the effect; certainly to the twentieth-century eye it is incredible that such wild inaccuracies got by.

The Graham Hudson Effect: this comparison pair shows Hastings, Sussex, as seen in a nineteenth-century commercial engraving and, more accurately, in a 1980s Hudson photograph. The 1840s rendering, modified by the original artist or the engraver, compresses the scene to fit the width available.

But they did. Graham Hudson has made a special study of the facts and fancies of the billhead engraving and has written much on the subject. He points out not only the matter of the pygmies, but a whole stock-in-trade of billhead deception. In 'Printed Ephemera and the Industrial Historian' (in *Industrial Archaeology*, Winter 1977) he writes: 'The fact is that artists responsible for making the actual engraving might never set eyes on the premises they depicted. Instead they worked from other people's sketches.' He goes on to recall the memoirs of Heber Mardon, son of the Bristol printer, who in the 1860s travelled into Wales making drawings of customers' premises for printing on the paper bags they had ordered from the company.

From these sketches, modest enough in themselves no doubt, the remote engravers concocted their images, adding passers-by and carriages to taste. It is not surprising, as Hudson puts it, that 'significant differences could creep in between image and reality'.

Hudson has researched a number of actual cases. He cites in one case (*Ephemerist*, March 1987) two billhead renderings showing the glass works at York, one in 1851, the other in 1855. The latter shows major additions to the factory. Rebuilding, perhaps? But another version, from 1842, shows yet another layout of the buildings. Not two rebuildings in 13 years, surely? No, each of the drawings is an unreliable rendering of an unreliable original, none of them fit for more than a pinch of salt.

There are certain cases where the deceit is all too obvious. It sometimes happens that a subsequent photograph renders a subject recorded up to then only by an engraving. The differences are immediately apparent; the engraver's flights of fancy are revealed.

The desire to 'improve' things was of course nothing new. With few exceptions, all of the early portrait painters and their clients were agreed on the need to put the best interpretation on the matter. The commercial engraver of the nineteenth century had his counterparts in those who worked for the publishers of *Seats of the Nobility and Gentry*, and other such tomes. These, greatly in vogue in the latter part of the eighteenth century, successfully fed the vanity of the aristocracy and the *nouveau riche* with 'enhanced' images of their properties. Though basically factual, the engravings owed much to the discretion and good taste of the artist. William Watts, mastermind of *Seats of the Nobility and Gentry*, made sure that the nobility would not only approve of his renderings, but would subscribe in advance to the publication, and indeed order two or three dozen unbound copies of their particular prints for family and friends. (In some cases he also made an extra guinea or two by selling them the artists' originals.)

The enhancement effect included the addition of imaginary features, as well as concealment of unsightly bits with luxuriant shrubbery. There was much fabrication of deer, and even, in the case of the affluent gentleman farmer, whole herds of cattle. As with the tradesmen and their tradecards to come, there was also the ubiquitous strolling family, she with crinoline and parasol, he with frockcoat and top-hat. Most vital and prestigious of all were the gentry in their carriage, briskly bowling up the drive to the *porte cochère*. As J.J. Bagley puts it in his *Historical Interpretation* (1971), 'the drawings vary in the degree of truth they convey'. He adds, more specifically, 'There was no sale for an unflattering picture.'

Both for the High Street and the stately home, there was a long-sanctioned tradition of untruthfulness. That we must accept. But that being so, how far can any such item serve as evidence? Are we not as likely to be taken in as our forebears?

There is indeed some risk of this. But on the whole, like our forebears, we make allowance for overstatement. The same pinch of salt that works for them works for us. And after all, we have our own overstatements. There must be few today who wholly believe in the families in our TV commercials and the never-never model girls in never-never fashion magazines. These too are expressions of aspirations rather than fact. It would be wrong to take them literally, but it would also be wrong to dismiss them out of hand. They are not actual evidence but, like the trout in the milk, they are not to be ignored.

The historian has a number of well recognized preoccupations. Among them are such matters as bias in the selection of facts, the reliability of witnesses, and the dangers of misinterpretation. But an over-riding concern is the need to go back to primary sources.

The concept of the primary source is crucial. As with the Anglo-Saxon legal system—where hearsay evidence is inadmissible because it is filtered through a third party—the historian seeks direct evidence. He wants what the jurist calls 'best evidence', the raw, untreated facts. That is not to say, as Marwick points out, that historians ignore the secondary evidence of history books; the whole range of secondary sources must be consulted before the real work begins. The real work starts with locating, analysing and organizing the primary raw material. It is completed when the historian has produced his own history book. Says Marwick, 'Simplifying slightly, one could say that the historian at work is engaged in converting the scattered, difficult primary sources into a coherent, intelligible secondary source.'

All are agreed that this scattered, difficult primary material is vital, but there is room for much discussion as to what is and what is not primary material. As the researcher appraises the secondary sources—books, journals, pamphlets etc.—there is an instinctive drive to delve beneath, to weigh the evidence on which they are based. And with that evidence, too, to delve beneath . . . at each successive 'layer' of research the question poses: is this necessarily more reliable than the last?

The quest for depth in many cases leads to material in manuscript—sometimes the personal testimony of a key witness—the very farthest back and closest anyone could get, as we might think, to the heart and soul of the matter. But this may not be true, of course; evidence is not more reliable because it is in handwriting rather than print. There are as many reasons why a single individual might fudge the record with a pen as there are for authors at the press. The truth is that evidence, manuscript or printed, primary, secondary, or whatever you please, is never quite above suspicion; the most we can say is that the closer we get to base the less likely is the risk of interpretative bias.

Sources may be wholly handwritten, part printed or wholly printed. They may be purely personal memoranda, inventories, wills, household accounts or correspondence, or they may be local or national documents of record—jurors' lists, gamekeepers' registers, churchwardens' accounts, Poor Law papers, selectmen's notes, registers of births, marriages and deaths, ordinances and proclamations. Sometimes, as we have already noted, they form part of an integrated body of record; sometimes they are found as part of a tattered miscellany, forgotten mish-mash at the bottom of an old chest. In either form they may be the historian's raw material.

Until recent times, it must be said, the historian's eye has tended to dwell on the primary papers of official and semi-official record, the registers and returns, the reports, minutes and pronouncements of authorities and private institutions. Toward the bottom of the pile, less noticed, have been the minor memorabilia—the miscellaneous ephemera of the primary source material.

Today there is an awakening of interest in these oddments, and it is recognized that in the main they fall within that vital designation, primary source. They are in some cases the historian's 'best evidence'.

Best or not, items of printed and handwritten ephemera appear increasingly among the notes and files of the social historian. In the published works of such writers as Asa Briggs, Eric Hobsbawm and Kenneth Hudson they are often a notable feature.

We may pause for a moment to consider the matter of handwritten, as opposed to printed ephemera—a subject still not fully resolved among collectors and curators. The question need not delay us unduly long, but for the record it must be said that there are two views; one that there is an essential difference in quality between the printed and the manuscript document; the other that handwritten ephemera may be as fragmentary and transitory as printed ephemera, and both are evidence.

The tendency to exclude handwritten material may be due in part to the persistent use of the expression 'printed ephemera', the word 'printed' originally apearing by way of explanation to those unaccustomed to the use of the word 'ephemera' on its own. In addition, there has in fact been a distinct typographic bias among early specialists (as in John Lewis's pioneering *Printed Ephemera—the changing uses of type and letterforms in English and American printing*, 1962). In any case, where the word 'ephemera' is intended to import handwritten as well as printed matter, the more precise 'printed and handwritten ephemera' is normally too cumbersome a designation. (Only in its more long-winded statements does the Ephemera Society describe itself as 'devoted to the conservation, study and presentation of printed and handwritten ephemera'.) And even in the case of this book, which by rights should include the word 'handwritten' in its title, accuracy gives way to brevity.

The case for including manuscript material is simple. It is best expressed by reference to those items of evidence which may appear in either form or as a mixture of both.

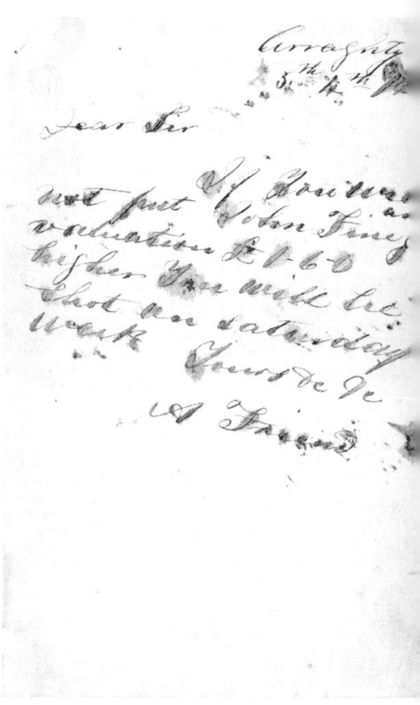
Dear Sir
If you will
not put John Finegan's
valuation £1-6-0
higher You will be
shot on Saturday
week Yours &c &c
A Friend

Handwritten primary source. Of indistinct dateline, a threatening letter informs the recipient: 'If you will not put John Finegan's valuation £1. 6. 0 higher, you will be shot on Saturday week. Yours &c &c A Friend'

THE RIOT ACT.

If any persons to the number of 12 or more unlawfully, riotously, and tumultuously assemble together to the disturbance of the public peace and being required by any Justice by proclamation in the King's name in the exact form of the Riot Act, I George I, Sess. 2 c. 5 s. 2, to disperse themselves and peaceably depart, shall to the number of 12 or more unlawfully, riotously and tumultuously remain or continue together for an hour after such proclamation shall be guilty of a felony.

The Form of Proclamation is as follows:—

"Our Sovereign Lord the King chargeth and commandeth all persons, being assembled, immediately to disperse themselves, and peaceably depart to their habitations, or to their lawful business, upon the pains contained in the Act made in the first year of King George the First for preventing tumults and riotous assemblies."

GOD SAVE THE KING.

rinted as a handy pocket folder, and bearing a formal preamble, an early ventieth-century version of the Riot Act Proclamation enshrines the principles of the law of 1714.

Our Sovereign Lord the King chargeth and Commandeth all Persons being assembled, imme-diately to disperse themselves, and peaceably to depart to their Habitations or lawful Business, upon Pain contained in the Act made in the first year of King George, for preventing Tumults and Riotous assemblies. God Save the King

Text of the Riot Act Proclamation, thought to have been written out by Penry Williams, Lord Lieutenant of Brecon, and proclaimed during the anti-toll-gate riots in South Wales in 1843.

Take for example that most homely of items of domestic record, the laundry list. This may appear in earlier times as a handwritten scribble or, in the era of the commercial laundry, as a printed listing with spaces for insertion of date and numbers. The wholly handwritten item is clearly an item of ephemera, a 'transient minor document of everyday life', as valid for our consideration as a printed or part-printed item.

Or take the document known as The Riot Act. This was a form of words set out by Parliament in 1714 as a means of dealing with disturbances. If rioters, twelve or more in number, did not peacefully disperse within an hour of its being read out to them, they ceased to be 'misdemeanants' and became guilty of a felony, punishable with imprisonment for life. In more recent times, though the Act has since been superseded, the form of words was available as a handy printed folder, but in the eighteenth and nineteenth centuries it was hurriedly transcribed from the Statute Book to a scrap of paper and rushed to the scene for declaiming. Such scraps of paper survive, as do printed folders. Both forms are ephemera (the MS version perhaps more ephemeral than the folder). To ignore the existence of one in favour of the other would be absurd.

Or another example, shown on page 180: a handwritten note instructs a gaoler to release a debtor if the prisoner hands over a promissory note for twenty dollars; while on pages 138–42 we have playing cards, used at the turn of the eighteenth century for written notes—invitations, invoices etc. These too are clearly candidates for conservation and study.

As documents of the human condition, handwritten notes are often more poignant, more immediate and more telling, than printed items. In the Collection of the Foundation for Ephemera Studies in London are the following specimens:

> *Lancaster, Philadelphia, Feb. 17, 1836: W. Bonner to B. S. Bonsall, US Marshall:*
> I have served those summons that you sent, but if you have many to serve it would be the best way to send a Deputy to do it and I will give him all the Information in my power for I find it a very unpopular act for me to serve them for the people heare have a notion that it is an Unlawfull procedure against them.
>
> *Stockton, Durham, August 6, 1810: William Stephenson to W. Kitching, Darlington:*
> I am Sorry to Inform you that my wife is in a very poor Situation and very much disordered in her sences and so very Silley that I can hardley wait on her or my Selph and our income is so very Small that it will hardley keep us with meat if we live ever so poorley so if you would be so kind as allow us a little more weekly . . . and if you cannot dow it of your selph if you will be so kind as mention it to the gentlemen at the meeting and dow what you can for us i should take it as a pertickler kindes and be in duty bound to acknowledg such a favor. So i must conclude my Selph your most humble servant Wm Stephenson

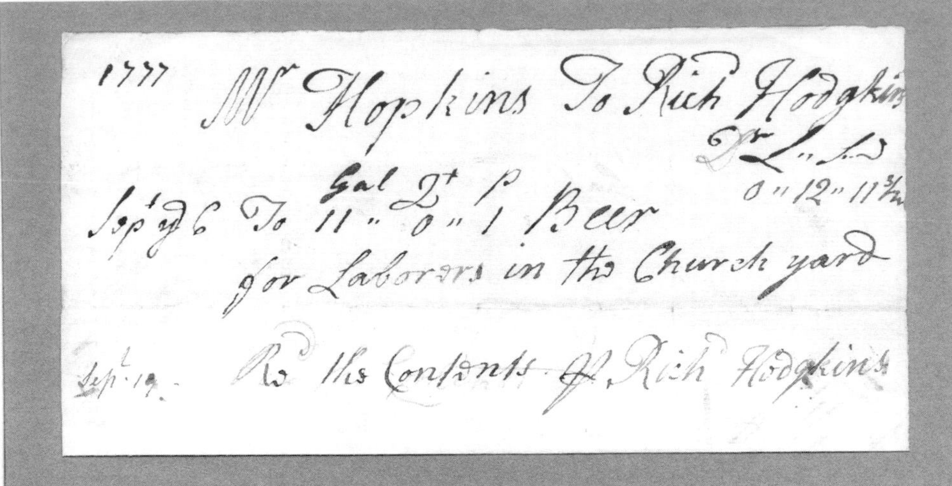

1777 Mr Hopkins To Rich Hodgkins
Dr £ " s " d
Sept 26 To Gal Qt P 11 " 0 " 1 Beer 0 " 12 " 11¾
for Laborers in the Church yard
Sept 19. Recd the Contents ⅌ Rich Hodgkins

Among the most common of wholly handwritten ephemera are the invoices and receipts of artisans, craftsmen and small shopkeepers. Many such items survive among parish papers, often recording the work of day labourers. Here Mr Hodgkins, churchwarden, claims reimbursement of twelve shillings and elevenpence three-farthings for some eleven gallons of beer for men working in the churchyard.

Dover, August 12, 1816: Val Hoile to W. Welch:
Sir, I shall be obliged to you to send me down a £1 note to buy myself Nourishment as I hav had another attack in my Head but am getting better. I am sir your very humble servant, Val Hoile.

Lancaster Gaol, Lancs., Dec. 26, 1863: A. Hansbrow, Governor, to M. Nelson, Matron:
Why was not the Christmas treat given yesterday to the Male Debtors on County allowance as ordered by the Visiting Justices. Reply hereon:
[*Answer*] When I make enquiries about last year of the officers (both male and female) they said it was not given to the Debtors, that they had pudding instead. I have some bread left but not sufficient and five or six pints of coffee. M. Nelson, Matron.

(Unlocated, undated) Jacob Pike, signwriter, to his client:
Will you Pleas to Send and Let Me Know What i am to Wright on the Wagon by Return of Post. it Would of Bin Writen to Day if i had of know Wot to Put on it.

(Off the Coast of New Guinea) 1793: G. Middleton, Midshipman, to 'Uncle & Anty'
This Day we have taken a very rich prize to the amount of about £50000 of a French vesel homeward bound From the Eas Indies Loaded with Indigo Sugar & Cotton, we was the first Ship that boarded, but there are seven othe India Ships that shares the same with us on that account there will be but little fore each mans Share but I hope we will have a good man more such like before we return—we are to send the prize to England & have taken the opertownity of informing you the particulars I am very well preasant thank God for hoping this will find you the same give my best respectes to the Dr & Mrs Livingston, I hope you did receive the guinea I sent you to the care of Mr Tower we are now in the Latitude of 8 South and Longitude 22 aboute 25 Degrees from the Lands end I hope you will take care of my Sister till I return—I shall write you the first opertownity I mus conclude as the prize is now going to set sail from us—we have taken all the Frenchman on board our Ship whill make a Large ships Company in all I like the busness very well, so I conclude & remayn
Your affectionate Nephew George Middleton

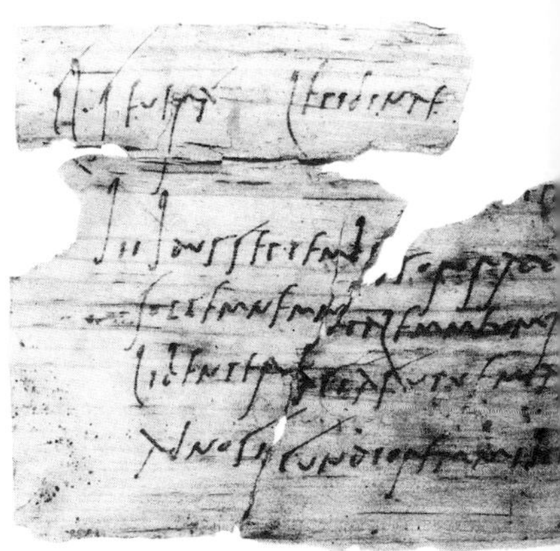

Documents like these survive in some quantities, often as unrelated strays among miscellanies. We may suspect that their survival stems in part from the fact that they are usually less legible than printed papers; they may attract less careful scrutiny.

Above all they remind us that in the long perspective of history, printing is relatively recent; for countless generations the record was set down as the personal work of individuals; methods, forms and materials varied, but the medium was handwriting.

The record—and indeed the ephemera record—goes back farther than we might think. Mary Greenland, Research Officer of the Foundation for Ephemera Studies, writes of the excavation work at Vindolanda, a Roman fortress near Hadrian's Wall. She reports (*Ephemerist*, September 1986) finds of first-century pottery, textiles, tools, finely decorated knife handles, jewellery and shoes. 'But the most exciting finds of all are . . . scraps of wood; thin, dark, and barely distinguishable from the earth that has protected them for nineteen hundred years.' Amazingly, these slivers of wood turn out to be letters and documents, written in pen and ink, faded, fragmentary, but in many cases legible. Says Miss Greenland, 'The writing tablets of Vindolanda are Britain's earliest ephemera . . . Their appeal lies in the extraordinary glimpses they present of the personal lives of the occupying soldiers and their families, and the insights into their day-to-day activities.'

These fragments of Roman ephemera include camp records, accounts of building operations, mentions of shoemakers, plasterers and the use of kilns. Among personal notes and memoranda is an invitation to a birthday party, and there is part of a letter about warm clothing sent from home to a soldier serving in the northern winter. (Garments include *udones*, socks made of felt, and *subligaria*, Roman underpants: 'I have sent you . . . pairs of socks . . . from Sattua two pairs of sandals and two pairs of underpants . . .'.)

Before the discovery of these tablets it had been thought that Romans in Britain had written on wax set in a recessed board, or on papyrus, both forms since perished in the British climate. But at a single archaeological stroke the Vindolanda tablets took Britain's ephemera record back some thirteen hundred years. Robin Birley, archaeologist in charge of the dig, was understandably impressed. 'If I have to spend the rest of my life working in dirty wet trenches, I doubt that I shall ever experience again the shock and excitement at my first glimpse of hieroglyphics on tiny scraps of wood . . .'

Oldest specimens of Britain's handwritten ephemera are the recently discovered wooden writing tablets from Hadrian's Wall, discarded as rubbish by the occupying Romans around AD 100. The example shown is part of a birthday party invitation from Flavia Severa Lepidina, the commanding officer's wife. Other fragments are from letters referring to gifts of winter woollies and there are disparaging references to the Brituncul̲i, or 'Little Brits'.

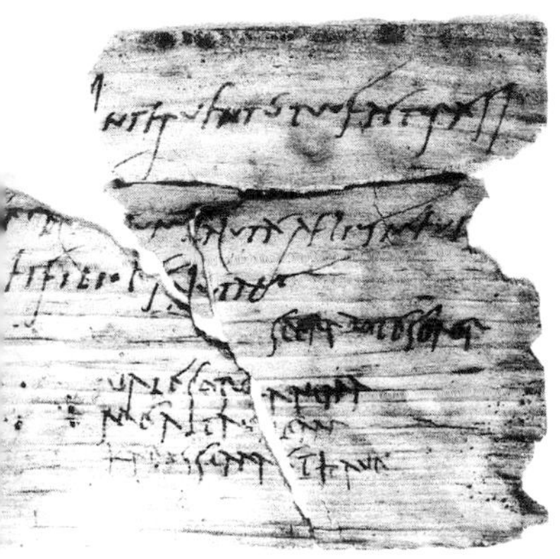

But the handwritten ephemera record goes back farther still—to the papyrus. Among those – noted below (page 28) are papyri dating from 300 BC, but it should be remembered that papyrus was in general use as far back as 3500 BC. It is perhaps not surprising that this material, the pre-eminent surface of day-to-day record in ancient times, should yield important information. What is surprising is that so many specimens have survived to tell the tale.

Its survival has in fact depended solely on climate. Of all the areas in the world where papyrus was used (and these extended to parts of Europe too) only the dry sands of Egypt offered protection. Excavated after some 5000 years in obscurity, the material brings us news of a period about which, by a quirk of climate, we know more than we do of many more recent times.

Papyri were made from a two-layer laminate of strips of papyrus leaves, the layers crossing at right angles. Soaked in water, the strips adhered to each other and were dried, pressed and hammered smooth. The result was a more or less satisfactory, but fragile, writing surface.

Papyrus was used for virtually the whole range of documentation, from dynastic histories and proclamations to personal missives and memoranda. As with paper in modern times, it was the major medium of government, bureaucracy and civic and regional control. Much of the administration of the Roman Empire depended on it. Books and literature at large were written on papyrus, the pieces being pasted together to form a continuous roll or *biblion* (book), and many of the great writers of the ancient world survive in part on papyrus.

It is remarkable that this great mass of documentation became known to the western world only as late as the 1770s—and then almost by accident. The first to reach Europe was bought from villagers by a traveller in 1778. It was an account of a compulsory labour scheme for irrigation in AD 192. It is said that the villagers who sold it offered a great many more at the same time, but the buyer felt that one was enough—so they burned the rest.

Since then, many thousands have been found. Some 40,000 have been translated and published, reportedly less than 20 per cent of those known to exist. Here, still awaiting human scrutiny, is a very Aladdin's cave of formal record and transient fragment.

For our present purpose, from Hunt and Edgar's *Select Papyri*, take these:

HERMIAS TO HORUS *112* BC
Lucius Memmius, a Roman senator, who occupies a position of great dignity and honour, is sailing up from Alexandria . . . to see the sights. Let him be received with special magnificence, and take care that at the proper spots the guest chambers be prepared, and the landing places to them be completed, and that the gifts be presented to him at the landing place, and that the furniture for the guest chamber, the titbits for . . . the crocodiles, the conveniences for viewing the Labyrinth, and the offerings and sacrifices be provided; in general take the greatest pains in everything to see that the visitor is satisfied, and display the utmost zeal . . .

PETITION OF A LENTIL COOK *3rd century* BC
I do my best to pay the tax every month in order that you may have no complaint against me. Now the folk in the town are roasting pumpkins. For that reason . . . nobody buys lentils from me at the present time. I beg and beseech you then . . . to be allowed more time . . . for paying the tax. For in the morning they straightway sit down beside the lentils selling their pumpkins and give me no chance to sell my lentils.

RECEIPT FOR A MUMMY AD *173*
I acknowledge that I have received from you the bandaged mummy of [. . .] whom I will transport to the harbour of Kerke . . . and deliver to Thakaris, funeral undertaker, and for freight and toll and all the expenses of the boat the fee agreed upon, which I have received . . .

ALYPIUS TO HERONINUS AD *256*
God permitting, expect us to pay you a visit on the 23rd. As soon therefore as you receive my letter be sure to have the bathroom heated, getting logs carried in and collecting chaff from everywhere, in order that we may bathe in warmth in this wintry weather . . . See that we are provided with every attention, and above all with a good pig for our party, but again let it be a good one and not lean and unfit like the last. Send word also to the fishermen to bring us some fish. I have sent a letter to Horion telling him to send you five hundred bundles of grass, and you may give him back the same amount; for my working animals are eating green fodder; and at all events have abundance of green grass brought in, in order that they too may have sufficient food. So send for the grass today without fail.

SARAPAMMON TO PIPERAS *3rd century* AD
I sent you a letter by the baker, and perhaps you know what I wrote to you. If you persist in your folly I wish you joy; if you are repenting, you yourself know. Let me tell you that you owe me seven years' rents and revenues, so unless you send remittances you know the risk you run.

APPIANUS TO HERONINUS AD *256*
When one despatches even the smallest load, he ought to send a letter with it stating what has been sent and by what carrier. And the goods which you despatched were not so many as to require a man and a donkey to leave their work for them, only four baskets of rotten figs. And it was evident from the poorness and dryness and parched appearance of the figs that the estate has been neglected. But about this we shall have an account to settle between ourselves.

HORUS TO APION *Late 1st century* AD
Horus to the most honoured Apion greeting. Regarding Lampon, the mouse-catcher, I paid him on your account eight drachmae as earnest money to catch mice in Toka. You will kindly send me this sum. I have also sent eight drachmae to Dionysius and he has not sent them back. This is to inform you.

Papyri are among the earliest of handwritten documents. Many are great historical or literary significance; others are true ephemera—'the transient minor documents of everyday life'. Few papyri are to be found in ephemera collections however, and the collection of the Foundation of Ephemera Studies has only a single specimen, the fragment shown here It is currently under examination at the British Museum.

INVITATION TO A FESTIVAL *3rd or 4th century* AD
Greetings my lady Serina from Perosiris. Make every effort, dear lady, to come on the 20th, the birthday of the festival god, and let me know whether you are coming by boat or by donkey, in order that we may send for you. Take care not to forget, dear lady. I pray for your lasting health.

THINGS TO BE DONE *c.250* BC
Ask Herodotus about the goat hair . . . The letter to Dioscurides about the boat. Make an agreement with Timaeus about the pigs. Draft the contract with Apollodorus and write to him to hand over. Load the boat with wood. Write to Jason to let Dionysius put wool on board and take it down the river when cleaned . . . Theogenes about twelve yokes of bulls.

NOTE FROM VICTOR TO THEODORE *6th or 7th century* AD
With your true brotherliness have the goodness to send me day by day some asparagus, for the vegetables here are rotten and disgust me . . .

A FLUTE-PLAYER'S CONTRACT AD *322*
I acknowledge that I have contracted and agreed with you the landlord to present myself at the village . . . at the vintage of the vineyards . . . and without fault assist the grape-treaders and other workers by my flute-playing and not leave until after the completion . . . And for the flute-playing and the entertainment I shall receive the prescribed fee . . .

For the average collector, papyri may seem remote and irrelevant. On the open market they are rare, and indeed it is only occasionally that they emerge at all. When they do show up their immediate appeal is largely in their antiquity; their message must await the often lengthy process of expert examination. But the trouble of finding out may well be worth it; as with some of the specimens cited here, a single fragment may convey a vivid image. The museum specialist is normally happy to be consulted, and may also be glad to come across something unusual. For the possessor of a papyrus fragment—even a fragment of no historical importance—it is no bad thing to establish how old it is, where it came from, and what it is about.

However old, however new, from the fragment of five thousand years ago to that of this very afternoon, the ephemera of daily life contribute an essential portion of the historical record. Their evidence may be 'best' (in the courtroom sense), bad, or merely doubtful; but they are not to be neglected. It is in their careful gathering, their orderly arrangement and study that the ephemerist gives them the accessibility they deserve.

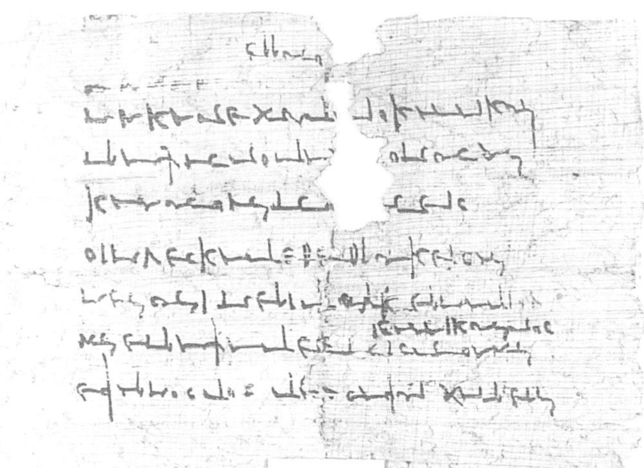

This Greek papyrus, one of many thousands in the British Museum, offers an engaging sidelight on the day-to-day troubles of our forebears. It says 'Please write again: your last was eaten by mice'.

Collecting

The collector in any field usually starts from a position of personal interest or special enthusiasm. The man with the world's biggest collection of corkscrews is on the whole unlikely to be a teetotaller. The big-time collector of dental instruments usually turns out to be a dentist. The collection is an expression of the collector.

It is unusual (though not unheard of) for anyone to be seen to be casting about 'looking for something to start collecting'. In general there is an existing basic interest in a given subject; then a first casual acquisition of a relevant item, then another and another. Shortly, without formal announcement, a collection has come into being—a spontaneous outcome of the owner's interest.

For the deeper motivations of the collector as a social species we might turn to the psychologist (perhaps even to the psychiatrist), but in the present context we may settle for a less clinical view. The average collector of ephemera, as with the collector at large, finds it difficult to be altogether clear about motives; some start collecting 'for fun', others for nostalgia, others for investment.

On the whole, it must be said, the investment group is smallest, least likely to sustain an interest (and certainly least likely to get rich). We shall be looking at the matter of markets and values in later pages, but at this point we need merely sound a note of warning: whatever the future holds for ephemera, today the sale-room is still only a side-arena. And the collector who sees no farther than the auction rostrum sees all too little.

The typical ephemerist is not, by and large, a natural-born tycoon; if collected items increase in value, that is fine; but that is not the object of the exercise. The true ephemerist is as committed to the smallest neglected fragment as to the spectacular 'collector's piece'. Normally, too, if the ephemerist parts with an item it is preferably by way of exchange rather than sale. It is the ephemera that matters, not a profit margin.

The collector for fun, or nostalgia, is the beginner most likely to succeed. In either case, consciously or not, here there is the approach to ephemera for its own sake—as the quarry in a hunting game, as evidence in a history trail.

At whatever level the collector operates, and whatever the individual motives, collections tend to sort themselves into special disciplines. They may concentrate on categories (billheads, admission tickets, share certificates, tradecards etc.), or on themes (sport, women's lib, air travel, medicine, crime, fashion etc.). They may combine both approaches. In many of the world's great ephemera collections, catalogue entries include such titles as 'rewards of merit' and 'education'—this notwithstanding that the 'education' section may well include examples of rewards of merit as well.

Whichever the approach, category or theme, for most collectors the essential is the 'history trail' effect, the piecing together, through actual examples, of an evo-

Elizabeth Greig's interest in the ephemera of civil flight stemmed from memories of planes stunting over Hendon aerodrome, visible fro[m] her nursery window and famous as venue for displays, race meetings an[d] other air events. As with many specialist ephemerists, her collection expresses a more-than-average enthusiasm for its social-history content. Her forthcoming book The Ephemera of Flight *is largely based on her collection.*

Ken Kittelberger, formerly an officer in the United States Army and much involved with the Boy Scout movement, has built his ephemera collection around Baden-Powell, founder of the movement. He sees Baden-Powell as a world influence, and the museum at his home in Maryland provides 'probably the world's most complete commemoration of this truly remarkable figure'.

lutionary process—the changing face of fashion, for example, or the changing face of the restaurant menu. Theme or category, the basis is the same.

On the whole, it may be thought, the category collector has the easier life. With only few exceptions, there will be little difficulty in deciding whether or not a prospective item falls within the collection's terms of reference. A school merit card, old or new, plain or coloured, manuscript or printed, has a claim to a place in a collection of such cards. For the theme collector however, life is an endless re-appraisal: does a school repair bill qualify for inclusion under the heading 'education'? Or a cycle-shed price list? Or a retiring teacher's pension claim? Decisions, decisions . . .

But for the category collector too, all this is not absolutely plain sailing. There is that first major matter: which category to select?

The list of possibles is breathtaking: a short list might include, in no particular order, the following:

> Labels, printed notices, tradecards, laundry lists, certificates, summonses, bills of lading, licenses, indentures, permits, rent demands, timetables, tax forms, wrappers and packaging, advertising material, menus, notices to quit, mobilization papers, membership cards, death warrants, school reports, mourning cards, greeting cards, magazines and newspapers, posters, stickers, stationery, parking tickets, touring maps, scraps, lottery tickets, library labels, bookmarks, banknotes, passports, share certificates, deeds, calendars, music covers, board games, insurance policies, programmes, permits, proclamations, notices, instruction sheets, aerial leaflets, price tags, dance cards, election badges, scholars' reward cards, cheques, book and record tokens, calling cards, ration cards, auction catalogues, battle orders, betting slips, folk recipes, tickets, invitations, compliments slips, telegram forms, final demands, bumper stickers and many, many more.

Each of these special categories has its own experts, its own folklore, its finer points and its own scene-stealers. Each is a collecting world of its own, but is open to everyone.

Each sector is also susceptible of thematic sub-division: the label specialist may focus only on chemists' labels—or needle- or button- or nib- or perfume- or stationers'- or tea- or cigar- or pin-packet-labels. The tax-fancier may favour tax forms for assessments on land, manservants, hair powder, armorial bearings, horses, salt or windows. The ticket specialist may ignore all institutions other than railways—or theatres, sports events, or concerts.

In a category of its own is packaging—a three-dimensional exception to a generally two-dimensional scene—by common consent admitted for its supreme ephemerality. Robert Opie's world-famous packaging museum at Gloucester, the product of 25 years' collecting (and still growing), is a monumental example of one man's deciding on a category and staying with it. Here, as much as anywhere, the passing trends of the social scene are graphically reflected. Packaging, among the most transient and easily destructible of ephemera, is a category to be reckoned with.

We may mention here two or three other categories of ephemera, close to the borderline of exclusion, if not beyond it. They are of two kinds: serial items, such as cigarette cards, and items forming major specialist fields of their own, such as postcards and postage stamps.

Serial items are of course as ephemeral as menus and calling cards. But they differ from these and from most other ephemera in one particular: they were produced specifically *to be collected*. Devised as a means of retaining customer 'brand loyalty', they were included with products as numbered giveaways; the inducement to the customer was to go on buying the product at least until the whole 'set' had been

Collecting 'shop ephemera' began as a pastime for Annette Buckley. After 15 years she opened the collection as a business, setting up a Museum of Shops in the High Street in Battle, Sussex, and backing it with sales of old-time items—skipping ropes, egg-timers and the like. 'It started just out of interest,' says Mrs Buckley, 'and that's how it grew . . .'

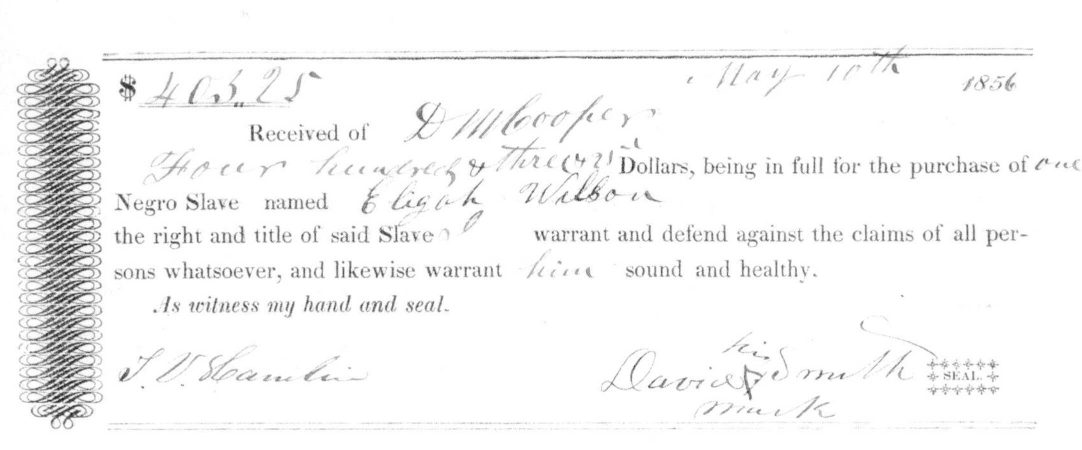

$ 403.25 May 10th 1856

Received of D M Cooper

Four hundred & three [illegible] Dollars, being in full for the purchase of one Negro Slave named Eligah Wilson the right and title of said Slave [illegible] warrant and defend against the claims of all persons whatsoever, and likewise warrant him sound and healthy.

As witness my hand and seal.

J. V. Hamlin

David his mark Smith SEAL.

Ephemera as teaching aid: few items of evidence could express the slave trade as concisely as this North Carolina receipt for $403.25 for a Negro slave, warranted sound and healthy. The selling price, and the printed form of words, suggest a routine sale by auction. (See also page 136)

Fumigating Ingredients,

To remove Offensive Smells, Foul, Putrid and Stagnated Air, from Halls, Chambers, Courts of Juſtice, diſtemper'd Gaols, (even more ſpeedy and ſucceſsful than the Ventilators), and to diſpel the Noxious Fumes of new painted Houſes, &c. &c.

It is well known to the World, that fœtid Smells, ſtagnated and putrid Air, are in general the Cauſe of many dreadful Diſeaſes; ſuch as, Malignant Fevers, putrid Sore Throats, the Plague, &c. &c. which ſo frequently prove fatal to whole Families, and even Kingdoms: by throwing a ſmall Quantity of the Fumigating Ingredients on a Chafing-diſh or Shovel, with clear Embers or Coals, thoſe noxious and offenſive Smells will inſtantly give way to a healthy, pleaſant and reviving Odour.

Captains of Ships, particularly thoſe in the [illegible] of *Guinea* Trade, ſhould not be without it; for a whole Cargo of Negro Slaves may be ſaved by the moderate Uſe of theſe Ingredients. Sold in Caniſters at 3s. 6d. each, at Mr. *Groote*'s, Apothecary and Chemiſt, *Naſſau-ſtreet, St. Ann's, Soho*; at Mr. *Rowley*'s, the *London Coffee-houſe, Ludgate-hill*; and at Mr. *Bailey*'s, Perfumer in *Cockſpur-ſtreet*.

Allowance will be made to ſell again.

To prevent Counterfeits, Mr. *Groote* has ſigned his Name at length to the Directions, and ſealed the Caniſters with his Arms.

G. Groote

'A whole Cargo of Negro slaves may be saved by the moderate Use of these Ingredients . . .' From the David Temperley collection, an early nineteenth-century expression of sound commercial sense.

collected, by which time a fresh set had been launched, and the process began again.

The cards appeared—and still appear—in a huge range of products, from cigarettes to bubble gum, chocolates to beef extract. It would be pedantic to deny them some sort of place in the canon of true ephemera, but for all that, the ephemerist may think twice about them. Many would claim that the essence of the appeal of ephemera is in its *unwitting* role as evidence, and the serial card must be seen to fall far short of actual artlessness. It may thus be less easily at home among the genuine waifs and strays.

As for the postcard and the postage stamp, these by their very profusion give them a separate and sovereign status in their own right. To profess to encompass them within the designation 'ephemera' would be to seek to include the greater within the smaller.

These 'fringe-area' categories may nevertheless happily appear as supportive incidentals in thematic collections. A postcard showing Lindbergh's arrival in France serves an evidential function in a collection of 'History of Flight' ephemera; so does an overprinted 'occupation' stamp in an ephemera history of warfare.

Thematic collections are on the whole more commonly met with than the collection by category. Long as a list of categories may be, a listing of human affairs is longer. And it is that very quality, the capacity to illustrate and illuminate every aspect of our existence, that gives thematic collecting its popular appeal. Such varied topics as medicine, sport, crime, conjuring, ballet, public health—these and literally hundreds of others may be expressed in collections of ephemera, each from an individually specialized viewpoint, each using a handpicked selection of rescued oddments.

The thematic collection may fulfil a variety of functions. It may be used in schools as a graphic teaching aid; in industry to illustrate company history or the development of special trades and processes. It may outline the growth of a town or neighbourhood, or trace the origins of institutions and organizations. The thematic ephemera collection has become not just a leisure interest, but a recognized tool of social-history education.

It is adaptable to the needs of everyone: the schoolchild may gather items bearing his or her birth-date, or the current output of the local shopping centre; the housewife may collect material reflecting new household technology, or inflation, or the history of cooking, or indeed, if the mood takes her, deep-sea diving.

Modern Times

Dowsing

Not a Theory Course or an Occult Study

Hands-on Experience of the Earths' magnetism. We will develope the basic skill of dowsing and then Explore Manhattan to see how we have responded to the magnetic element, chiefly with respect to the ideas of path and center as seen in the layout of the city and its architecture.

Dowsing is curious, fun, feels good. It makes space palpable. It is great for the skeptical, pragmatic, show a link, even diologue, we all share with the earth.

Just the same we will try not to make a spectacle of ourselves. This is an endless subject, as everything has a certain magnetism, so part of our direction will be determined by the class interest.

David Houston learned dowsing from a water witch in upstate New York. He has a B. A. from Bard College, is an artist, illustrator, billboard painter, dock builder and dance teacher. Classes starting the end of February, eight hours for $25.

Single lesson arranged as well. Telephone: 873-7182

A souvenir of Boston, Massachuse in the 1970s, this item reflects just one portion of the range of tod ephemera—most of it available fre of charge, much of it rich in social-history content.

Ephemera need cost the collector nothing at all. For most of the throwaways of our own day—certainly for the Niagara of advertising and promotional material that engulfs us—there is no charge whatever. Even with the item that does incidentally involve money, the ticket, the rent demand, the notice to quit or the IOU, the piece of paper itself comes as a bonus—a free gift, with society's compliments. Cheap as it is, it may turn out to be a collector's item.

Present-day ephemera makes its appeal on any or all of a number of counts. It may attract purely as printed design, as souvenir, as history-in-the-making, as curiosity, or simply as an expression of the collector's personal interests.

For the design-conscious, the field is vast. Whether as typographer, graphic designer, printer, publisher, layout specialist, student of graphics or plain amateur printed-matter-watcher, the design collector has plenty to choose from. Letterheads, billheads and general business stationery; tickets, invitations, notices, leaflets; packaging and point-of-sale display material; cigar labels, betting slips, lottery tickets, menus, bookmarks, printed serviettes—the list is endless.

In each category the connoisseur discerns the rise and fall of design trends, the changing use of layout and typography. These items mirror exactly the graphic fads and fancies of the day. One distinguished designer has a colourful collection of horse-race betting slips. Another collects orange wrappers. And a lecturer in graphics collects 'underground' leaflets and stickers.

But design awareness is by no means confined to experts. For specialist and layman alike the collecting criterion is purely personal: 'I collect them because I like them' is the classic comment; a housewife collects printed paper serviettes; a schoolboy collects banana labels; a librarian collects compliments slips; a hospital nurse collects lottery tickets. Each in a short time becomes an expert, a connoisseur in a chosen field. Variants, re-designs, re-issues, 'first editions'—all of the finer points of the collector's world apply.

At whatever level they appear, most items of ephemera aim to please. Decorative labels, attractively designed promotion items—it is but a step from noticing them in ones and twos to enthusing over them in numbers.

In the souvenir category of ephemera come all those oddments that evoke our yesterdays. Trips abroad, seaside holidays, family jaunts and excursions are all productive of their quota of memorabilia. A complete holiday can be chronicled by its yield of printed miscellany. Tickets, travel folders, price lists, itineraries may bring back—sometimes even more vividly than photographs—the pleasures and adventures of time off. (And we may note in passing that it is not the made-on-purpose souvenir that is necessarily most appealing. Formal souvenirs may not be as evocative for us as our own old luggage tag.)

Other souvenir aspects of ephemera are expressed in neighbourhood and world-of-my-youth collections. Here the collector gathers local or birth-date items. Among the simplest and quickest to acquire is a complete collection of local shop-keepers' tradecards or billheads. These, assembled over a period of a few weeks or months, may in a very few years acquire considerable local-history interest. Not only does their design and presentation reflect a specific period; the information they convey, in terms of addresses and trading details, may rapidly become a matter of history. Changes occur more rapidly than we realize. A complete documentation of a shopping area, perhaps unobtainable from other sources, may form the nucleus of a local-history archive.

Another neighbourhood theme could be one's own city or town. A single year's output of municipal pamphlets, leaflets and other odds and ends provides a telling expression—easily acquired at the time, but afterwards perhaps unobtainable—of the local social scene.

In Britain in the latter part of this century the propaganda sticker has un riot. Used as a mini-poster—in ts own right, or as an addendum to osters of the established order—the sticker is handy and cheap, easy to apply, difficult to remove. Its small size makes it easy to conceal until needed (an advantage over yesterday's brush and bucket of whitewash) and its message is necessarily to the point. As a social-history collector's item it presents a special challenge: its public life is often brief, and it rarely appears in fresh editions. It may be removed if required, by a judicious application of surgical spirit.

These items carry a vast amount of factual information on neighbourhood affairs, social services and other such matters. Like most ephemera, they also convey a between-the-lines picture of trends and attitudes. An information booklet for the London Borough of Camden has entries on Abandoned Vehicles, Adoption, Control of Advertising, Burials, Dental Health, Pest Control, Drains, Elderly Persons, Factory Inspection—and so on through to Unmarried Mothers' Vaccination, Water Safety, and Workshops for the Handicapped.

World-of-my-youth items of ephemera, only slightly more difficult to come by, make a special appeal to the younger collector. The ephemerist gathers material dating, for example, from the first year, or the first decade, of his life. Here again, in a quickly changing world, the very recent bygone may gain remarkably in interest as each year passes. For the ten-year-old collector, newspaper front pages that appeared on the day of his birth may convey a world of unimaginable remoteness.

The category of 'curiosity' ephemera, more specialized than others, and requiring greater tenacity, can be no less rewarding. Here the criterion is mere quirkiness—an appeal to the collector's personal sense of the odd, the ridiculous or amusing. One specialist collects incomprehensible instruction leaflets. Another has an eye for the quirky notice. (A catering exhibition displaying fine foods carried notices saying 'Please Do Not Eat the Exhibition'.) Yet another collects examples of fractured phrases on foreign products: 'Close the point of contact with a humid stuff, in order that the steam goes up to the couscous'.

Another collector specializes in computerized accountancy claims for gigantic sums for electricity bills. Another has a world collection of refuse-men's Christmas cards. These, in their respective languages, are mailed or left with householders as a hint as gift-time draws near.

Further offbeat collectibles include editors' rejection slips, telegram forms, summonses, final demands, ships' newspapers, lodging-house tickets, misprints, and printed toilet paper.

Among only-just-bygone ephemera (now, alas, not available free of charge) are the colourful crate labels, till recently inseparable from fruit and vegetable marketing; and hotel and resort labels, the promotional stickers that only a short while ago appeared on travellers' luggage. Equally evocative, and only just not contemporary, are record sleeves from the 78 rpm era; one collector has amassed some fifteen hundred of these newly nostalgic items.

It is in the area of social history that collectors of present-day ephemera stand strongest. Whatever the charms of graphic design, of curiosities, personal souvenirs and misprints, the long-term value of today's material is in its implicit chronicle of the times. The social-history collector concentrates on subject matter, regardless of form or category. A collection on a given theme may include items as disparate as a sticker and a government proclamation, a bookplate and a honey-jar label.

For the most part, not surprisingly, it is the major issues reflected by historical ephemera that claim attention. Urban violence, contraception, inflation, race equality—these are typical of the more obvious themes that today's ephemera may illustrate. Less obvious, but no less readily depicted, are such subjects as illiteracy, the changing church, medical ethics, computerization, radioactivity, worker participation in industry. Thoughtful ephemerists take their choice.

Marcus McCorison, Director of the American Antiquarian Society in Worcester, Massachusetts, has aptly described ephemera as a 'window into the centre of a culture'. The phrase is as valid for contemporary specimens as it is for bygones.

Present-day items of ephemera cost little or nothing; viewed individually, they are often too insignificant to attract much notice; they are in the main so common that nobody normally thinks of preserving them. They are produced, by common consent, to be thrown away. It is in this very quality of triviality and transience that their potential value lies. Salvaged, and presented coherently, they form part of a story that speaks for itself.

In 1977 a call went out for items for a commemorative display featuring the 1951 Festival of Britain. All that was required was minor ephemera, a few examples from among the many millions of the items that the event had generated. To the nation's surprise, little or nothing had survived. It had been so common at the time, everyone had thown it away.

'Modern' ephemera may date back some years, depending on the age of the beholder. For the older collector this early 1930s record sleeve is an 'only-just-bygone', still possibly folded away in attic or lumber room. As with the records themselves, sleeves from the 78 rpm era are attracting interest from collectors of all ages—as old friends or new curiosities.

John Selden (1584–1654), English historian and antiquary, is remembered by ephemerists for his collection of street literature and his famous comment on the role of ephemera as 'straws in the wind' (see page 42). He is best known for his scholarly studies and for his controversial views on the Church's claim to divine right of tithe.

The ephemerists

Not all ephemerists are collectors of ephemera. Some are 'ephemera fanciers', content to take notice of the existence and importance of the material, and to commend it to the attention of others. Some simply consult ephemera, using the collections of institutions or individuals as research material. Others are dealers in ephemera, well-informed and enthusiastic appraisers and purveyors. In each of these categories a small number may collect as well—just a *little* (as the honey-seller occasionally licks his finger-tips). But for none of these is collecting an activity in in its own right; for them, collecting—and the collector too—is simply a means to an end.

For the classic collector, the collection itself may be seen as nine-tenths of the case. It is the gathering, the analysis, ordering and control of the material, that matters; the use it may be put to is just a bonus. Many collectors see it this way from the beginning, finding satisfaction in the simple exercise of growth. Others take on this role from positions on the side-lines, and from being fanciers, researchers or purveyors, they become custodians.

Certainly the impulse to amass and organize material, whether for oneself or on behalf of an institution, is common, and collectors throughout history—as well as their friends and relations—have pondered its implications. What kind of people are we? What makes us do it? How about the Great Ephemerists—Selden, Pepys, John Johnson, Bella Landauer—what were *their* motives? And is there any essential difference between the ephemerist and, say, the book collector, or the fine-art collector, or the bug collector?

Collecting at large was looked at (along with everything else) by Sigmund Freud at the turn of the nineteenth century. He diagnosed it (along with everything else) as being almost wholly sex-propelled. For details the reader is referred to the *Psychopathology of Everyday Life* (1904); suffice it here to say that Freud's works, after those of Copernicus and Darwin, were described as 'a third blow to man's self-esteem'.

How did the ephemerist fare? Writing in *The Ephemerist* (September 1987) Dr Neil Johnson, of the Department of Psychology at Lancaster University, said that there may be something in what the master said—and then again, there might not. He discusses Freud's theory that the urge to collect is another form of *retention*—a resistance to parental encouragement in the nursery functions. It is a form of protest, of possession, says the theory, classically expressed in the older child's cry 'That's mine . . . *mine*!'

Says Neil Johnson, 'Certainly one can detect a degree of obsessionality, even pedantry, in the way in which some collectors catalogue and index their collections, but beyond this there is little support to be found for the Freudian view . . .' Similarly with other well-worn propositions—for example that there is an underlying human desire for the act of acquisition (as opposed to simply possessing); here too

Neil Johnson is dubious: 'A man may wish to own a new house, or to acquire a wife, without wishing to start a collection of either'. Or again, that such human activity reflects the hoarding instincts of animals: but animals, though they may acquire, do not *collect*; that is, they do not *order, categorize and arrange* their acquisitions. The making of collections is peculiar to humans.

Another theory suggests that collecting represents a re-direction of love, a lavishing of affection on inanimates, objects incapable of disappointing or rejecting the lover. Yet another proposes that there is some symbolism in the subject matter itself. Is there some secret significance in stamps, coins, postcards—false moustaches and Victorian ladies' underwear? Or what about the idea that we need to dominate some aspect of our environment? Proving our ability to organize and control things—even stamps or false moustaches—shows that we are not wholly the victims of the outside world.

These and other theories have been propounded by psychologists, professional and amateur. In a lecture session of The Ephemera Society of America in the early 1980s one speaker described a number of additionally recognized collecting syndromes. Among these were the *Golden Past* syndrome: the collector escapes from today's instability by means of bygones; the *Cannibal* syndrome: acquisition not only of the collector's piece but of the former owner's prestige; *Top Dog*: 'My collection is the greatest'; *More is Better*: sense of security derives from added volume; *Social Passport*: access to a sense of common ground; *Instant Egghead*: the collector knows more about his field than anyone else; in no time is 'an authority'; *The Connoisseur*: cultural and aesthetic one-upmanship; *Show-off*: 'Admire my collection, admire me'; *Hen and Chicks*: the collection as a family—'My treasures'; *David and Goliath*: the self-imposed collecting challenge—'I'm going to get every hotel matchcover ever published'; *Immortality*: survival by collection; the collection as monument.

Though not to be taken over-seriously, the above listing may bear a passing thought. Certainly there are ephemerists who would admit to recognition of some of the characteristics described—both in the psychologist's comments and in the layman's lecture.

Still we may pause at this point to ponder the need for such analysis. Does anyone seriously think that the world's great ephemerists, the John Johnsons and the Bella Landauers, the Samuel Pepys's and the Isaiah Thomas's, were somehow disturbed in this respect? We shall shortly be looking at these 'greats' and their collecting motives.

But for a moment let us glance at those other fields: books, art and bugs.

Little appears to have been written on the matter of the psychology of the bug collector, but for art and books we may turn to the experts. The collector in these areas has in fact had professional psychological attention, and it must be said that analyses are more or less unanimous—and discouraging. For details the reader may refer to two opinions: Dr Norman Weiner's 'On Bibliomania' (*Psychoanalytic Quarterly*, Autumn 1966), and Dr Frederick Baekeland's 'Psychological Aspects of Art Collecting' (*Psychiatry*, February 1981). All the syndromes outlined in the Ephemera Society lecture appear in detail, together with others less flattering.

Weiner and Baekeland see the art and book collector, respectively and jointly, as, on the whole, unscholarly, sly, superficial, aggressive, competitive, autistic, power-hungry and crypto-lecherous. Above all, say these professionals, the collectors in question are seen to be concerned more with the status of their quarry than its inherent content. Weiner quotes Holbrook Jackson's dictum: 'The glory of possessing a manuscript of Cicero seems to approximate that of being its author'. Baekeland quotes Otto Fenichel's 'Trophy and Triumph', in which possession brings not only the thing itself, but the prestige of the previous owner: the relationship, says Fenichel, reflects the feeling that '*I have acquired something* ... [*which*] *originally belonged to someone more powerful, but which is a talisman for me, or which connects me magically with the previous possessor.* It is as if merely by having [it] the current owner were imbued with the fame, riches, power or special abilities of a former owner ...'. The writer also points out that objects that have belonged to a famous collection are always more expensive and sought after than those that have not.

To-day's ephemerists may wince slightly at some of this. But only slightly: for on the whole, at whatever level they collect, their hearts are with the material itself, and not with the power and glory it may bring. Whether it be football programmes or eighteenth-century tradecards, laundry lists or labels, reward cards or billheads, the addiction almost always springs from genuine interest in the subject matter, very rarely from sale-room attributes of provenance and status.

Certainly no thought of personal gain impelled the early ephemerists. However apparently eccentric, the pioneers were clearly neither investors nor status-seekers. They simply perceived the role of ephemera as evidential record—and rescued it. Far from being sly, power-hungry and competitive, there was about them an engaging naivety. Here were full-grown men, each distinguished in his field, concerned to collect and consult the throwaways of their own time and times past. It was a novel proposition.

Samuel Pepys (1633–1703), Secretary to the Admiralty and celebrated diarist, was also the first general ephemerist. His collection embraced tradecards, boardgames and labels, as well as ballads and other street literature. This portrait, based on a carving in ivory by Jean Cavalier (1688) was drawn for the Ephemera Society by Graham Hudson. It has formed the centrepiece of the Society's emblem since the mid-1980s and was adopted by the Foundation for Ephemera Studies in 1987.

Pre-eminent among them, though only marginally in respect of his career at large, was Samuel Pepys, Secretary to the Admiralty, diarist and distinguished man-about-town. As his diary proves, here was one enthusiast for whom collecting ephemera was certainly not a substitute for sex. Nor was it a substitute for anything else; it took its place among a multitude of pleasures—Greek, Latin, Spanish and French; singing, and playing the viol, the violin, the lute and the flageolet, books and their bindings, maps and prints; history, science and mathematics; the theatre, clothes, politics, conversation, dining, wining and wenching.

Pepys's ephemera collection is preserved in the Pepys Library at Magdalene College, Cambridge, housed in twelve specially fashioned bookcases. The library comprises 3000 volumes—no more, no less, by Pepys's firm decision—among them the diary itself, a million and a quarter words in six volumes.

The library is in a special sense a monument to the man. It was designed, he said, to be very different from other such collections, which he dismissed as the 'Extensive, Pompous, and Stationary Libraries of Princes, Universities, Colleges and other Public Societies'. It was to comprise 'in fewest Books and least Room the greatest diversity of Subjects, Stiles and Languages its Owner's Reading [would] bear'.

It is indeed different from other libraries, and its diversity is as wide-ranging as the man himself. Apart from a selection of contemporary books there are some 200 early printed books (25 of them dating from before 1500) and a collection of maritime titles. There are also special collections: albums of prints (twenty large volumes); printed ballads (more than 1700 in five volumes); specimens of calligraphy (three volumes); and a collection of systems of shorthand (five small volumes).

There are also two large albums entitled *London & Westminster*. These, to the ephemerist, are of the greatest interest, both for themselves and for the light they cast on their owner. Pasted in the two volumes are some one thousand items—street literature, tradecards, pictorial prints, playing card wrappers, funeral cards, tobacco labels, boardgame sheets, bills of mortality, invitations—a throwaway conspectus of the life and times of a remarkable Londoner.

We can only speculate as to how these items were gathered in. Nowhere, not even in the diary, does Pepys refer to his collecting activities or to the appeal of such items as tobacco labels and playing card wrappers. But these were undoubtedly part of his everyday concern, and we may visualise him, wig, walking-staff and all, not above stooping in the street for a likely item.

Nor was his collecting merely a gentlemanly pastime: it is clear that he was personally involved and committed, as the manuscript title-page of volume 1 of the *London & Westminster* collection implies: 'My Collection of Prints & Drawings relating to London & Westminster &c. put-together Anno Domini 1700'. It is true that the handwriting is not his, and we may assume that someone else did the actual pasting-in for him, but this was no lordly arm's-length amusement; the man was an astute observer, an instinctive social historian, and this was part of his evidence.

Among the 40 or so tradecards included in the collection are some of the earliest surviving examples of their kind. Drawn from addresses within walking distance of the owner's home ground, they cover a period of nearly half a century. Trades include a sword cutler, woollen drapers, milliners & haberdashers, tobacconists, stationers, a silk dyer and a colourman. Wording on the cards is in classic style:

> John Cooke. At the Signe of the Shears in little Lombard Street. Maketh Razors, Sissars, Launcets, Pen knives. And all sortes of Chirurgeons Instruments. Also by him are sold ye best Hoanes.
>
> Roger Tucker. Bookseller at the Signe of the Golden Legg. At the corner of Salisbury Street in the Strand. Sells all sorts of Printed Books and all manner of Stationery Ware at reasonable Rates. Where also one may have ready mony for all Sorts of books.
>
> Will[m] Peery (and Caleb Hooker late of Norwich) at the signe of ye Golden Wheat Sheaf and Crown in New Round Court in the Strand over against York Buildings. Selleth all sorts of Norwich Goods, as Grogorums, Barragons, Bombazins, Serge de Nimms, Camletts, Calemancoes, Barrateens, Antherines, Tammies, Tammins, Tammarines, Damask, Grazetts, all sorts of Crape. Choice of Druggets, Shalloons, Padua and other Serges, Plushes, Alamodes &ct all at reasonable rates.

For us, three hundred years later, these items have the appeal of the archaic; in both style and subject matter they are engagingly out of our world. But we must remind ourselves that for Pepys they were in no wise quaint. They were as commonplace and unremarkable as our own ephemera, and his keeping and caring for them must be put down to a special far-sightedness.

As we have noted, a major element in the Pepys library is the collection of printed ballads. We cannot leave those upper rooms at Magdalene College without a closer look at these, some of the earliest examples of collectible ephemera.

The popular ballad had been a feature of daily life in Britain long before Pepys's time. As with modern popular music ballads reflected everyday basics: love, sacred and profane; life, death, fame and fortune; crime and punishment; romance, wit and bawdry. At first a purely oral tradition, the birth of printing had brought it wider currency and continuity. Though much of it was scurrilous—often frankly obscene—it was early the subject of serious study as a form of social-history record. (It was also the subject of much official displeasure; the street ballad-monger was at various times classed with beggars, idlers and rogues as gaol-fodder.)

The output of printed balladry was enormous. Sold in the streets, at fairs and country markets, they were everyone's pleasure. As well as being 'read to pieces' from hand to hand, they were pasted up in cottages and pubs, and used in the end as firelighters. They were the one universally available item of printed matter produced and consumed in quantity.

True to his nature as a collector, Pepys classified and arranged his ballads by theme: *Devotion and morality; History, True and Fabulous; Tragedy—viz Murders,*

Playing cards were among the firs[t] products to require packaging. Th[e] wrapper design, dating from the la[te] seventeenth century, is among the items in the Pepys collection of ephemera at Magdalene College, Cambridge.

The Pepys Collection includes numerous early advertising items, including (above) a broadside for a new suction pump 'for the speedy and easy quenching fires and draining ponds' and some 40 tradecards, of which a typical album page appears on the right. Note the compiler's effort to accommodate the twelve items within the sheet: the Virginia tobacco item in the top row has been turned sideways to fit the space available.

Executions, Judgments of God; State and Times; Love-Pleasant; ditto Unfortunate; Marriage, Cuckoldry, etc; Sea-Love, Gallantry & Actions; Drinking & Good Fellowshipp; Humour, Frollicks, etc. mixt. All human life was there . . .

Until about 1700 the popular ballad had been printed in the ubiquitous 'black letter', a printer's version of the broad-pen lettering of pre-printing times; the change from this to 'white letter' (type substantially the same as the book type-face of today) was a watershed. The black letter quickly became a symbol of the 'olden times', and even at the time ballad connoisseurs saw it as a mark of special collectibility. Also much appreciated was the use of the woodcut illustration, a convention which was in fact to continue for another two hundred years; though Pepys, for one, was under the impression it was on the way out. His title-page to the ballads reads:

> *My Collection of Ballads. Vol. 1. Begun by Mr Selden; improved by ye addition of many Pieces elder thereto in Time; and the whole continued to the year 1700. When the Form, till then peculiar thereto, viz^e^. of the Black Letter with Picturs, seems (for cheepness sake) wholly laid aside, for that of the White Letter without Pictures.*

The words 'begun by Mr Selden' convey an important truth: Samuel Pepys's interest in collecting ballads was unusual but not unique. John Selden had got there before him. Selden, jurist, historian and antiquary, is famed as a scholar and controversialist, but for the ephemerist his abiding memorial is a single, if wordy, aphorism, a remark he is said to have made shortly before his death in 1654. It is recorded by his secretary, Richard Milward, in *Table Talk* (1689), under the heading 'Libells'—the name given to transient matter of all kinds:

> *Though some may make slight of Libells, yet you may see by them how the wind sitts; as, take a straw, and throw it upp into the aire, you shall see by that w[ch] way the wind is. W[ch] you shall not doe by casting upp a stone—More solid things do not show the complexion of the times so well as Ballads and libells.*

This passage has beome the very touchstone of the ephemerist's philosophy (and indeed is enshrined in the motto of The Ephemera Society, *E stipula ventum*: From the straw, the wind), and Selden's collection of such *stipulae*, his own Ballads and Libells, ranks first in the annals of the care and study of ephemera.

First though he was, Selden's role remains a shadowy one. Though a man of incisive mind and method, a man above all of antiquarian and historical interest, he seems to have left no record of his collection or of any evidential use he may have put it to. Nor is there any record of how the collection found its way to Pepys.

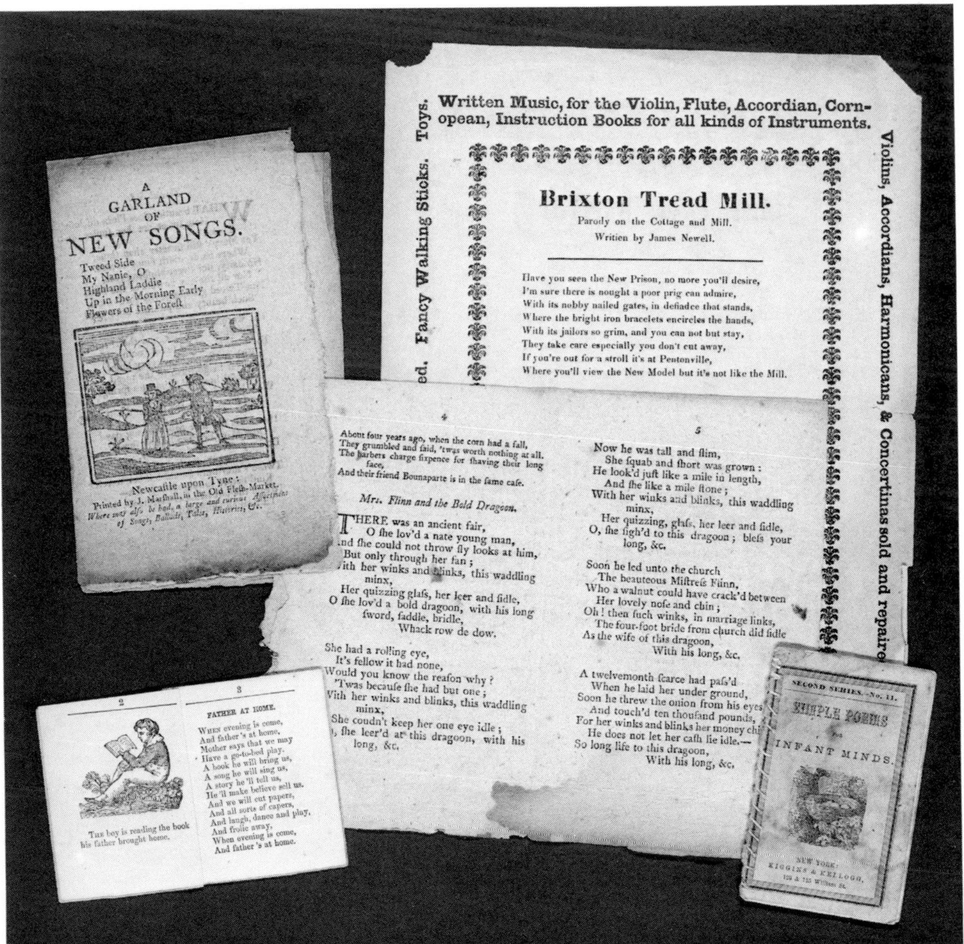

Street literature, in the form of ballads, 'garlands' and children's chapbooks, has attracted the attention of scholars from an early date. Examples are found in the collections of Selden, Pepys, Bagford, and in later times John Johnson and Leslie Shepard. The tradition is unbroken, from the collected garlands of the seventeenth century to the advertising parodies of the 1840s and 50s. Chapbooks and ballads were also popular in America: the little book Simple Poems for Infant Minds *(below right) appeared as one of a series, in New York in the 1850s. It was customary, as in this case, for the reader to sew the loose pages together with thread.*

John Bagford (1650–1716), addicted 'rescuer' of ballads, title pages and general ephemera, was described by bibliographer Dibdin as 'the most hungry and rapacious of all book and print collectors . . . He spared neither the most delicate nor the most costly specimens'. His collection is at once remarkable and deplorable.

When Selden died at 70, Pepys was just 21; it is unlikely that they met and Pepys must have acquired it, we must assume, in his later years of affluence, perhaps in the 1670s or 80s.

Also unrecorded is the proportion of the whole Pepys ballad collection that was Selden's portion. The expression 'begun by Mr Selden' in Pepys's title-piece suggests perhaps a few hundred out of the final total of some 1800. Of these, a substantial number would have been in black letter, the total figure of black-letter items in the ballad collection is 1376. It is said that more than half of this collection consists of unique surviving specimens: again, it is not certain how many of these came from Selden.

Though Selden clearly came first, it is to Samuel Pepys that the ephemerist turns for a father figure—Pepys the ephemera generalist, the dedicated collector of social-history evidence, the snapper-up of tradecards and serving girls, the engaging hero-scallywag. It must come as no surprise that, regardless of his foibles, The Ephemera Society in 1980 named their Gold Medal after him. The Society's Samuel Pepys Medal for Outstanding Contributions to Ephemera Studies is a tribute to the man as well as to its modern-day recipients.

Not quite so well-treasured is the memory of another seventeenth-century collector, also a ballad-fancier, and also in some senses of the word, an ephemera generalist. His name was John Bagford. He is the man least likely to have a medal named after him, though all are agreed that he made his mark.

Brought up as a shoemaker in Blackfriars in the 1650s and 60s, he early acquired a taste for books, a taste which was to lead him to fame in two capacities. One was as compiler of the Bagford Ballads, and the other as the book-world's all-time *bête noire*. The one, as Richard Garnett has it in the *Dictionary of National Biography* 'entitled him to the gratitude of all antiquarians and lovers of English verse' and the other, the enormous collection of title-pages and other fragments in sixty-four volumes folio, 'procured him the no less emphatic maledictions of all who object to the mutilation of books'.

Bagford, a man of virtually no education, became a free-lance book scout. Working on commission for dealers and booklovers, he ferreted out volumes from bookshops, antiquarians, attics and cupboards. In the course of his travels, which took him a number of times to the Continent, he became acquainted with the world of literature, bibliography, publishing and bookselling at large; his interests extended to prints and literary curiosities and printed ephemera. He became well-known as a self-educated but honest and reliable bibliophile. Before long he was undertaking commissions for such luminaries as Sir Hans Sloane, the Bishop of Ely and the Earl of Oxford, and he was among the eminent group that revived the Society of Antiquaries in 1707. He was reputed to have an extensive knowledge of paper and binding and was also thought to have had some practical experience as a printer. (This last, however, may have been confined to setting up a hand-press in a booth on the ice at a frost fair.)

Like Pepys, he became fascinated with the social-history content of the printed ballad. He collected them in the 1670s and 80s for his clients and for himself. In course of time, it is said, he may even have stolen them. Gordon Gerould, in his book *The Ballad of Tradition* (1932) refers to the collection of another balladeer of the period, Anthony Wood, whose collection, housed in the Ashmolean Museum, had become curiously depleted. Says Gerould; quoted in Leslie Shepard's *The Broadside Ballad* (1978):

> The only rival of Pepys as a collector in his own time was . . . Anthony Wood, who died in 1695. Wood was less happy than Pepys, however, in the fate of what he garnered, for only 279 items remain in his collection. The evidence is fairly clear that

> one John Bagford, in the service of Robert Harley, the first Earl of Oxford, stole on a grand scale from the Ashmolean Museum, to which Wood had bequeathed his ballads. Harley's acquisitions . . . filled two volumes, while Bagford had three volumes of his own. Towards the end of the eighteenth century the third Duke of Roxburghe, who at the time owned Harley's collection, added another great volume, largely made up of material likewise abstracted from Wood's papers. Who served the Duke in this ignoble business has not been discovered. Presumably he did not soil his hands by stealing the broadsides for himself . . .

It is clear that Shepard shares Gerould's view, as do other experts. Bagford is not above suspicion. (It is interesting to note, by the way, that among Bagford's many customers, as reported by Robert Latham in his Companion Volume to the Diary, was Samuel Pepys. Could Pepys too have acquired stolen property?)

Whatever the truth about Bagford's ballads, there are no two ways about his other collecting interest, his material for a comprehensive history of printing.

In 1707 he published his *Proposals for printing an Historical Account of that most universally celebrated, as well as useful Art of Typography*. This was to be illustrated by actual examples, principally of title-pages, removed from some hundreds of published books. Additional material would be bookplates, engravings, decorative printer's initials, tailpieces, rules, borders—all the ingredients of the printer's art from Gutenberg to Bagford's own day. It was to be a truly monumental work, never before attempted.

In point of fact, he had been collecting material for the book in the 1690s. Assiduously, ruthlessly, Bagford laid about him. From libraries, bookshops, rubbish tips, he culled his title-pages, illustrations, frontispieces, end-papers, bindings—anything remotely relevant to this most exciting *magnum opus*. He has been described as 'a literary monster'; 'the scourge of the book world'; 'the most hungry and rapacious of all book and print collectors'. William Blades, in *The Enemies of Books* (1888) described him as 'a wicked old biblioclast . . . one of the founders of the Society of Antiquaries who . . . went about the country from library to library tearing away title-pages . . .'.

Title-pages, conceived quite rightly as a book's 'vital organ', were Bagford's main quarry. These he sorted by nationality, town, period, printer etc., interlarding them with a wild assortment of printed and handwritten ephemera. The result, some centuries later, is a number of volumes of seventeenth- and early eighteenth-century printed matter, a miscellany almost too painful to behold. 'That they are of service as materials in compiling a history of printing cannot be denied,' says Blades, 'but the destruction of many rare books was the result, and more than counterbalanced any benefit bibliographers will ever receive from them . . . You cannot bless the memory of the antiquarian shoemaker John Bagford.'

It is certainly difficult to assess Bagford's reasoning in his selection of material. Cheek-by-jowl with the rarest of early title-pages are the most irrelevant of commercial oddments, lottery puffs, bale labels, playing cards and price lists—material far removed, it seems, from the history of printing.

For the bibliophile the collection is at once fascinating and disturbing. For those intent on the ephemera among the plunder, it is strangely compelling. The miscellany includes items of predictably bookish interest—type-sheets, bookplates, paper specimens and price-lists, ream labels, specimens of end-papers, watermarks etc.—but the range of general material is extensive. There are indulgences, proclamations, auction catalogues, maps, tradecards, handbills, almanacs, 'lost' notices, writing books, quack medicine items and specimens of music paper—a goodly haul of everyday oddments of the turn of the seventeenth century. (We may also note an item in support of the image of Bagford as practical printer—a frost-fair keepsake, printed on the Thames by J. Bagford.)

As we peruse the collection we seem to see the compiler seduced from the particular to the general, from an impossibly unmanageable project to one even more unruly.

It must be said that although there were many who marvelled at the Bagford phenomenon, and some who sorrowed at the failure of his Grand Design, many more were horrified at the enormity of his enterprise and depredation and were

The tradecard collections of Pepys, Bagford and Heal show close identity of interest. These early examples, common to all three, are rarely found elsewhere.

greatly relieved that it came to nothing. Bagford's grasp of history, grammar and spelling left much to be desired, and it was the general opinion that he was the one enthusiast wholly incompetent to write *The History of Printing*.

But whatever his shortcomings, Bagford showed tremendous single-mindedness and tenacity. His collection of printed ballads, in three volumes, vies with that of Pepys and other major collectors, and his title-page collection—albeit a bibliographical breakers' yard—has saving graces. It enshrines the existence of volumes otherwise unknown.

Among other notable collectors of ballads was Thomas Percy (1729–1811). Bishop Percy, poet and churchman, came upon the ballad by accident. While visiting the house of a friend, one Humphrey Pitt, he noticed a bundle of old papers 'lying dirty on the floor . . . in the parlour'. It turned out that the maids had been using the papers as fire-lighters, so Percy rescued them, and took them home to study. He discovered that they were manuscript copies, in early seventeenth-century writing, of ancient poems.

A man with some historical sense, and himself a poet, Percy became keenly interested in his find, and began casting about for other such works, handwritten or printed. Numerous friends, among them Garrick and Goldsmith, came up with contributions, and he and a colleague researched the college libraries (not least, we note, the Pepysian Library at Cambridge).

The upshot was the publication in 1765 of *Reliques of Ancient English Poetry*, a transcription of some of the earliest ballads in English, edited (and in some cases 'improved') by Percy. The work was severely criticized for its want of academic integrity, the editor's interventions proving too much for the purists. But it went to a second, third and fourth edition, marking an epoch in the history of English literature.

The Percy papers surfaced again in 1865, when the original folio from which Percy had his material was re-edited—minus percyisms—by Professor Hales and Dr Furnivall. The papers themselves were returned to their private resting place in family archives. They were to re-emerge when, as we shall see, Percy's great grand-daughter, Constance Meade, brought them to the attention of John Johnson, Printer to the University of Oxford.

America's first great ephemerist was born a generation or so after Percy. He was to become not only the country's Grand Old Man of ephemera, but founder of one of its most illustrious institutions. Isaiah Thomas (1749–1831) was taken from his mother at the age of six by the Overseers of the Poor at Boston and apprenticed to a printer. It was a good move: the child grew up to be a first-class printer, an astute editor and publisher, and a dedicated patriot. His newspaper, *The Massachusetts Spy*, was a leading voice in the conflict with the British, and he was profoundly aware of

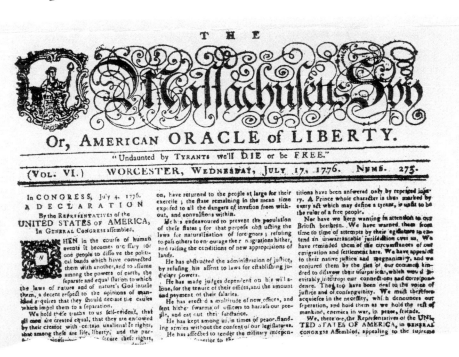

THE

Massachusetts Spy

Or, AMERICAN ORACLE of LIBERTY.

"Undaunted by TYRANTS we'll DIE or be FREE."

(VOL. VI.) WORCESTER, WEDNESDAY, JULY 17, 1776. NUMB. 275.

In CONGRESS, July 4, 1776.

A DECLARATION

By the REPRESENTATIVES of the

UNITED STATES OF AMERICA,

In GENERAL CONGRESS assembled.

WHEN in the course of human events it becomes necessary for one people to dissolve the political bands which have connected them with another, and to assume among the powers of earth, the separate and equal station to which the laws of nature and of nature's God intitle them, a decent respect to the opinions of mankind requires that they should declare the causes which impel them to a separation.

We hold these truths to us self-evident, that all men are created equal, that they are endowed by their creator with certain unalienable rights, that among these are life, liberty, and the pursuit of happiness—That to secure these rights, [illegible]

[illegible] on, have returned to the people at large for their exercise; the state remaining in the mean time exposed to all the dangers of invasion from without, and convulsions within.

He has endeavoured to prevent the population of these states; for that perpose obstructing the laws for naturalization of foreignors; refusing to pass others to encourage their migrations hither, and raising the conditions of new appropriatons of lands.

He has obstructed the administration of justice, by refusing his assent to laws for establishing judiciary powers.

He has made judges dependent on his will alone, for the tenure of their offices, and the amount and payment of their salaries.

He has erected a multitude of new offices, and sent hither swarms of officers to harrass our people, and eat out their substance.

He has kept among us, in times of peace, standing armies without the consent of our legislatures.

He has affected to render the military independent of and superior to the [illegible]

[illegible] titions have been answered only by repeated injury. A Prince whose character is thus marked by every act which may define a tyrant, is unfit to be the ruler of a free people.

Nor have we been wanting in attention to our British brethren. We have warned them from time to time of attempts by their legislature to extend an unwarrantable jurisdiction over us. We have reminded them of the circumstances of our emigration and settlement here. We have appealed to their native justice and magnanimity, and we conjured them by the ties of our common kindred to disavow their usurpations, which would inevitably interrupt our connections and correspondence. They too have been deaf to the voice of justice and of consanguinity. We must therefore acquiesce in the necessity, which denounces our seperation, and hold them as we hold the rest of mankind, enemies in war, in peace, friends.

We, therefore, the Representatives of the UNITED STATES OF AMERICA, in GENERAL CONGRESS Assembled, appealing to the supreme [illegible]

Isaiah Thomas's Massachusetts Spy *had a major propaganda role i the drive for independence. The iss for July, 1776, under the motto 'Undaunted by tyrants, we'll die o be free', carries one of the earliest printings of the Declaration of Independence. The paper was published in Boston until April 1775; after that date it appeared in Worcester, which became Thomas'. home and later the home of the American Antiquarian Society, Thomas's legacy to the nation.*

the historical role of the press at large, both as influence and record.

By the time he retired, in 1802, he had set himself to locate and preserve the record of the origins of the nation he had helped to make. One of the first things he did was to make the rounds of the newspapers of revolutionary days, buying up their files. He extended the idea: one day he walked into Boston's biggest music shop and bought a copy of every ballad on their shelves. In time the range extended to printed matter of almost every description.

In 1812, the year of the Anglo-American war, with the British cannon menacing Boston harbour, he smuggled his press out of town and set up beyond their range at his home in Worcester, some 40 miles inland. There he founded the American Antiquarian Society, the country's first national historical repository. With 27 like-minded men, its first members, the Society resolved to 'collect and preserve every variety of book, pamphlet and manuscript that might be valuable in illustrating any and all parts of American history', and to make this material available 'for the enlightenment of future generations'.

Future generations have not been slow to profit from the vision of the printer's apprentice. Not only in the field of newspapers and music, the Society provides scholars and students with access to an immense store of printed and manuscript materials. Its collections include almanacs, bookplates, songbooks and music, type-specimen material, stereocards and postcards, menus, theatre posters, rewards of merit, watchpapers, ballads, proclamations, lottery tickets, booksellers' labels, telegram forms, valentines, sailing cards, watermarks and tradecards.

The American Antiquarian Society is the nation's largest institution of its kind. Today, with five miles of shelving, two million newspapers and countless hundreds of thousands of items of general ephemera, it is a realization beyond even the dreams of Thomas himself.

Though separated by a hundred years and 3000 miles, Isaiah Thomas and John Bagford had two points of identity. Both were instrumental in setting up a society devoted to the preservation and study of 'antiquities' (Thomas's society bore the name 'Antiquarian' in emulation of Bagford's Society of Antiquities in London). And both were involved in writing histories of printing. Bagford's did not appear, Thomas's did. Isaiah Thomas's *History of Printing in America* was published in 1810. It went to a new edition in 1875 and another in 1952 and remains today the standard work on the subject.

; a printer, Isaiah Thomas saw the nportance of epehemeral printing as part of the evidential record. Like arlier collectors he saw the value of the popular ballad, and as a ewspaper man a major interest was the weekly and daily journal of ecord. His scope rapidly broadened, and today the collection embraces ephemera from watchpapers to telegram forms.

But for the ephemerist, Thomas's real strength is in his view of the value of transient printed record. In the Valhalla of ephemerists there are many who brought their enthusiasm to institutional status but few, if any, whose vision is enshrined in an organization of the size and standing of the American Antiquarian Society. Apart from Isaiah Thomas himself, the Society has had a distinguished roll of membership, among them twelve Presidents of the United States, as well as such magical names as Alexander Graham Bell, Robert Fulton, Henry Cabot Lodge, Daniel Webster and Calvin Coolidge, who was president of the Society in 1933. For a pauper apprentice, quite a following.

As we have seen in the cases of Selden, Pepys and others, a common interest has been the popular ballad (Thomas too counted balladry among his fields), and we should not leave the matter without at least a passing glance at the poet and novelist Sir Walter Scott, much of whose output was concerned with the ballad form, and who was himself as keen a collector of printed ballads as anyone. As it turned out, however, his collection achieved neither renown nor, apparently, survival. There is no record of what became of it; it survives only by reflection in the writer's work. (Scott showed his hand, though, in his novel *The Antiquary* [1816], whose central character collects 'broadsides and old black-letter ballads'; here the Walter Scott collection is obliquely aired—a concession to the collector's pride of ownership.)

There were other enthusiasts. The British Museum and the British Library between them bear evidence of their enterprise. The names of Fillenham, Ames, Franks, Fielden and Francis Place have left their mark. Many of these collections are extensive. The tradecards of Sarah Banks, for example, run to some 6000 items, and the Joseph Ames collection, hard on the heels of Bagford, includes 7425 title-pages.

It was toward the latter part of the nineteenth century before the more generalized collections of ephemera began to emerge, at first in Britain, later in the United States.

The early 1920s brought two remarkable figures to the fore, Bella Landauer in New York, and John Johnson at the University of Oxford. More or less simultaneously, though unknown to each other, the two individuals began to collect ephemera.

For Mrs Landauer, a widowed New York housewife, the story starts with her acquisition in 1923 of a collection of bookplates. Though she had no interest in bookplates she bought them out of sympathy for the vendor, a hard-up youth who desperately needed a hundred dollars. It later emerged that the bookplates had been stolen, but by the time Mrs Landauer had made her peace with the rightful owner she had become irretrievably addicted, not only to bookplates but to an ever-extending range of printed ephemera.

Bella C. Landauer (1875–1960), New York housewife and First Lady of American advertising ephemera. 'I still marvel that the ephemera, which for so many years has been spurned, now has finally become important and desirable.'

In the course of time she became a well-known browser in antiquarian bookshops. Dealers and friends began to offer her items, and she came to know a number of curators and librarians to whom she shortly began to present duplicate material. Her circle of acquaintance expanded. So did her collection.

It was soon a collection of collections. It included tradecards, advertising fans, valentines, membership cards, almanacs, labels, invitations, telegrams, lottery tickets, rail passes, posters, catalogues, music—as well as thematic collections on journalism, fashion, politics, aeronautics, medicine, theatre, New York City, and so on. There was no stopping her.

Her success was her problem. Where to store it all? At length, from among her many friends in the field, Alexander Wall, director of the New-York Historical Society came up with an offer of a disused kitchen under the eaves of the Society's building at Central Park West. She accepted.

In that room for many years she struggled on her own with the task of soaking off and washing specimens by the hundred and thousand, sorting, mounting and annotating in a one-woman collector's marathon. A major concern was the patience of the Historical Society guards, who toiled up the stairs of the three-storey building with endless buckets of hot water for the work of soaking. With only occasional lapses, they stayed with it. It was a lonely task: 'There was no telephone in my scant quarters,' she recalls, 'and except for two exhibitions in the spring of 1929 and summer of 1930, no visitor ever examined my collection or saw my pathetic domain ...'.

But the Bella C. Landauer collection was to become a world-famous institution. In 1939, when extensions to the building allowed, she was given more space, and research and educational visits became easier. The collecting process continued, however, and it became logical to hive off certain portions of the material to specialist bodies elsewhere. It was thus that a large quantity of early aeronautical material—one of Mrs Landauer's major interests—found its way to the Institute of Aeronautical Science (thence, later, to the Smithsonian Institution). Other portions are lodged in the Metropolitan Museum of Art, at Dartmouth College Library and the Baker Library, Hanover, New Hampshire.

Mrs Landauer was not content to gather material. As well as making it available for research and study, she published small selections from the collection. These, on

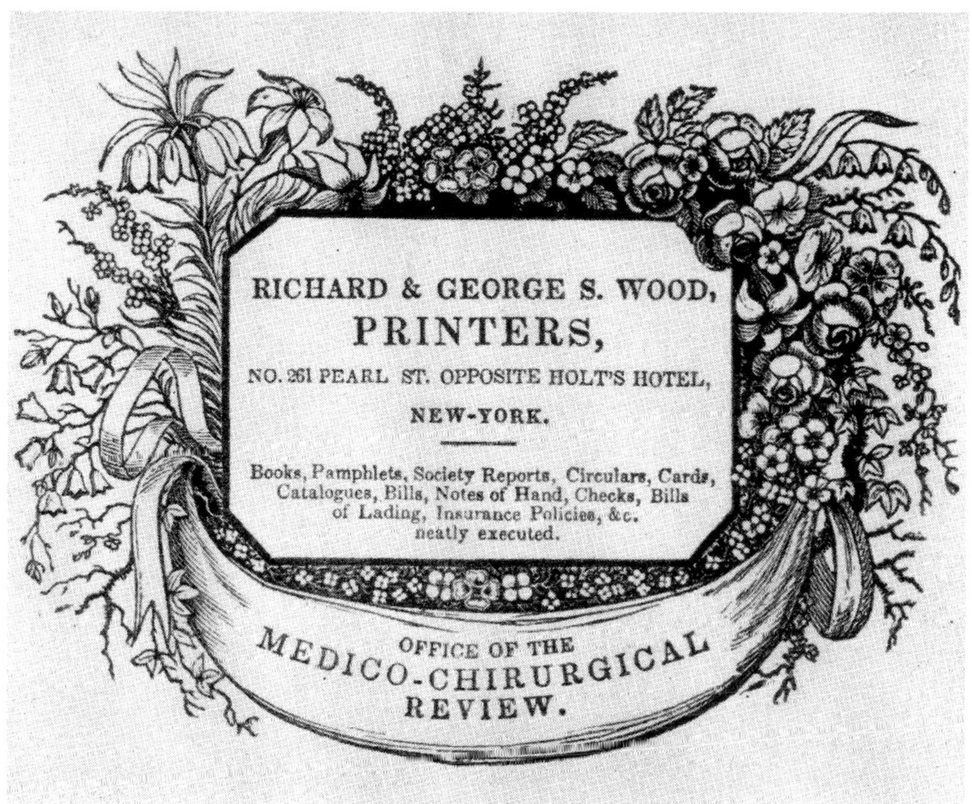

With its hyphenated town name (retained to this day in the title of the New-York Historical Society), is 1840s tradecard recalls America's re-chromolitho advertising era. It is among the earlier specimens in the hundreds of such items in the Bella Landauer collection.

a variety of themes, and each introduced with a few paragraphs of enthusiasm, presented two or three dozen illustrations. Typical titles are *Some Alcoholic Americana* (1932) and *Pre-Frigidaire Ice Ephemera* (1943). The booklets appeared at more or less yearly intervals over 30 years. Published privately (or latterly by the New-York Historical Society), they present a fragmentary view of a collection which, by the mid-1950s numbered some 400,000 items.

Bella Landauer was a woman to be reckoned with. She is recollected, in her collecting hey-day, as an irrepressible driving force—warm-hearted, dominant, single-minded—of independent means and boundless enthusiasm.

Her collecting bout lasted in all 40 years. Luckily, it was very early on—just five years after she had started—that she had a letter from John Johnson, Printer to the University of Oxford. It was the beginning of a long correspondence and a close collecting association.

And it is to John Johnson, the Oxford ephemerist, that we now turn. Johnson's collection of printed ephemera had started, almost casually, at about the same time as Bella's. In his case, however, there is no identifiable occasion, no purchase of a collection of bookplates or anything else, by which to date it.

Its origins may be seen as three-fold. One component came from the sands of ancient Egypt, the other two from within the University.

It was in Egypt, excavating on behalf of the Egypt Exploration Society, that Johnson found at first hand the excitement of ephemera as historical evidence. Based at Magdalen College, Oxford, as assistant to the papyrologists Grenfell and Hunt, Johnson spent the summers immediately before World War I digging rubbish mounds in the desert, and the winters writing up his finds in Oxford. The work in the desert was exacting; the Society had virtually no funds, and he served as organizer, manager, caterer, banker, paymaster, photographer and digger all in one. His health suffered. But in the meantime he had become aware of the broader significance of what he was doing: in a letter in later years to Strickland Gibson, Bodley's sub-librarian, he wrote:

> ... I was spending my winters with large gangs of fellahin, digging the rubbish mounds of Graeco-Roman cities ... for the written materials—the waste paper—of those ages ... Often I used to look over those dark and crumbling sites and wonder what could be done to treat the background of our own English civilization with the same minute care with which we scholars were treating the ancient.

Embellished with objects of art and antiquity, this was the view throug the series of four compartments or 'cabins' in which John Johnson established his collection of ephemera. Starting as a more or les unofficial sideshow to his work as Printer to Oxford University, the collection came to dominate his life. Throughout the war years, 1939–45, he slept nightly on a truckle bed among the exhibits, working on the collection night and morning, and sometimes appearing in the mornings in dressing gown and pyjamas.

Further health troubles, and in 1914 the outbreak of World War I, brought him back to Oxford, unfit for military service, but available. He was appointed Assistant Secretary of Oxford University Press, a post for which his academic and administrative background alone fitted him. He knew no more than the next man about publishing.

He went to it with a will, however, and was soon involved in the printing and production of new titles for the press. A special interest was the educational field, and he found himself collecting items of printed ephemera as illustrations for school books. The more ordinary these items, the more compelling they were in their new context, he found. Soon, a school history illustrated in this way caught on, selling some 40,000 copies a year. Ephemera had entered Johnson's life not just as an academic concept, but as a professional instrument.

In a passage quoted in Michael Turner's exhibition catalogue *The John Johnson Collection* (1971) we have an insight into the impact of ephemera on Johnson's personal life, 'At that time in my house, let me confess that there was the growing material of illustration for a book under each bed, a primitive and not unsatisfactory dodge for keeping the material apart . . .'.

John de Monins Johnson (1882–1956), Printer to the University of Oxford, and founder of the John Johnson Collection of Printed Ephemera, Oxford. Now the richest collection of jobbing printing in existence, it was moved to the Bodleian Library in 1968.

We have seen two of the three contributory factors in the inception of the John Johnson collection—Egypt and educational publishing. The third element was Johnson's appointment in 1925 as Printer to the University, a post as prestigious as it must have been daunting. It was another appointment for which on the face of it he was wholly unqualified, but, as soon appeared, eminently suitable.

It came about then that it was in the context of printing history, and the history of the Press and the University as a whole, that Johnson began to acquire further printed matter. Imperceptibly, collecting themes and categories widened to encompass not only printing and Oxford but virtually the whole of human experience.

He pursued his duties in the printing works (bringing it, incidentally, from the candle-lit nineteenth century into the 1920s), and as a more or less unofficial side-show he built up the Collection of Ephemeral Printing. He installed it, little by little, in spare space on the premises of Oxford University Press. He was well placed. With the facilities and informal help of a great institution at his elbow he availed himself of resources that few private individuals could have matched. For the construction of shelving, cupboards and other such furnishings he was able to call on carpenters and joiners; file boxes and folders were covered and labelled in spare moments in the bindery—even the paper and paste for mounting specimens came from the stores of the University Press.

It should be said at once that the collection was never seen as anything but University property. The collector's use of the Press's facilities was 'unofficial', but it was in no wise covert. If there was a division of interest between the collector and the Press, it was in the matter of priorities. Collecting and storing ephemera had not been part of the original Johnson job-description, and the Press viewed the growing collection with something less than enthusiasm.

As the collection's reputation grew it attracted interest and support from outside. Johnson had a special knack of appreciation: visitors were welcomed, gifts were warmly acknowledged, acolytes encouraged. By the early 1930s the collection had a personal circle of well-wishers around the world. Specialized subject collections were acquired (watchpapers, calling cards, banknotes, postal history etc.) and in a number of cases people contributed money.

Notable among benefactors was Constance Meade, one of a group of ladies who in 1930 visited the collection while attending a conference in Oxford. Miss Meade's visit proved almost providential. She was greatly impressed, both by the collection and its custodian, and later bethought herself of some old family papers, items belonging to her great-great grandfather, which might be of interest. As we have seen, Miss Meade's great-great grandfather was none other than Thomas Percy (he of the ballads and the intrusive pen).

The 'family papers' proved to be part of the fall-out of the bishop's collection, and Johnson was delighted to accept a portion of the material, the rest of it going to the British Museum and the Bodleian Library. Perhaps more importantly, Johnson acquired a life-long supporter and benefactress. She was still devotedly committed to the collection when he died, a quarter of a century later. He named the collection after her (though it was to be re-named after him when it was moved from the Press to the Bodleian in 1968).

Through Bella Landauer, with whom he started to correspond in the late 1920s, the collection profited from a lively injection of transatlantic enthusiasm. She also contributed ephemera—and, as time went on, minor gifts to Johnson and his family. In the years of World War II, mindful of shortages in Britain, she sent parcels of vitamin pills, chocolate and winter woollies. Though she visited the collection two or three times, their relationship, and their interchange of information and ephemera, was largely postal. It represented, however, an early Anglo-American link in the field of ephemera, a link that was to remain undeveloped until the emergence of Britain's Ephemera Society, and its offshoot The Ephemera Society of America, some half a century later.

Lilian Thrussell, Johnson's lifelo assistant, is seen here on the occas of her acceptance of the Samuel Pepys Medal of the Ephemera Society in November 1987. Mrs Thrussell received the medal on h own behalf and as a posthumous award to John Johnson for their jo work in setting up the Johnson Collection. She continued to look after the collection until the late 1960s, some 20 years after Johnson's death.

Not least of Johnson's supporters was Lilian Thrussell, the gardener's daughter who graduated from tending the Johnson family's rockery at Old Headington to looking after the collection. Now famed as 'the girl who came in from the garden' (*Ephemerist*, June 1986), she was eventually to share with Johnson The Ephemera Society's Samuel Pepys medal, accepting the award on her own behalf and that of Johnson, 31 years after his death.

Mrs Thrussell's introduction to ephemera had been through a casual chat with Mrs Johnson. Over a cup of coffee the lady of the house confided that she had again been unable to take a bath; the bathtub was afloat with soaked-off labels, tickets, stationery and other oddments.

The gardener's daughter took over the job of washing, drying and mounting the material. Forsaking the rockery, she became the collection's personal guardian and, over the years, its expert and enthusiast. She stayed not only as unofficial custodian, but as guide and counsellor to visiting scholars. In the course of time, dozens of writers and researchers were to avow their debt to her knowledge of the collection and her readiness to help with their projects. Her name appears among the acknowledgements in numerous publications.

She was perhaps Johnson's least expected and, as it turned out, most valued personal asset, and she remained with the collection under the successive curatorships of Harry Carter, Charles Batey and Michael Turner, until the late 1960s, some 20 years after Johnson's death. Her name takes its place in the Roll of Honour of pioneer ephemerists.

Dr John Johnson, who set the scene for so many enthusiasts and helpers, was a unique phenomenon. His success came not only from his single-mindedness but, as we have seen, from his ability to gain the interest and loyalty of others. He moved in a world where, in general, the systematic collecting of such items as menus and turnpike tickets was seen to be—at least—eccentric. Within the precincts of an ancient university it was scarcely credible. And yet this solemn-faced man, well-known for his ill-assorted and ill-fitting clothes, a man of whom the more timid were actually frightened, won friends and influenced people in a remarkable way.

In the specially built 'cabins' which housed the collection, and in which much of the work of sorting and mounting was carried out, he received notable visitors from the world of graphic design, printing and social history, regaling them with his enthusiasm. It was here in the cabins that the word 'ephemera' began to gain currency and it was from here, in a letter to Gerald Morice in February 1940, that Johnson appears to have used the word 'ephemerist' for the first time in its present sense. Referring to the need to help a collector in distant Malvern, 'a poor old chap in his ice-box on the Malvern Hills', Johnson says 'real ephemerists are rare and are worthy of support'.

The cabins were not only, as Holbrook Jackson called them, 'a Sanctuary of Printing', they were a haven of civilization. Into it came, as well as printed waifs and strays, rescued panelling, pieces of carving, a corinthian pilaster or two, and lettering pieces. To this quiet setting Johnson at length brought some two and a half thousand leather-labelled boxes and portfolios of ephemera. The cabins had started as a single unit, a room built into a spare space in the printing works—then another and another, as the collection grew. In 1968 there were four such rooms. They formed a unique hall of ephemera studies, a place of pilgrimage and a memorial to the man. But by the end of 1968 the cabins had gone; the collection was moved to the new Bodleian building and the space reclaimed for the Press.

The monument remains however, as does the continuing pilgrimage. In the new Bodleian, today's curators carry the Johnson vision forward, tending the collection, guiding visitors. Writing to a friend, a contributing collector, in the 1950s, Johnson said, 'Sometimes I feel a little disheartened. But more often than not I feel heartened, and believe that you and Lil and I and some of the others will some day have created a history of the ordinary English people . . .'. The day has surely come, and now the rest of us know it too.

At a different level, and in a more restricted sense, another major institutional collection serves as monument. The institution is the Metropolitan Museum of Art, and the monument is to Jefferson R. Burdick.

Burdick was employed in the 1930s and 40s in an electrical company in Syracuse. A lifelong sufferer from arthritis, which seriously afflicted his fingers, he nevertheless carried out delicate manipulations in the assembly of specialized switching equipment. He also collected 'trade and souvenir cards and other paper Americana'.

Unlike Johnson, he had started collecting as a child. He had begun at the age of ten, with 'insert cards', the pictorial series cards given with cigarettes, chewing gum, coffee and other products, but he later broadened his range to include other types of card—advertising cards, tradecards, postcards, playing cards, greeting cards, 'clipper cards' (sailing notices), stereo cards, visiting cards and poster cards (large advertising cards used in public service vehicles).

Jefferson Burdick, schoolboy collector of cigarette cards and other modern-day items, was the first such enthusiast to be taken seriously by one of the world's great museums. These match folders are typical specimens from the Burdick Collection at the Metropolitan Museum of Art. They date (l to r) from c.1930, 1953, 1937 and c.1935.

Later the scope of the collection increased further still until it also embraced pin buttons, poster stamps, rewards of merit, matchfolders, calendars, labels, tobacco tags, sheet music, paper dolls, weighing-machine cards, paper money and cigar-packaging material.

Burdick lived on his own, spending all his time and most of his meagre earnings on his collection, while his health continued to deteriorate. He took to writing small publications based on the collection, and with a group of colleagues in the 1960s produced *The American Card Catalog*, a compendious listing and price guide. In a further indication of the author's widening scope, the guide carried a brief appendix on yet other forms of ephemera. This included bookplates, bookmarks, illustrated envelopes, song sheets, almanacs, business stationery, menus and programmes and other miscellaneous Americana. We perceive how, over the years, the schoolboy collector of cigarette- and chewing-gum-cards grew into the general ephemerist.

As with Bella Landauer, John Johnson and many other collectors, Burdick found himself obliged to have his collection 'adopted'. In Burdick's case, failing health made the matter doubly pressing.

A. Hyatt Mayor, then director of the Print Department of New York's Metropolitan Museum of Art, has described the arrival on a day in 1947, of Jefferson R. Burdick, requesting the Museum to take over. Arthritis had so stiffened his joints and warped his fingers that 'even so simple an act as putting on his hat cost him a painful minute to contrive'. In spite of his infirmities, it was clear that no-one else had Burdick's ability to continue the mounting and cataloguing that remained to be done. They came to an arrangement, not unlike that of Mrs Landauer at the New-York Historical Society: 'He brought his little oak desk from home and installed it in the only available corner of the crowded Print Department, which at once became the American headquarters of cartophiles from everywhere . . . We bought him more and more scrapbook binders . . . more and more pots of paste . . .'.

For upwards of fifteen years, Burdick was a fixture at his new post, struggling with his illness on one hand and the challenge of his task on the other. He just managed to complete the job in time. 'On the 10th of January 1963 he told us at five o'clock that he had mounted his last card. As he twisted himself into his overcoat he bade us goodbye . . . He added "I shan't be back".' The next day he walked from his lodgings to nearby University Hospital where, two months later, he died.

Hyatt Mayor said of him: 'On first meeting, one felt sorry for this racked, frail man . . . but pity quickly gave way to admiration—even envy—at his making so much of so bad a bargain. All in all, he triumphed more than many.'

Burdick's monument (and in a sense Hyatt Mayor's too) is a collection which is by far the largest section of ephemeral printing in the Print Department of the Metropolitan Museum of Art. It has been augmented by European material from the Landauer collection and by a substantial gathering of American manufacturers' illustrated catalogues of clothing, furniture, tableware, carriages and other products, bought by the Museum to round out the picture. Starting with Burdick's first cigarette cards, the collection has become a continuous record of promotional iconography in the United States.

Another collector whose interest started in a small way was Ambrose Heal, great grandson of an early nineteenth-century London furnishing tradesman. The original Heal establishment moved in 1840 from Rathbone Place, just off Oxford Street, to Tottenham Court Road, where it remains some 150 years later. The firm became famous for its furniture, and under Ambrose was developed into the country's foremost name in the field. Among ephemerists the name is doubly significant.

Ambrose Heal became interested in the history, not only of his own firm, but of

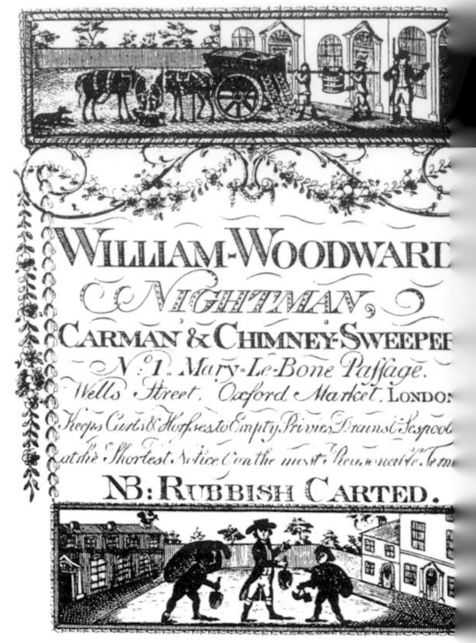

Ambrose Heal was fascinated by t many fragments of information to gleaned from tradecards. A typical example is this card for William Woodward, who 'keeps carts and horses to empty privies at the shortest notice . . .'

Famed as a furniture designer a manufacturer, Sir Ambrose H (1872–1959) was als distinguished student and collector the London tradecard. His intere extended to billheads, sh signboards and calligraphy, and wrote widely on these subjec

the furniture trade as a whole. Casually, he began to acquire historical evidence of early craftsmen, their firms, addresses and specialities—largely in the form of tradecards, billheads and labels. Soon he was collecting London tradesmen's material at large. In 1925 appeared his *London Tradesmen's Cards of the Eighteenth Century*, and this was followed in 1935 by *The London Goldsmiths*, a listing of the craftsmen's names and addresses, their signs and tradecards. In 1953 came *London Furniture Makers 1660–1840*, a lifetime's compilation, again with scores of tradecard illustrations.

Each of these books features tradecards from Heal's own collection which, by the time he bequeathed it to the British Museum, numbered some 1900 items. Apart from their interest as examples of eighteenth-century trade engraving, the cards provide frequent 'missing links' in the chain of historical detail, proving in some cases the only means of solving key problems of identification, succession, changes of address and so on.

The Heal collection is one of the most extensive of its kind in the world. It was brought together not simply as a collector's fancy but as a research instrument. In its present lodgement in the British Museum it is accompanied by many related items, including news cuttings, letters, manuscript shop bills, headed paper and reproductions, and the mounts of the specimens bear copious notes in Heal's hand. There are also boxes of his original lecture notes and general research material—not to mention four boxes of portraits of London shopkeepers and tradesmen, and 24 folders listing shop signs in eighteenth-century London.

Sir Ambrose (he was knighted in 1933) was the classic scholar/collector, fascinated by the material itself, assiduous in its analysis and organization, academically equal to the task of interpreting and presenting it.

Just as assiduous, if less well organized, was Heal's contemporary, Walter Harding. Born in 1883 'in a cottage on a little street just off London's Old Kent Road', Harding was taken by his parents at the age of four to Chicago. He never returned. However, he did send back the collection he amassed in his 86 years in America. It was shipped to the Bodleian—all 25 tons of it—where it now resides as his gift to the land of his birth, a unique collection of popular ballads, street literature, songs, poems, chapbooks, sheet music, song books, opera scores, and general musical ephemera.

Harding's first love was the song book—the popular song and the printed ballad. Like Pepys and Percy and Bagford before him, he saw these as the quintessence of the human condition. His collection started with a chest-high stack of loose music and ten bound volumes, which he bought in 1929 for four dollars. By 1973, when Bodley's experts arrived in Chicago to get its final measure, it had become a four-bedroomed houseful. Harding's detached house in a Chicago suburb was stacked from basement to roof with musical material of every conceivable kind.

There were estimated to be 6000 English chap-books, 5300 opera scores, 2000 French song books and 60–80,000 sheets of music. It took Michael Turner, then curator of the John Johnson collection, seven months to organize and supervise the removal of this acquisition of 60 years. It arrived at Oxford in 884 boxes; its value (anybody's guess) was put at 'maybe a million dollars'.

Lifetime collections of the Harding kind are by no means rare. The Warshaw Collection, housed in the Collection of Business Americana at the National Museum of American History, the life gatherings of Isadore Warshaw, a New York bookseller. Over decades, Warshaw accumulated American advertising of the nineteenth and twentieth centuries, finally selling the million-item collection to the Smithsonian Institution in 1967. It is still being sorted and catalogued.

Other collections, not necessarily lives' works, are no less redolent of their originators. In Britain's Guildhall Library there is the Roland Knaster collection of binders' and booksellers' tickets (the tiny labels formerly fixed to the inside covers of 'quality' volumes); the collection of watchpapers, and the Noble Collection, formed in the 1860s and 70s by the impressively named Theophilus Charles Noble, sometime Warden of the Ironmongers Company, historian, genealogist and ephemera-jackdaw. His gatherings are housed in some 40 solid box files, a major ingredient in the Guildhall's great London holdings.

On a high shelf in the Metropolitan Museum of Art in New York is a set of three handsomely bound volumes of British and European ephemera of the eighteenth and early nineteenth centuries. This fifteen-hundred-item collection provides a conspectus of everyday life of the period, including such offerings as shop lists, invitations, pin-papers, frost-fair keepsakes, tobacco papers, Gretna Green marriage certificates, sale catalogues, labels, and tickets.

The volumes are part of a major collection of ephemera made by Baron Leverhulme of Bolton le Moors (later Viscount Leverhulme), which was shipped out for sale in America on his death in 1925. Other portions of the collection are still to be found in private hands, but the three volumes in question, bought by Mrs Morris Hawkes in 1926, were presented by the purchaser in 1927 to the Metropolitan Museum of Art. By such tenuous links do eighteenth-century London tradecards appear in New York, and American songs and ballads make their way to the Bodleian.

Lodgement for today's private collections remains a matter of speculation: where, in 50 years' time will the researcher look for the collections of the latter part of the twentieth century? We think particularly of the notables: the Laura Seddon Greeting Card Collection; the Gardiner-Malpa collection of Rewards of Merit; the Peter Jackson London Collection; the Brian North Lee Collection of Bookplates and Labels; Brian Love's Charity File; the William Helfand Pharmaceutical History Collection—these and numerous others await the verdict of time.

From this brief review of ephemerists and their collections we may distil a number of common factors. Chief among these is the addictive nature of the activity. For whatever reason it begins—psychological imbalance or the coolest of socio-scientific curiosity—the collection appears sooner or later to take on an independent existence. Not only does it drive itself; it drives its curator.

The collection may bring out the best or the worst in the owner. It may induce unheard-of heights of discipline and tidiness, or depths of chaos and confusion. It may turn the collector into a shameless show-off, or into an inaccessible recluse. It

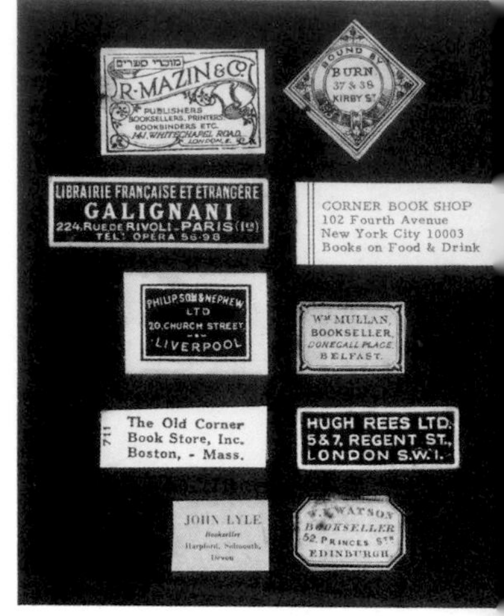

For London bookdealer Roland Knaster the tiny labels used by binders and booksellers had a speci charm, and in the latter years of hi life he made a point of rescuing the from stray binding boards. His collection, now in the Guildhall Library, is among the largest of its kind.

may spring vibrantly to life as a study and research resource, or it may moulder unseen and unappreciated.

But whatever happens, three factors are always present. One is the sense of personal investment contributed by the collector; another is the problem of continuing growth; the third—a corollary of these—is the question 'What is to become of it?'

For most collectors, the desire for safe lodgement is paramount. As with all the persons of our drama, from Samuel Pepys to Isaiah Thomas, from Bella Landauer to John Johnson, the objective is some form of *attachment*—preferably to some immortal institution: Magdalene College, Cambridge; The American Antiquarian Society; The New-York Historical Society; The Bodleian Library, Oxford.

ypical of the 'immortal institution' is the American Antiquarian ociety, founded by Isaiah Thomas safe lodging for his collection. The picture shows a small section of its five-mile stretch of newspaper holdings, the current outcome of its founder's vision.

But the world's great libraries and museums, once affluent enough to welcome the burden of acquisition, are today hard-pressed. Like the collector, they have not room, time, assistance or revenue enough to cope with offerings already bursting at the seams. For the ephemerist who sees the national museum or library as the automatic recipient of a lifetime's accumulation, there may be bad news ahead.

For all that, the true ephemera collector, waiting at the end of the line to harvest the legacies of the individual, must be the institution. As in the past, so going into the twenty-first century, the library and museum remain the final haven.

In the foregoing pages we have looked at ephemerists and their collections. There is however a class of ephemerist so far neglected—the non-collector. Over the years, certainly since the middle years of the nineteenth century, there have been writers and commentators whose vision has helped to set the scene for collectors to come.

We find for example in *Notes and Queries* (January 26, 1856), over the pseudonym 'Handbill', the following plea:

> *Handbills &c.* There are, I am sure, several of the readers of "N. & Q." who, like old Pepys, take pleasure in collecting handbills, placards and broadsides—frailest of the children of the press; they are valuable as expressions of popular opinions and doings of the hour.
>
> The historian of the social and domestic life of the nineteenth century will find such sheets his most valuable aids next to a file of *The Times*: the latter is frequently found; there are not that I am aware of, any public collections of the former.
>
> I wish to suggest that now the postage on printed matter is reduced, there is every facility for the exchange of such papers. Will the editor of "N. & Q." give collectors' names . . . in his pages?

Or consider this, from Samuel F. Haven, Librarian of the American Antiquarian Society, in his semi-annual report for 1872:

> . . . *Broadsides*, embracing all sorts of posters, advertisements, notices, programmes, and indeed whatever is printed on one side of a sheet of paper, large or small. Ballads and proclamations usually come within the definition. They are the legitimate representatives of the most ephemeral literature, the least likely to escape destruction, and yet they are the most vivid exhibition of the manners, arts and daily life of communities of nations . . . They imply a vast deal more than they literally express, and disclose visions of interior conditions of society such as cannot be found in normal narratives.

ompany-label files, kept for nmercial reference, may often olve into an historical study irce. In the picture on the left elen Wilkins of the Foundation for hemera Studies selects items from e label file of Price's Patent Candle ompany. The work, carried out in sociation with the company, serves illustrate both the history of the m and the changing role of the ndle. The labels shown below are om the period 1890–1920. Carriage candles continued to be arketed until 1926.)

In both these passages we have as clear a foreshadowing of the philosophy of the ephemerist as it was oblique in Selden's reference to straws in the wind (page 42).

The twentieth century has brought forth a number of distinguished non-collectors—librarians, writers and commentators whose enthusiasm for ephemera has influenced opinion. Not least of these was Holbrook Jackson, writer-advocate of John Johnson and his works ('One man's litter is another man's literature'), and no less influential was Vivian Ridler, whose 'wants list' entitled 'Desiderata for the Sanctuary of Printing' played a notable part in bringing gifts to the Johnson cabins. In America, Alexander Wall and A. Hyatt Mayor, of The New-York Historical Society and Metropolitan Museum of Art, were pioneers in advocacy, and in Britain in 1966 appeared Michael Twyman's study *John Soulby, Ulverston*, a review of the ephemeral output of a provincial printer of the 1790s and early 1800s. The 1970s brought two more titles, Twyman's *Printing. 1770–1970* and Michael Turner's exhibition catalogue *The John Johnson Collection* (1971), both of which served to focus public attention. In West Berlin in 1983 Christa Pieske's catalogue of her exhibition *Das ABC des Luxuspapiers* did much the same for German ephemera.

In another context, a major non-collector contribution came in the mid-1970s, when Dr Robin Alston, Director of the British Library's ESTC (Eighteenth-century Short-Title Catalogue) operation, was instrumental in securing the inclusion of printed ephemera in the system. As a result of Alston's efforts ESTC now gives research access not only to the books for which it was at first conceived, but to a broad range of single-sheet ephemera. A quarter of a million such items—Graham Pollard's 'ragged edge' of the bibliographical field—may now be located at a computer keyboard.

Robin Alston, here seen at the ESTC keyboard, brought a fresh perspective to ephemera studies by his successful advocacy of the inclusion of single-sheet items in th British Library's computerized Eighteenth-century Short-Title Catalogue.

But in the latter half of the twentieth century by far the most significant non-collector contribution comes from designer and typographer John Lewis. His book *Printed Ephemera*, published in 1962 and today still in world-wide demand, marked a watershed in ephemera studies. It also established the expression 'Printed Ephemera' (Lewis's own) firmly in the public mind, and brought to the subject the imprimatur of a senior lecturer at the Royal College of Art.

Printed Ephemera displayed for the first time virtually the whole spectrum of ephemeral printing, featuring some 700 items culled from the great British and American collections, and from friends. Though not specifically a collector himself, the author nevertheless conveys the ephemerist's pleasure at finds by the way: 'The greatest excitements of the chase . . . were in finding things for myself . . . in antiquarian bookshops and in printing works, factories, businesses and shops, in waste-paper baskets and even garbage bins. One beautiful hardware label I found in a muddy Ipswich gutter.'

PRINTED
EPHEMERA

JOHN LEWIS

Publication date: 26th October 1962

W.S. COWELL

John Lewis's book Printed Ephemera *sparked a new wave of interest in the subject in the 1960s, trend undiminished in the 80s. Shown here is Lewis in his Royal College of Art days and the title page of the prospectus for the book (now a collector's item in its own right).* Printed Ephemera *was republished in 1988, 25 years after i first appearance.*

Sources and values

Among a multitude of sources, the nineteenth-century spike-file is a more than likely starter. Blackened with dust and grime, untouched for decades, these early filing systems ften yield collector's items. The file iown here was part of a haul found in the attic of a Wakefield general tore in the early 1970s. It contained material dating back to 1842.

Most collectors of ephemera have heard the mystified query: 'How do you *find* all this—where does it come from?' The superficial answer is easy. It comes from attics, basements, rubbish dumps, junkshops, old business files, flea-markets, dealers, auctions and so on. But there is more to it than that, as the collector really knows. The question needs a proper answer: Where *does* it come from?

Starting, literally, from the ground up, the ephemerist sees a major source in 'rubbish'. Today, as in the unenlightened past, huge quantities of evidential material disappear daily; for most of those who are concerned with it, it is manifestly trivial—and before long, thankfully, gone. It passes, perhaps within a few hours, from one status to another; the menu becomes a bygone, the ticket merely litter.

Society's capacity for throwing things away is remarkable. Even books (never mind ephemera) have been burnt, scattered, torn up, re-pulped by the cartload, as Mayhew's Rag-and-Bottle man testifies: 'Waste-paper I buy as it comes. I can't read very much, and don't understand about books. I takes the backs off and weighs them, and gives a penny and a penny-farthing and twopence a pound, and there's an end . . .'

The destruction of books and papers has proceeded at an extraordinary rate, and the waste-paper man has been only one of the classic targets of the browsers. History is full of last-minute rescues, from theological libraries where pages had been used to light vestry fires, from parochial registers, where documents had been cut up into tailors' measures or used for kettle holders; and monasteries where monks used strips from books to light candles.

It was not always a case of rescue. A correspondent in *Notes and Queries* (December 17, 1859) writes: 'I remember a book slaughterers, as it was called, at the Drury Lane end of Wych Street, where the most valuable books were constantly being cut up for the butter shops and waste paper wants . . .' Other writers report papers being used as book covers, for singeing a goose, for pulping into sugar-paper, for firing bakers' ovens, and for wrapping tobacco and snuff. Among the more notorious predators are housemaids, reputed to favour 'old documents' as firelighters. It was John Stuart Mills's servant who used the MS of the first chapter of Carlyle's *French Revolution* for this purpose, and we have already noted the role of the maids in the case of the Percy ballads. More original, perhaps, was the reported use in the 1630s of manuscript paper for pie bottoms.

To the ephemerist, who seeks only the most modest of throwaways, these stories are especially chilling. For if books and manuscripts were served like this, what of the day-to-day oddments, items actually *intended* for destruction? Could any of these survive at all? It seems unlikely.

And yet they did—and still do. Historically, much has depended on the economic climate. In times of scarcity, paper may be used for a succession of different purposes (printer's proofs for trunk linings, paper bags for book wrappers); at other times it may be salvaged and re-cycled; sometimes it is just thrown away. Waste-paper collection services, municipal and private, wax and wane; at some periods the commercial disposal agency will pay for waste; at others it makes a charge for removal ('for confidential shredding'). The ephemera record gains or loses accordingly.

In World War II, paper shortages all over Europe brought a huge rise in 'salvage'. Enforced clearance of papers from attics as an anti-fire-bomb measure re-doubled the effect. The period saw one of the greatest paper clear-outs in history, and this, added to the directly destructive effect of the war itself, greatly diminished the record. (Though even at the height of it all there were still self-appointed paper-rescue squads. We spare a thought for Ethel Stokes, 70-year old acolyte of the British Records Association, whose air-raid forays in London's docks are remembered still. To the sound of sirens, it is said, she rummaged through mounds of 'salvaged' paper, bringing trophies back to the Association's offices in Charterhouse Square. Like John Johnson in his collector's lair in Oxford, who slept each night on a camp-bed in the midst of his collection, Ethel Stokes slept most nights on her office floor.)

Peace-time rubbish mounds—latterly laced with plastic—are safer, and certainly no less worthy of attention, and an arrangement with the local refuse team, or the waste-paper dealer, or the demolition-and-scrap man, is well worth while. It is to be remembered that today's rubbish may contain not only the throwaways of today, but those of times gone by—items stored away, perhaps for generations, and suddenly disposed of. If the rubbish of our time seems on the face of it unattractive (and much of it is) it may still bear pockets of reward.

A giant among waste-paper fanciers was Joe Bryson, whose story Iain Campbell has told (*Ephemerist*, March 1980). Bryson was by any standards a remarkable character (he is described as 'artist, sculptor, naturalist, philatelist, writer and beachcomber'), but he also had a consuming passion—the rescue of printed and handwritten ephemera. His example is not necessarily to be followed in detail, but it is certainly worth noticing.

Joe Bryson was one of a number of men from the Scots Guards, who in the 1920s were ordered to clear out a number of attics in Whitehall. He came upon a bundle of old papers among the rubbish and began to take an interest in them. The sergeant in charge told the young guardsman he could snaffle a few 'if he didn't make it too obvious'. Iain Campbell relates the crux of the story: 'A few days later a guardsman took some papers to Francis Edwards, the London booksellers, who paid him £25 for them. Francis Edwards thus happily acquired a list of all the soldiers fighting at the Battle of Waterloo, and Joe Bryson acquired the knowledge that old bits of paper could be worth a lot more than a soldier's weekly pay.'

Twenty years later, (after a spell as artist, sculptor, naturalist etc.) Joe Bryson returned to the business of old papers. Gathering items of ephemera, he took them round to waste-paper merchants as specimens, offering at least double their scrap value for similar items.

The material began to come in. Soon it became unmanageable. When he ran out of space, he built a shed in the garden and when that was full he built another.

To finance the collection, he sold off portions of it to booksellers, collectors, libraries and museums. His valuations, and his business style, left a trail of complications. He was unpredictable, abrupt and quixotic. And when he moved house he had the problem of what to do with his shedfuls of paper.

He offered seven tons of the collection to the Merseyside County Museum for £25,000, but finally settled for £5000. The museum took on three extra people for a year to sort the material.

BEAVERBROOK
WANTS YOUR
WASTEPAPER

Wastepaper is needed now more urgently than ever for munitions of war. A special drive to meet this appeal is being made in Horsell, and your co-operation is earnestly requested. A lorry will visit your road on

28 NOV. 1941

to collect wastepaper and cardboard: you are asked to make a special effort to turn out all your old BOOKS, LETTERS, BILLS, INVOICES, MAGAZINES, MUSIC, CARTONS, ETC., by having them ready for the collector on that day.

Turn out your cupboards and libraries

NOW

A.V.N. PRODUCTIONS LTD., PRINTERS, WOKING

Leave it on your doorstep

Vast quantities of ephemera vanish in World War II. Much w forcibly removed from lofts as a f precaution; much went for re-cycli as a war economy measure and f use in munitions. In this 19 appeal, Lord Beaverbook, Minist of Supply, calls on the people Horsell, Surrey, to 'turn out yo cupboards and libraries'. ('Leave on your doorstep', adds neighbourly hand

In the meantime Bryson was settling in at his new address. One of his first tasks, says Campbell, was to build a large shed in the garden and to plan how many more sheds the area would hold: 'He could never look at a garden without estimating its capacity for sheds.'

Odd as he was, Bryson was no fool. When the collection was finally analysed it revealed a treasure trove of evidential papers—material relating to the slave trade, inventories of houses and businesses, items from the American Civil War, the Californian gold rush; family papers and autograph letters, and a manuscript account of a school mistress's married life with a drunken sailor in the 1860s.

After his death in 1978 the Bryson haul found safe lodging. From a clutter of garden sheds it moved into the care of museums and libraries throughout Britain—among them, in addition to the Merseyside County Museum, the National Maritime Museum at Greenwich, the National Library of Scotland and the City of London Museum.

WASTE PAPER
Is More Vitally NEEDED Than Ever!
HAVE IT READY AND ON THE CURB FOR THE
City-Wide WASTE PAPER Drive-
SUNDAY, OCTOBER 15th
Please Have Bundles Tied Securely — Please Do Your Part on Oct. 15th
The war effort demands this be our biggest drive. The money received from
is drive will be used as follows:
First $100.00 to Boy Scouts
Balance of profits divided as follows:
½ to Medford War Service Fund (used for Servicemen's monthly newspaper, send-off gifts, etc.)
¼ to Youth Fund (used for youth activity of Medford) ¼ to Medford Red Cross
ION. WALTER E. LAWRENCE, Mayor JAMES C. GILLIS, Chairman

ated October 1944, the waste-paper ve in Medford, Massachusetts vides its proceeds between Boy outs, the local War Service Fund, Youth Fund and Medford Red oss. In both Horsell and Medford, is clear, the appeals themselves aped.

As with other addicts before him, Bryson began to acquire for the sake of acquisition. Typically, he ran out of space—and of common sense. But he proved beyond a doubt the value of the waste-paper dump, even in these latter years of the twentieth century.

Huge quantities of waste paper, confidential government documents and other 'sensitive' material, are firmly denied to the Brysons and Stokeses. In Washington and Whitehall, in the world's embassies and consulates, in public and private research establishments, in banknote and general security printers, the shredder reigns.

This is no new thing, as we learn from *Chamber's Journal* (November 21, 1896). Under the title 'Government Waste-Paper', the writer describes 'the enormous Government Stationery depot' which distributes a constant stream of paper products, printed or plain, to government offices all over the country. A prodigious output, indeed. But almost equally great is the return of the tide. Home to roost, in the reception centre half a mile away, comes an annual intake of two thousand tons of waste.

Here in the Waste Branch the material is tipped out over gratings for sifting and sorting. Some of it goes to dealers ('old account book covers . . . are destined sooner or later to do duty as leather for ladies' shoe-socks'). But many categories, such as letters, documents, and confidential reports cannot be sold off:

> At one time such things used to be sold to manufacturers, who were required to enter into bond to pulp them at once. This arrangement did not prove very satisfactory, and for a time government waste-paper was sent to Westminster prison, or the one at Coldbath Fields, to be torn into fragments by the prisoners. This was continued till 1885, when the Home Secretary came to the conclusion that 'as a matter of policy' this arrangement was undesirable, and eventually a gas-engine and powerful guillotine cutting machines were set up in the premises . . . and all sorts of letters and confidential documents are now passed down from the upper floor, by means of 'hoppers' and 'shoots', to the machines, where they are sliced up into fragments too small for any sort of information being garnered from them.

Security was a factor not only in Government offices. The legal profession was also much concerned. A handbill put out by the Wholesale Waste Paper Warehouse, Edinburgh, in 1887 assured its lawyer clients that all law papers were bought for re-manufacture only 'and are sent out of the kingdom immediately after purchase, thereby rendering it impossible for any person here to have access to the same'. The firm further assured its customers that it was 'the First House in the United Kingdom to introduced Machinery for the destruction of all important Written and Printed Papers'.

Today's shredding companies are in the same tradition. They offer not only assurances but formal 'certificates of destruction'.

The assault on waste paper has intensified. Where once the material was merely discarded, the trend has been toward positive destruction. And yet things still escape. By Bryson or by accident, items of ephemera do somehow survive.

The classic 'accident' is the firm going out of business or changing address. To the observant ephemerist the signs may become apparent some time in advance of the event, and a quiet enquiry can often secure a preview. In a long-established business, with possibly a generation or two of paper fall-out, much may be culled before the crucial day. It may well happen that the approach comes as a relief to the owner, either because the material is an embarrassment of bulk, or because it has some sentimental compulsion, or both. Certainly a removal may be seen as a chance to shed unwanted weight, and closure provides a last challenge of conscience. As with our end-of-the-road collectors, the cry goes up: 'Won't *somebody* take it and look after it?'

If the proposal be put with tact, and if it is clear that the material would be 'going to a good home', the owner may welcome the opportunity to solve a problem. The arrangement might be for the collector to acquire the whole of the material, disposing of it as appears appropriate, or for a selective culling before it goes for refuse. Either way, the matter may be a friendly arrangement or a cash transaction. On the whole the friendly arrangement is best, not only because it favours the collector, but because it relieves the affair of the image of the predator picking over the spoils. Ordinarily, in any case, the matter will be seen as too marginal for big-deal treatment.

It is helpful if the enquirer can establish his, or her, bona fides as a collector or curator, preferably with a visiting card or a Society membership card. The friendly arrangement has a better chance if the owner of the papers knows who and what the enquirer is. (If the enquirer is in fact a dealer, this too should be made known: it is still possible that an offer to clear the whole of the material—free of charge—may be cheerfully accepted.)

The going-out-of-business syndrome has occasionally spectacular effects. Known to the popular press as 'time capsules', these long-term closures may suddenly come to light in a property sale, a demolition order or an accidental break-in during reconstruction. Shops, offices, private apartments, are revealed, exactly as they had been left, sometimes decades before. Their contents, dust-covered but intact, provide a stop-frame image of their day. In some cases, instead of removing items for display elsewhere, the entire setting is preserved intact—sometimes on site, sometimes as a reconstruction in a museum.

Such finds are commonly less than perfectly preserved. Often it is a case of selective salvage, and here the serious ephemerist may have the privilege of picking and choosing from among assorted debris.

Sometimes, though rarely, the capsule effect applies to premises still in business. Lilian Thrussell, assistant curator at the John Johnson collection, recalls a research visit to Tewkesbury in the mid-1940s: it was a drapers-cum-children's shop, kept by a Mrs Reeves:

> It was a tiny little shop, and she was a tiny little old lady in a long black dress with a high button-up collar. It was a sort of toy-shop, but it sold other things as well, trinkets, little children's story books, chapbooks, classroom ABCs, and various kinds of old-time juvenile printed ephemera. It was really Dickensian. She served only one person at a time, latching the street door behind you so as to concentrate on you alone. The place was an Aladdin's cave of lovely things—all hopelessly old-fashioned and charming. Behind her, as this little figure stood at the counter, were boxes, stacked one on the

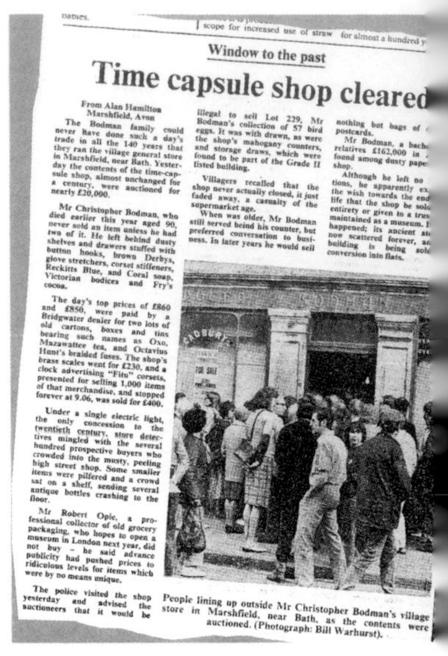

Window to the past

Time capsule shop cleared

From Alan Hamilton
Marshfield, Avon

The Bodman family could never have done such a day's trade in all the 140 years that they ran the village general store in Marshfield, near Bath. Yesterday the contents of the time-capsule shop, almost unchanged for a century, were auctioned for nearly £20,000.

Mr Christopher Bodman, who died earlier this year aged 90, never sold an item unless he had two of it. He left behind dusty shelves and drawers stuffed with button hooks, brown Derbys, glove stretchers, corset stiffeners, Reckitts Blue, and Coral soap, Victorian bodices and Fry's cocoa.

The day's top prices of £860 and £850, were paid by a Bridgwater dealer for two lots of old cartons, boxes and tins bearing such names as Oxo, Mazawattee tea, and Octavius Hunt's braided fuses. The shop's brass scales went for £230, and a clock advertising "Fitu" corsets, presented for selling 1,000 items of that merchandise, and stopped forever at 9.06, was sold for £400.

Under a single electric light, the only concession to the twentieth century, store detectives mingled with the several hundred prospective buyers who crowded into the musty, peeling high street shop. Some smaller items were pilfered and a crowd sat on a shelf, sending several antique bottles crashing to the floor.

Mr Robert Opie, a professional collector of old grocery packaging, who hopes to open a museum in London next year, did not buy – he said advance publicity had pushed prices to ridiculous levels for items which were by no means unique.

The police visited the shop yesterday and advised the auctioneers that it would be illegal to sell Lot 229, Mr Bodman's collection of 57 bird eggs. It was with drawn, as were the shop's mahogany counters, and storage draws, which were found to be part of the Grade II listed building.

Villagers recalled that the shop never actually closed, it just faded away, a casualty of the supermarket age.

When was older, Mr Bodman still served beind his counter, but preferred conversation to business. In later years he would sell nothing but bags of … postcards.

Mr Bodman, a bach… relatives £162,000 in … found among dusty pape… shop.

Although he left no … tions, he apparently ex… the wish towards the end … life that the shop be sol… entirety or given to a trus… maintained as a museum. … happened; its ancient st… now scattered forever, a… building is being sol… conversion into flats.

People lining up outside Mr Christopher Bodman's village store in Marshfield, near Bath, as the contents were auctioned. (Photograph: Bill Warhurst).

The 'time-capsule' effect, in which long-closed business at length revea its contents, has much popular appeal. At the sale reported here, typical of many, local and national interest was high and villagers crowded in among collectors and dealers. It was said that the shop h never actually closed: 'It just faded away, a casualty of the supermarke age'. Among the dusty papers foun in the shop was the will of the owner, who had died at 90. He left £162,000. He had hoped that the place might become a museum, but no-one took up the idea. The contents were dispersed.

> other from floor to ceiling, each with a label—*lace*—*battledores*—*beads*—*chapbooks*—*tapes*—and so on.
>
> But the most extraordinary thing about it was the prices, everything had the original price tags—from maybe 25 years back. A ha'penny and prices like that. I selected a lot of things for the collection, but I hadn't the heart to pay those absurd prices. She wouldn't have it though. She insisted I pay 'the proper price'. I was almost ashamed, but there it was . . .

The Tewkesbury case is not unique. In London's Euston Road in the late 1970s an elderly general dealer continued to sell 1930s packaged gas mantles and other goods at pre-decimal prices: 'That's the price, Sir: three shillings and sixpence, if you please.' Shillings and sixpences had disappeared some eight or nine years before.

Allied to the going-out-of-business syndrome is the household auction, where the complete contents of a home come under the hammer. Auctioneers are today more aware of ephemera than they may have been in the past, but even so there is some uncertainty about bundles of miscellaneous papers. They have no clear-cut market value, and they may seem something of an embarrassment among the wardrobes and chamber pots. Even unexamined, they are often worth an ephemerist's nod.

Not quite an-end-of-the-line situation, but not far removed, is the institutional re-shuffle. Libraries, museums and other bodies must now and then re-think their holdings, discarding some items in favour of better ones, sometimes whittling down to make space for more important material. Such occasions are rare, but they do happen. In the mid 1930s, when museums and libraries everywhere were waking up to the space crisis, some boards of trustees decided on 'programmes of elimination'. It is thus that private collections today may legitimately include items bearing the identification stamps—cancelled or not—of great institutions.

The matter was much discussed. In Britain in 1930 a Royal Commission on National Museums and Galleries came up with a recommendation that the British Museum's 'all-in' policy (of receiving and preserving 'everything printed') should be modified to exclude such items as were preserved elsewhere (registers of voters, patent specifications, railway and steamer timetables), as well as wall diaries and instructional wall sheets for schools. It had also been suggested that children's toy books and games be excluded. The commissioners jibbed at this, however: 'There is no more interesting exhibit in the Graeco-Roman room of the museum today than

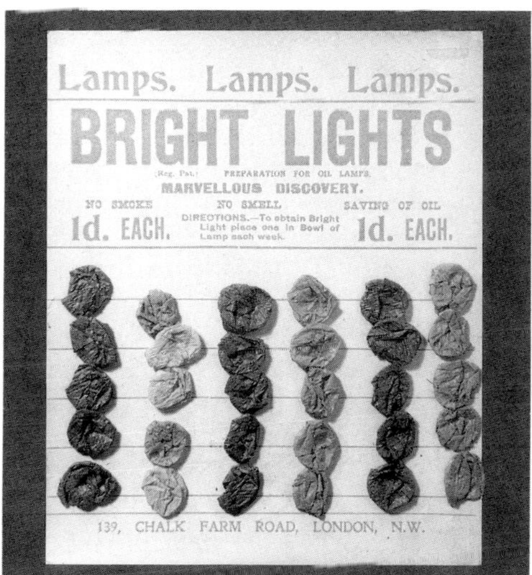

Time-capsules may disclose little-known facets of early commercial enterprise. This display card, found intact in an abandoned corner shop, proffers a 'marvellous discovery'—packets of an unspecified powder, to be placed in bowls of oil lamps for a brighter light. The nature of the powder, and the supposed chemistry of its effect, remain to be researched. Takers appear to have been slow.

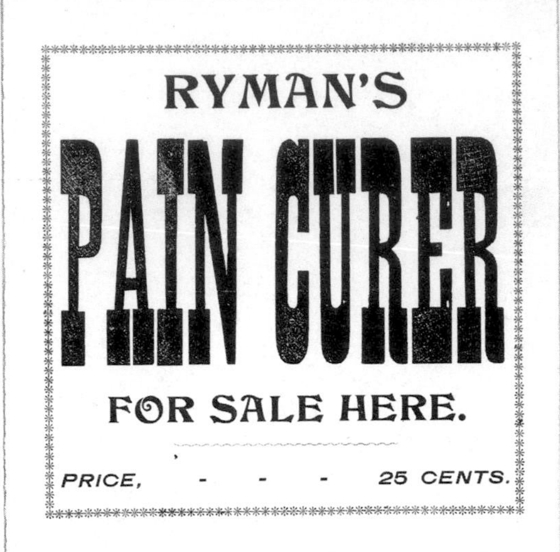

The early pharmacy and drugstore thrived on the use of showcards, a relief of pain is a dominant theme among survivals. These two specimens are typical in their uncompromising simplicity of sale pitch. Both were rescued from long term closures.

that devoted to children's toys and games.' The outcome of the recommendation is unavailable.

In another case, also in the early 1930s, the outcome was unmistakable. The *Bodleian Library Record* carried an article under the solemn title 'Elimination'. It pointed out that a new clause of the Statute now enabled the curators 'to eliminate . . . material of no literary or artistic value or of an ephemeral nature . . .'. The article went on to justify the decision on grounds of savings in bulk and curatorial time and labour. It finished with the words 'When a valueless item offends in both these respects, it is only reasonable to grant to the Library authorities power to "liquidate" it.'

Liquidation of many items did in fact take place. Among categories rejected were almanacs, calendars, diaries, fiction magazines, sheet music, books for young children, religious and temperance tracts and publishers' lists. In the 1930s and 40s the Bodleian thus suffered notable losses, a great many items bearing cancelled Bodley stamps got out into the wider world. But it is also a matter of record that many got back. Bodley's librarian, Strickland Gibson, steered as many items as possible into the Johnson 'Sanctuary', so that today the collection, now housed in the Bodleian, also contains items bearing a cancelled Bodley stamp.

As a general rule the great libraries and museums are reluctant—if not constitutionally unable—to let things go. For many of them acceptance of items as gifts carries with it the responsibility, implied or specified, of curatorship for all time. Such items may not be disposed of. In the case of printed ephemera, many examples of which may be held in duplicate, triplicate or more, even the supernumerary copies must be retained.

This means that in many cases where private collectors might be happy to exchange their duplicates for museum or library duplicates, both parties lose out. It should be said, however, that not every institution is thus tied, and indeed there now begins to emerge the concept of the 'duplicate sale', an innovation popular on all sides.

Institutional codes of conduct vary considerably. So do circumstances. In a personal memoir, pharmaceutical historians William Helfand and David Cowen relate a research visit to a New York College of Pharmacy in the 1970s. The college was being closed down, and the two specialists were invited to take their pick from a rich accumulation of papers. 'We took it,' says Helfand, 'we came away with some hundreds of significant items—files of nineteenth-century correspondence on engraved and lithographed letterheads, large numbers of 'miscellaneous' box files, and quantities of early advertising material. It was an Aladdin's cave . . .'.

The Aladdin's cave image is popular among ephemerists.

For the down-to-earth ephemerist, whose connections may not run to museums, colleges, or rubbish mounds, one good connection is the world of the antiquarian bookshop. Here, where a decade ago the word itself may have needed explanation, ephemera is increasingly forthcoming. The book *This is Ephemera*, referred to in earlier pages, has much to say for the bookshop:

> Here, in an odd volume (if you are lucky) you will come across a slipped-in fragment—an ancient ticket, a bill, an advertising card, a shopping list—dropped in on some forgotten day to mark the place. Or you may even find a full-blown bygone bookmark. Or a nineteenth-century school report, or a wartime ration card. Or, tucked away on a shelf, an errant pamphlet, a birth certificate, a catalogue for an eighteenth-century auction, a prospectus for a long-dead goldmine. Booksellers' shelves, at first sight offering books alone, may nevertheless yield minor trivia. They must be observed minutely: the smallest smitch of protruding paper may indicate a find. The dustiest, most dog-eared corner may prove to be the tip of a collector's piece. *Behind* the books is a good place to look. Crushed and crumpled, items have been known to remain unnoticed for decades.
>
> The difficulty—and the advantage—with items of this sort is that long before the browser discovers them the bookseller has found them himself, and been puzzled. The item he has tucked away is not quite his stock-in-trade. Uncertain how best to handle it, he parks it somewhere, temporarily.
>
> Bookmarks, formal and otherwise, are a particular problem. Are they part of the book or cuckoos in the nest? Often the bookman's decision will be in the ephemerist's favour.
>
> In addition to the bookshelf ephemera, most booksellers also maintain an unofficial hideaway where oddments accumulate. Here again, items are preserved 'because it seems a shame to throw them away'. Tact, and a becoming diffidence, may induce the proprietor to reveal the presence of this *cache* and even to open it up.

Today, some ten years on, tact and diffidence are no longer to the point. The *cache* is open to inspection; the shelves—even the spaces behind the books—have been cleared; books have been flipped through for fall-out. Bookshop ephemera, still a sideline but now formally recognized, is *available*. But in spite of this general change, pockets of adventure still remain; in book byways and outbacks, the ephemerist may still find things in corners.

For the bookmark collector, books and bookshops are obvious hunting grounds, and increasingly the bookseller's fall-out box is becoming a recognized institution. But the world's bookshelves, public, private and commercial, must still hold undiscovered temptation. Crises of conscience—to filch, or not to filch—are for the collector's own resolution.

Ephemera may also be found in the general antiquarian shop—again as a sideline, but here too at least the word is understood, and the enquiry raises no eyebrows. On the whole, however, prices here tend to be higher. A little further out of their depth than the bookman, antique shops play it safe and charge more. The ephemerist is commonly better off in a genuine junk shop, where a bundle of old papers is just a bundle of old papers—too much trouble to read and sort, and going cheap.

A further source is the print dealer, whose files of eighteenth- and nineteenth-century engravings may sometimes harbour a ticket or a tradecard. But, here, as with the antique shop, the fancy context calls for fancier prices, and bargains are few. Moreover, we are up against the printseller's incurable habit of mounting and framing. Even if a likely item should emerge, it will almost certainly have to be disinterred for inclusion in the buyer's collection.

The ephemerist is perhaps best served by the extremes of the market—the very top, where the great auction houses and dealers offer the certified cream, or the very bottom, where street traders and their customers shiver on dark mornings in the rain.

The street market, or flea-market (not to be confused with the more respectable indoor 'Antiques and Ephemera Fair') is truly the ground floor of organized ephemera sources. Here it is that raw, untreated ephemera gets its first airing, direct from house clearance and rubbish dump, ready for the home run to dealer, collector or curator. There is commonly some small excitement at these events, early birds competing for a first look in. Not that all is ephemera, however. On the contrary, paper usually takes second or third place in the hierarchy of miscellany. The vendor, disengaging papers from among coalplates and smoothing irons, may even damage material in the very act of selling it. Nor is the down-market setting a guarantee of bargains: a soggy paper compost may masquerade as 'valuable documents'. For the ephemera hunter, the situation calls for a clear head, tenacity and warm underwear.

And below the lower end of the market lie the primary hunting grounds, Aunt Emily's trunk and granny's attic—the very sources that feed the flea-markets and fairs. These, if they can only be located, are the true source.

This is Ephemera again:

> It is after all a matter of finding the right attic, the likely cupboard, the possible valise. With experience, the ephemerist develops a nose for these things. The search may lead to wild and savage places. Barns, out-houses, abandoned warehouses, lofts and basements, ruined mansions, derelict cottages—with tenacity, and a disregard for dirt and discomfort, these hiding places may yield their hoards.

One compendious source of ephemera, to be found at almost any level, is that most common of Victorian hoards, the scrap album. Some collectors search for these alone. From granny's attic, rainy market or ephemera fair, the album specialists bring back bookfuls of ephemera—tradecards, chromos, transfers and diecuts, culled and pasted at the time of their first appearance, and cold-stored till now.

These miscellanies, mounted higgledy-piggledy, and admitting anything from rewards of merit to perfume labels, epitomize the Victorian Sunday afternoon and the parlour pastime. In the detail of their content, in their presentation as a whole, and by the fact of their compilation, they are prime exhibits.

The middle-class miss had little enough to do. Music, drawing, needlework and the scrapbook were her chief creative outlets—and the scrapbook, we suspect, came easiest. With scissors and paste and a handful of printed oddments she composed an unwitting montage of her time—a drawing-room time-capsule. The album later accommodated the die-cut 'scraps' of the chromolitho trade, the albums themselves finally took charge (with the Bible and the photograph album) of everyone's parlour table.

The Victorian scrap album housec much more than chromolitho die-cuts, and collectors of series cards c alert to its potential as a source. T card is from a series given with packages of Buchner's chewing an smoking tobacco in the 1890s. It shows the scene at what is today t northernmost end of New York's Central Park. Traces of glue on th back of the card confirm its provenance.

ELEVATED R.R. 110th St.
One of these cards are packed in every package
"ONE OF THE FINEST" TOBACCO.

ı unusual time capsule emerged in :he 1980s in London's Ritz Hotel. panning a period of over 80 years, the material was found in an erlooked recess in the hall-porter's desk. It included the items shown re—a 1930s charity match-folder, 916 theatre ticket, a 1930s car-hire iff, and promotion cards for shows ı London (1912) and Paris (1950).

The albums form a ready-made collector's source. They are marred only by the attentions of the original compiler's scissors: to vary the monotony, and to mark her creative aptitude, she invariably trimmed the items close, cutting off surplus margins and sometimes—a bold creative gesture—chopping off the corners. The exhibits thus doctored are often beyond the point of no return. But many collectors are happy to leave them, and the album as a whole, as found. Others, regardless of the scissor-work, soak the exhibits off. (See page 75)

For the well-heeled ephemerist the top of the market is clearly the place to start. Through the portals of the auctioneers and dealers pass the world's most beautiful ephemera, and the best-shod collectors.

We may see these institutions in two lights. On the one hand they appear as arenas for upward spiralling prices. On the other they serve as supremely efficient focal points for bringing forward material that would otherwise remain in limbo. They raise standards of quality, and levels of appreciation; they employ expertise and experience beyond the ordinary, and they engender the work of search and rescue that the collector can rarely do personally.

Certainly prices have risen, and doubtless will continue to rise. But for the collector the effect, if cash values are a prime concern, is also beneficial. Items acquired a few years ago may now have doubled or trebled in value, and the value of items acquired today will similarly rise. It should be remembered too that prices rise not just by decision of the seller; the buyer is also part of the deal. Without the buyer's demand no one could sell at all.

For the less affluent collector the solution is a philosophical attitude and a concentration on less rarified collecting finds. If the world's first Christmas card now fetches four-figure bids (when until recently it was only two or three figures), why worry? Try another kind of card, still within ordinary reach, but becoming rare. Wartime cards for example, or pre-revolutionary Russian cards. In time to come, perhaps before very long, a selective collection of these too will run to double or treble figures. It is, as the expression has it, 'all in the mind'—initially, the individual collector's mind. But as we have noted earlier, the collector whose sights are set only on investment is rare. Market values are not the real point.

We do well to remember in any case that, whatever its price tag, any given item of printed ephemera is only in the rarest of cases actually unique. By its very nature, as the product of a printing press it must surely have had at least a handful of fellows—perhaps hundreds or thousands. It is only in the field of part-printed items, indentures, certificates etc., that the unique item occurs. For the most part—even with the rarest American clipper sailing-card, or the coveted first Christmas card—somewhere there must lurk at least one identical copy. At the turn of the 1980s Laura Seddon had identified and located 15 surviving copies of the Cole-Horsley Christmas card, published in 1843 in a run of one thousand. Even at auction, where such items attract heavy bidding, no-one can be sure that another specimen will not appear in the next catalogue.

Indisputably unique are those items that reveal an unexpected second ingredient. Among many such examples are the plain brown book-wrapper that turns out to have been improvised from an early printed pin-paper, and the eighteenth-century tradecard used as a bundle tag. Handbills and printer's type-proofs may carry notes or printed matter on the back, and an unwound spool of thread may disclose a recipe or a laundry list.

Also serendipitous are the items that reveal a famous signature, unnoticed at the point of purchase. An example is the 1842 admission ticket to the workings on Marc Isambard Brunel's Thames tunnel; a closer look reveals the hand of Brunel himself (page 124). A ticket in the Helfand Collection admits the bearer to the medical lectures of one Joseph Lister; it is signed by the lecturer. In the collection of The Foundation of Ephemera Studies is a '*carte pneumatique*'—a memento of the pneumatic postal system in Paris in the 1890s. The card bears the cancellation marking its passage through the air-tubes, and is signed by the composer Gabriel Fauré. In a class by itself, in the Barbara Rusch collection in Toronto, is an 1840s London chemist's bottle label: under the royal appointment coat-of-arms it bears the manuscript note *Lotion for the Eyes: to be used three times a day: The Queen*. A similar item appears on page 121.

Whatever the hunting ground—auction, fair or flea-market—ephemera springs surprises on even the most expert and experienced collector.

In the matter of markets, most ephemerists go for the middle ground, avoiding both the rigours of the flea-market and the temptations of the saleroom. They settle for the indoor ephemera fairs and bazaars, now firmly established as collectors' hunting grounds, and valued for their secondary role as meeting points. Many of these events are run by collectors' societies. Among them, in Britain, the Ephemera Society, and similar events are staged by the Ephemera Societies of America, Australia and Canada. Here, in the friendly atmosphere of a members' bazaar, with the general public partaking, collectors' items of all kinds change hands. For many long-term collectors, formerly accustomed to a gruelling round of bookshops, markets and rubbish dumps, these concentrated events are a great relief. To the newcomer they are a handy introduction.

Ephemera Society membership is in itself a useful form of collecting contact. In addition to bazaars and fairs, there are meetings and lectures, a quarterly journal and a cross-reference members' list to open up new sources for collectors old and new. (See page 220)

Some major sources come by chance and most rewarding among these are local printers' files, the long-neglected archives of family printing businesses, whose work records the doings of their neighbourhood for miles around, sometimes over two or three generations. Billheads, notices, tickets, sale catalogues, these and the whole spectrum of local printed matter are contained in albums ('guard books') or impaled on spike files. The practice of filing was induced not by efficiency but by force of law, the printer being required to keep specimen copies of everything he

From the store-room of Scottish printers Robert Smail in 1984 the author rescues specimen files. The haul, housed in 40 heavy guard-b covered a period of some 90 years, reflecting the history of the localit in notices, tickets, invitations and wide range of jobbing printing.

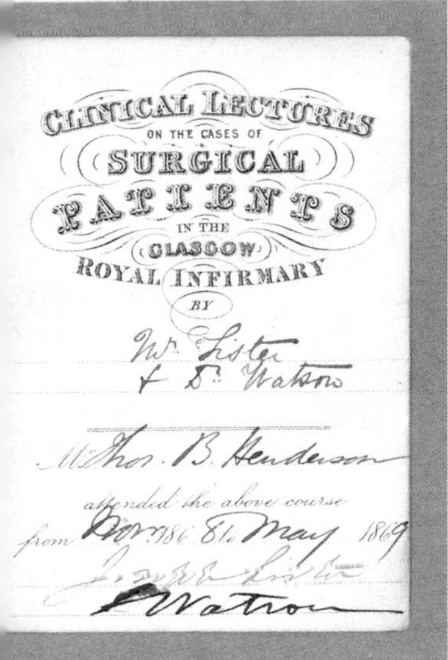

For the most part the collector is interested in ephemera for its own ake. Some items, however, reveal an added feature—and an added dimension—in a distinguished signature. This lecture attendance :rd is signed by lecturers Lister and Vatson. The first-named, father of ıtiseptic surgery, was Joseph, later ,ord Lister, President of the Royal ociety and the British Association.

produced. The result, in our time, is an occasional treasure-trove.

Best-known among such finds have been the Soulby collection, already noted (page 58) and the Robert Smail files, located by the Foundation for Ephemera Studies in Innerleithen, Peeblesshire, and now in the keeping of the National Trust for Scotland.

The classic case is that of the Procter spike-files, located by schoolmaster Robert Wood in Hartlepool in the late 1950s. They were later to form the basis of his *Victorian Delights* (Evans, 1967), and their content is today shared by the Music Hall Museum in Sunderland and the Hartlepool Museum and Art Gallery. They cover the period from 1834 to World War I, and number about a quarter of a million items, ranging from visiting cards to broadsheets and posters.

Writing in *The Ephemerist* in January 1979, their curator, Henry Middleton, described the collection's subject catalogues as covering the whole range of public and private activities of a Victorian provincial town and seaport: 'agriculture, auctions (from ships to furniture), coal-mining and exporting, dock and harbour administration, insurance, printing, religion, sport, shipping, shipbuilding, marine engineering, iron and steel making, entertainment, transport (including much local railway material), municipal and parliamentary elections, law and order, hospitals, education, local societies, temperance, as well as miscellaneous local trades and industries, from music-sellers to cement works, and from chain-testers to waterworks'. There were several vanloads of the material. 'It took two people, working full-time for several months, just to sort it into categories,' says Middleton.

Today, as the organization of the material approaches completion, we may visualize its initial discovery and rescue. In a letter to Graham Hudson in 1973 Robert Wood himself described how it happened. It started with a conversation with an elderly printer about local history. The printer peered at the stranger over his spectacles. 'You're interested in history?' Wood admitted he was, 'I've got something for you,' said the man, 'Wait a minute.'

The old man disappeared within for a moment and came back with a small

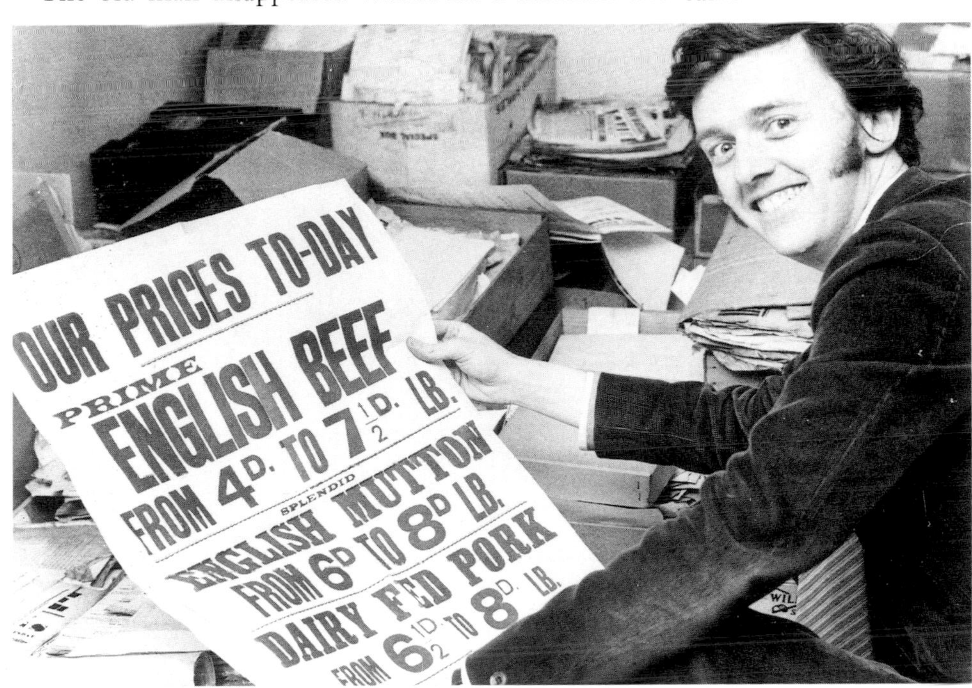

In the Hartlepool Museum in 1977 ırator Henry Middleton carries out first sorting of an estimated quarter a million items in the John Procter ɔllection. Salvaged by a Hartlepool schoolmaster, the material ranges from announcements of rabbit coursing to handbills advertising phrenologists and bonesetters. The butcher's poster is from the early 1920s (6d = 2½p).

broadside. It was an 1860s Visitors List from Harrogate—typical of those published at resorts at the time, partly to flatter the tourist, partly to alert the trader. It was just the sort of thing that Robert Wood had always found fascinating:

> I admired it. I said I hoped he would take care of it, because some day someone would be writing a history of Harrogate, and the list would be useful. He laughed. He said he had a houseful of stuff like that. I told him he was a lucky man. 'Not at all', he said, 'it's a damn nuisance'.
>
> He told me how he had bought this old printing firm shortly before 1939, and when the war came, with its fire-bomb threats, the Fire Brigade had insisted that the attics should be cleared of all the old files stored in them.
>
> The files were thrown out of the attic windows into a courtyard, and left to be picked up by corporation lorries for paper salvage. But then he discovered that some of the drivers were handing out the more curious posters in the local pubs, so he allowed no more to be taken. He had the remainder bundled into a ruined house in the courtyard—and, he said, they were still there.

Woods was not slow to respond: could he see the papers—even possibly select some of them for local history research?

> He told me that if I wanted to use any of the material I was welcome to it. But he warned me that I would find the stuff in a terrible condition. I arranged to go over the following Saturday morning.
>
> When I got there the sight was almost indescribable. Spike-files like Christmas trees, black as soot, had been thrown into a large room till it was full to a height of about four feet. Most of the tiles were off the roof, and the rain had seeped through and the plaster of the ceiling had fallen down. To add to the mess, seagulls had nested in the place and there were two or three dead ones laying about.
>
> It was a cold, wet, windy February morning. I dragged the nearest file out through the window and took it along the courtyard to the warmth of the boiler-house, where I began to peel off the top layers of jet black paper until I could find something readable. Three or four layers down, the paper was clean. I found I was gazing at the proof sheets of the paper tickets issued on the Hartlepool railway in *1837* ...
>
> That find decided the course of my spare-time occupation for the next ten years. I spent every available minute extracting and preserving the contents of the spike-files.
>
> The original printer, John Procter, had started in business in 1834, and had clearly been a compulsive hoarder. The spikes carried not only his printing proofs but his personal correspondence—even the weekly butcher's bills. All these had to be carefully peeled off these sodden piles and sorted out.
>
> Obviously it couldn't be done indoors, and in our short summers I used to sit on my lawn with a spikeful before me and two boxes, one on either side, into one of which went what had to be retained, into the other what had to be discarded ...

We picture Robert Wood in his summer garden, the retired schoolmaster contentedly peeling off layers of Hartlepool history. His is the classic collector's story, the epitome of the ephemerist at work. As we admire his single-mindedness—and envy his luck—we may remind ourselves that elsewhere in the world there is surely such treasure still to be found.

An example of the work of the onservation laboratories of Britain's Public Record Office. The lower icture shows a single sheet from the decaying bundle above. Ultra-violet hotography has completed the work of reclamation by intensifying faded writing. It must be stressed, owever, that the amateur's scope for epair is limited; work of this calibre equires special techniques and many years of experience.

Conservation and display

Collectors at every level, from the cheese-label specialist to the British Museum and the Smithsonian Institution, share a four-fold problem: storage, conservation, filing and display. The elements are interlinked; no single aspect of the whole can be solved without complicating another.

It is clear, for example, that display is incompatible with both conservation and storage. Display means visibility, which means light; which, in general terms is harmful to exhibits. Display is therefore conservationally undesirable. Display also means some form of fixing, mounting, framing or encapsulation—all potentially harmful processes, conservationally undesirable. As well as all this, display complicates both filing and storage: items on display are not in store, and their absence and location have to be registered in an infinitely flexible filing system.

No one has so far come up with a viable solution. As cynics have said, the only sure answer is to put everything in deep-freeze in the dark in perpetuity.

There is in fact a tendency for institutions to do almost that. Time and again we have the complaint of the benefactor whose gift has vanished from sight, apparently for good. The story is told of the collector who was asked about the lodgement of his material in the National Museum. 'It's there all right,' he said, 'as safe from danger as it is from human scrutiny.'

Somehow, there has to be a compromise. For the ephemerist the problem may be slow to develop, but as the collection begins to burst its way out of its first folder or shoebox home, and bits of it start coming adrift, it suddenly becomes a real concern.

Conservation is our first priority. Under this heading come three major tasks: to halt the progress of any present deterioration, to repair tears or other damage, and to protect the collection from damage or deterioration in the future. Until recently—the 1970s and 80s—these processes were considered to be matters for the expert alone. (In some quarters the view remains.) But recent years have brought new products and techniques for amateur use, as well as a bold new sense of enterprise in the beginner.

For amateur or professional, there are underlying principles that govern the whole of this work, and we must consider them carefully before getting down to detail.

Writing of manuscript archive repair (*The Principles of Archive Repair,* 1951), Roger Ellis describes the document as 'first and foremost a vehicle of evidence, of impartial evidence; it is for this quality, in the first place, that it has been preserved, and it is this quality above others that any process of repair must respect.'

Ellis goes on to explain what this means in practice:

> . . . no process of repair may be allowed to remove, diminish, falsify or obscure, in any way, the document's value as evidence . . . Repair must never become tampering, and

> never can become so provided that it obscures nothing of the original, and is itself clearly distinguishable . . . The repairer . . . will also be at pains not to conceal by his operations any portion or feature of the document which is part of, or could shed light upon, its evidential value; and this means not simply that he will not paste new paper over old writing . . . but also that he will observe, preserve, and on occasion reveal such other incidental features as original sewing-holes, dustings of pounce, marks of folding, traces of seals, watermarks, old end-papers, even on occasion stray blobs of wax or old stains—and a great many more . . .

To the simple ephemerist, concerned perhaps with nothing more portentous than a soup ticket or laundry list, the archivist's approach to repair may seem a little over-fussy. But if items of ephemera are to justify a claim to evidential status, if they are to command the same sort of respect as the conventionally accepted historical document, it is clear they must be seen to be above suspicion of 'tampering'.

At another level, but in the same vein, are the comments of David Ellen, of Scotland Yard's Forensic Science Laboratory, speaking to the Ephemera Society in London in the early 1980s:

> The smallest scrap of paper—printed, handwritten, or even apparently blank—is a possibly fertile source of information, not only in its written content (which may also disclose more than at first sight appears) but in many other attributes, folds, tears, holes, creases, erasures, alterations, indentations, it may serve as vital evidence. However apparently trivial, it is in some measure a document of evidential record . . .

Here again, the warning is implicit: whatever may have to be done to preserve an item must be the minimum consistent with the need to retain its validity as best evidence. The less the item is worked on, the greater its evidential value.

For the ordinary collector this may come as bad news. Is it not, after all, natural and reasonable to want to smarten up the collection—to bring exhibits back to mint condition? It is, but 'smartening up' is more than just rescue and repair. It is restoration.

The distinction between repair and restoration is fundamental, and the ephemerist does well to decide which policy to adopt. To repair is 'to arrest decay and protect from further damage'. To restore is to add missing elements—paper, print, writing etc.—bringing the item back to a semblance of its assumed original condition.

In a properly repaired document *the work of mending is apparent*, though more or less unobtrusive. Typically, holes and ragged edges are neatly filled in with comparable, but not exactly matching, paper. The observer sees clearly where the damage was—which is the original document and which has been added. The outer limits of the original are also retained, frayed edges and all. It may thus be possible to assess the overall size of the item, an impossibility if the sheet had been 'tidied up' by trimming. In all, the document is presented as found—nothing added or taken away, and saved as evidence.

In a restored document, on the other hand, *work on the item is as far as possible invisible*. The paper is cleaned, holes are filled; margins are added, using exactly matching paper; broken borders, defective images, missing writing, are 'made good', and the whole is refurbished to a point where the item is indistinguishable from an untouched original. The work is often unbelievably convincing, an exercise in high skill and low cunning. Frankly, it may come perilously close to the counterfeit—real in parts, but mostly fake.

Most ephemerists compromise, repairing where they can, restoring hardly at all.

One other underlying principle in repair, observed by amateur and professional alike, is that of reversibility. No operation should be carried out on an item if it cannot be reversed without damage. Nothing should be affixed to it nor applied to

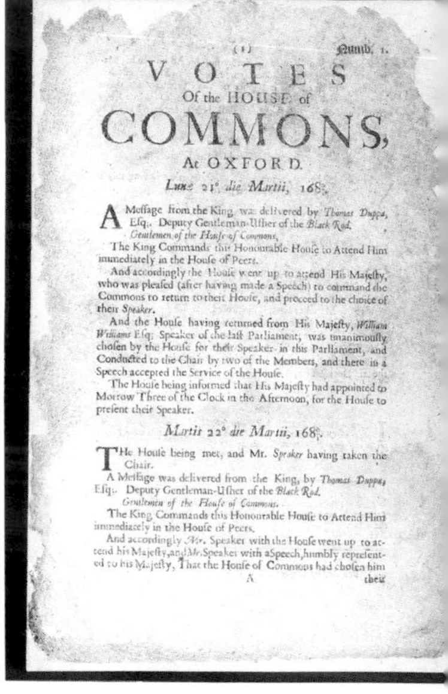

(1) Numb. 1.

VOTES
Of the HOUSE of
COMMONS,
At OXFORD.

Lunæ 21° die Martii, 168$\frac{0}{1}$.

A Meſſage from the King was delivered by *Thomas Duppa*, Eſq;. Deputy Gentleman-Uſher of the *Black Rod*.

Gentlemen of the Houſe of Commons,

The King Commands this Honourable Houſe to Attend Him immediately in the Houſe of Peers.

And accordingly the Houſe went up to attend His Majeſty, who was pleaſed (after having made a Speech) to command the Commons to return to their Houſe, and proceed to the choice of their *Speaker*.

And the Houſe having returned from His Majeſty, *William Williams* Eſq; Speaker of the laſt Parliament, was unanimouſly choſen by the Houſe for their Speaker in this Parliament, and Conducted to the Chair by two of the Members, and there in a Speech accepted the Service of the Houſe.

The Houſe being informed that His Majeſty had appointed to Morrow Three of the Clock in the Afternoon, for the Houſe to preſent their Speaker.

Martis 22° die Martii, 168$\frac{0}{1}$.

THe Houſe being met, and Mr. *Speaker* having taken the Chair.

A Meſſage was delivered from the King, by *Thomas Duppa*, Eſq;. Deputy Gentleman-Uſher of the *Black Rod*.

Gentlemen of the Houſe of Commons.

The King Commands this Honourable Houſe to Attend Him immediately in the Houſe of Peers.

And accordingly *Mr.* Speaker with the Houſe went up to attend his Majeſty, and *Mr.* Speaker with a Speech, humbly repreſented to his Majeſty, That the Houſe of Commons had choſen him

A their

In this expertly treated document, the work of mending is clearly apparent; missing paper is replace by comparable—but noticeably different—paper, and the outer limits are untrimmed, leaving the original dimensions of the sheet to the judgement of others. Note that this double-sided document is legib from both sides: the added paper is shaped to fill out the area and is he in place by an overall facing of transparent repair tissue, back and front.

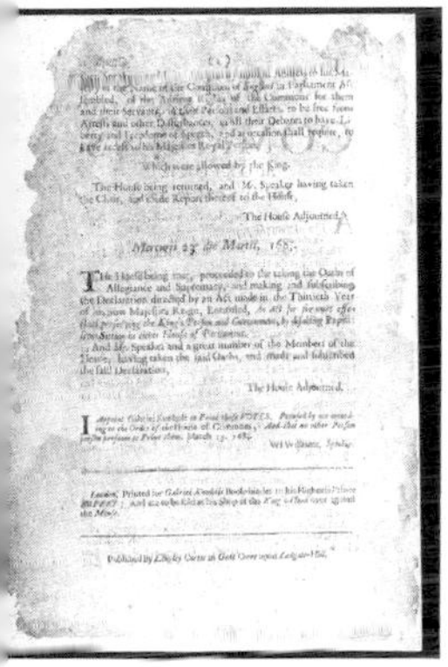

it that cannot be removed safely. Nor should it be washed, bleached, tinted or otherwise treated, if the effect of such treatments cannot also be reversed without harm.

A further principle relates to restraint. As in major surgery, it is generally agreed that the number of operations carried out on a subject should be kept to a minimum; most operations involve an element of risk, and in any case, unwanted side-effects may call for yet further remedial treatment. As a general rule the collector is advised to let well alone.

There is an additional reason for leaving well alone, unrelated to risk. Many forms of treatment, apart from the most urgent of first-aid repairs, are more or less cosmetic in effect, designed to rejuvenate the ageing exhibit, and there is a temptation to avail oneself of these as a matter of course, replacing folds and wrinkles with a schoolgirl complexion. But this is to tamper with evidence. The crumples and creases of a life-time are essential components of the item; it has, in fact, a *right* to them. Without them, it is not only a fraud, but an aesthetic offence.

For the amateur collector/repairer there is one final reason for letting well alone: however adept the amateur, the professional does it so much better. Professional skills and experience always win the day.

But there are still certain basic treatments and observances that the beginner may practise at home.

The first of these is cleaning—dry and wet. Dry-cleaning may be carried out with the traditional india-rubber eraser, using as soft a substance and as light a touch as possible. The eraser may also be applied as a fine powder, sprinkled on the surface and lightly rubbed with the fingers or a pad of soft material. Both methods involve a measure of abrasion of course, and inevitably they remove a small portion of the surface as well as dirt. Also available are non-abrasive cleaners made of kneadable rubber. These are permanently tacky and may be formed and re-formed as pressure pads for lifting dirt without rubbing. They do not smear, nor do they leave clinging particles. They are merely dabbed on the surface, removing extraneous matter, but leaving surface and image intact.

Another form of dry cleaning is carried out with a fine scalpel. Patches of surface dirt may be lightly abraded, using the point of the blade for small particles and the edge for larger areas. Large-area work is best done under a magnifier, using a succession of gentle shaving movements rather than trying to remove the whole of the deposit in one stroke.

In these processes, as in all treatment where items are handled or held in place with the fingers, care must be taken to shield the surface from damage by skin moisture. A protective paper should be used, not only beneath the finger-tips that hold the item but at the point of rest of the scalpel hand.

For the amateur, wet cleaning is a slightly more daunting job, though with a little practice on test items, this too is a manageable home process. The document to be treated is laid on a larger sheet of Melinex, Mylar, or other flexible transparent film, the film having first been wetted with tap water. With the item so placed, and the film resting on a suitable flat surface, the document is gently moistened by dabbing its surface with a wet sponge. The paper, fully moistened, will become soft and floppy. No attempt should be made to lift or manipulate the paper as a whole, but very gentle dabbing with the sponge will induce crease-lines to flatten out. Dog-ears or other such irregularities may be lightly touched back into place with a camel-hair brush.

Continued sponge-dabbing—*dabbing*, not rubbing—will release surprising quantities of surface dirt, though the effect will become fully apparent only afterwards, when the document is thoroughly dry. If desired, the document may

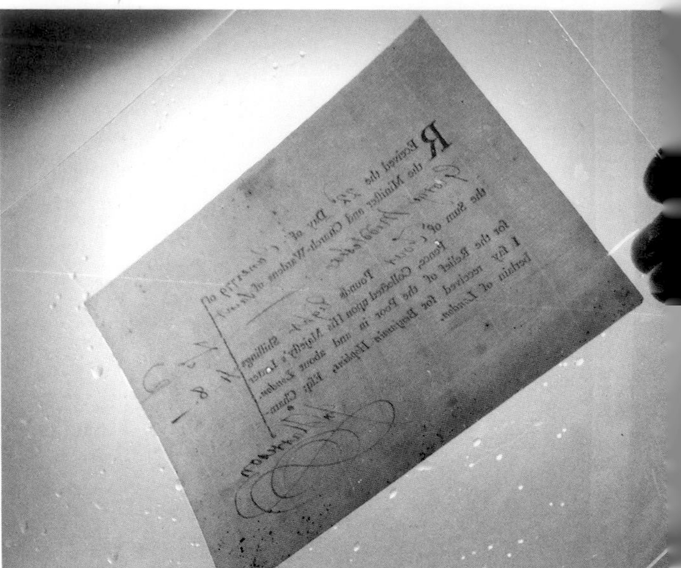

Items of ephemera may be cleaned b washing in plain water. The specimen is laid on a sheet of film (left) and gently dabbed with a wet sponge. The soaked paper adheres t the film (above), allowing the item to be turned over and laid down on second sheet of film for treatment of the reverse.

also be laved under a gently running stream of tap-water, though this must not be so strong as to dislodge it from contact with the plastic film.

The other side of the item is now to be washed. A second sheet of plastic film, pre-moistened as before, is laid over the wet document, forming a sandwich, the paper held between the two sheets of plastic. The whole sandwich may now be turned over and the original sheet of film carefully rolled away, leaving the paper adhering to the lower sheet.

The reverse of the document, now uppermost, may be washed and treated as before. Finally, surplus water is drained off. The plastic film, still bearing the wet document, is held vertically for a few minutes until the trickle of water stops. It is then laid flat, document uppermost, and the whole is covered with three or four sheets of super-absorbent white blotting paper. The sandwich, at this point consisting of film/document/blotting paper, is turned over as before, the film, now uppermost, is rolled back as before, and replaced by more sheets of blotting paper. This new sandwich is now placed under a heavy, evenly-distributed weight to dry out. Drying time will depend on the thickness of the document, the absorbency of the blotting paper and the temperature and humidity of the workplace. If all has gone well, the dry document will be absolutely flat and noticeably cleaner.

The sandwiching technique is far less complicated than it sounds, and it allows safe handling of even the most fragile and unwieldy items. At no point is the document actually waterborne, and its weakest portions are not strained by its own waterlogged weight. The method lies at the heart of many of the more radical repair and conservation processes, and time spent in its mastery is well repaid.

The technique as described applies in general terms to the run-of-the-mill item of printed ephemera, a broadside for example, printed in black on white paper. An item printed in colour, however, or on a colour-tinted paper, may need special attention. It is as well to check specimens for colour fastness before starting. A corner of blotting paper dipped in a single drop of water on the surface to be checked will reveal whether or not colours will run. If the blotting paper picks up any trace, dry treatment is indicated.

As it happens, a very large range of paper material—plain, coloured, printed, handwritten—withstands water well. (And papers themselves, particularly those produced prior to the wood-pulp processes of the 1850s and 60s, may sometimes seem indestructible.) But colour fastness cannot be relied on. Handwriting in ink is surprisingly rugged, but here again confidence should be tempered with caution. The blotting-paper test is always worth the trouble. Pencil writing, wet or dry, is at risk only when rubbed.

Two more wet processes are to be noted—bleaching and sizing.

Printed documents may be whitened with a weak solution of ordinary household bleach. An eggcupful added to a litre of plain cold water will be enough to experiment with. A photographer's developing dish or a household baking dish should be used. The item to be treated, already soaked in plain water, should be slipped into the solution, and fully immersed. The dish is gently rocked to ensure even coverage. (Here, it must be noted, the item is unsandwiched, free-floating, and at risk of falling apart if not handled with extreme care.) Before long the tone of the paper will be seen to be lightening. The process will be fast or slow, depending on the strength of the solution. It will stop when the solution is poured off and replaced with clean water. Printing will remain; all else—*including ink handwriting*—will have faded. After a 20–30 minute rinse in running water, the item is sandwich-dried and pressed as usual.

The bleach effect may be startling. The paper is reduced to a snowy whiteness (some would say an unhealthy pallor) and the item may even be taken at first glance for a modern reproduction. The process is to be used only sparingly, if at all.

Sizing, designed to restore paper to its former crispness, may be carried out as a separate operation or as an addition to other wet treatments. All that is needed is a final immersion for a few minutes in a weak solution of good-quality decorator's size (one teaspoonful to a litre of water will do). After a final brief rinse in plain water the item may be sandwich-dried.

There is one wet operation that sooner or later every ephemerist encounters, the process of soaking items from album pages or other mounts. Here again, a precautionary colour-fastness test is advised before work begins.

Floating items free is sometimes easy, sometimes maddeningly difficult. Much depends of course on the nature of the adhesives concerned, on how liberally they were applied, and how porous or otherwise are the papers involved. Only trial and error will guide the operator, but there are a few general points to remember. Broadly speaking, warm water is more effective than cold (though colours run more readily in warm). Warm water may work in minutes, where cold may take hours. Temperature may also affect the amount of glue or paste adhering to the item when it is dried. It is a good plan to leave things to soak for some time after they

onze brought to light.—

have observed on board
, an invention which,
urselves competent to
us as being worthy of
'ater Tank, measuring
and 3 feet in diameter,
gallons of water, con-
ust and companionway,
e the deck. Its supe-
on account of the ex-
d in it to the open air,
ed in a higher state of
casks; secondly, the
stock of water can be
e time of rain by the
appeared more conve-
m than casks, and as
where it was least in
.]

the leaves of the com-
hem, without pressing
good spirits of wine
nd let it stand until it
incture will keep for
tle inferior to attar of
suffice to impregnate
h a delicious odor.—
proved by a very small
erman paper.]

row the capital which their business may require; while persons of these classes *know*, that through the agency of the Bank of the United States, the rate of interest has been practically reduced in the State from seven to six per cent.; that the currency, not only here, but throughout the United States, owes its equality, and hence property, its stability, to this institution; that it has now out on loan millions and tens of millions which cannot be called in without creating one wide scene of desolation; and therefore, that it is a beneficial institution, which, instead of being destroyed, should be protected; the sycophants who swear by a master—the money changers at Albany—the monied oligarchy of the Farmers' and Mechanics' Bank, and all its subsidiaries—the owners of stock in the State banks, and others who have a common interest with the State banks in depressing a rival that furnishes money cheaper than themselves,—all join in the cry of *Veto! Veto!*—and though claiming to be democrats, friends of the people, yet applaud an act of passion of the Executive—of a single man—which neutralizes, by the simple word "*I forbid,*" the deliberate act of the representatives of twelve millions of people and of twenty-four sovereign States!!

Such are the materials, such the democracy, such

An appropriation was obtained, (as is stated in the Official, &c.,) a few years since for erecting a Light-house at the mouth of Duck Creek; but no Light-house ever has been erected there. The obvious superiority of Mahon's Landing as a location for a Light-house, was apparent to every one, and a petition was preferred to Congress, praying that this appropriation should be diverted from its original object and applied to the erection of a Light-house at Mahon's Landing. It was ordered by Congress, and a Light-house was built at Mahon's Landing, which is now deemed by waterman the most useful one in the bay.

This Light House and the Harbor are separated from the main land by a large extent of marsh and a branch of the Delaware, and is inaccessible from the main land but by a boat. The appropriation in the Harbor bill of 9000 dollars, was to connect this isolated improvement and the Harbor, with the main land. Without this road, it is believed, that the Light House will not be tenantable for another year—and it is essential to the utility of the Harbor that the communication should be open in the winter season, to enable the keeper of the Light house and the crews of the numerous vessels which are often shut up there by the ice, to get to land where they may procure the necessaries of life to save themselves from starvation. We are informed, that last winter, the crew of a southern vessel, which had sought shelter in the Harbor, nearly perished from frost and famine, from inability to get to the shore—their hands and feet were so severely frost bitten, that the flesh dropped from them. It is to

New-York in agriculture, commerce and manufactures, which justly entitles her to pre-eminence in the Union, is mainly attributable to those great arteries of inter-communication, canals, which an enlarged and liberal policy has constructed, and which will long remain sources of opulence and glory to the State.

Resolved, That in the judgment of this meeting, neither justice nor policy required that the march of internal improvement should be arrested, until those portions of the State hitherto neglected, are allowed to share that prosperity which the erection of public works has produced in more favored districts.

Resolved, That it be recommended to the friends of the Chenango canal, wherever resident and especially to those living in the valley of the Chenango, to remit no honorable exertion to obtain the sanction of the legislature to the construction of the Chenango canal.

On motion, Resolved: That the committee appointed to draft resolutions, be requested to draft and publish an address to the people of this State; and also to draft a memorial to the legislature praying for the passage of an act authorizing the construction of the Chenango canal, and the said committee affix the names of the members of this convention to said address and memorial.

On motion of Charles P. Kirkland,

Resolved, That this convention entertains a grateful sense of the enlightened zeal and valuable exertions of the late Wm. H. Maynard, in behalf of the Chenango canal, and that the friends of this improvement in common with their fellow citizens at large,

This demonstration piece shows the effect of 'improving' an item by bleaching. The left-hand portion is admittedly more legible, but suffers ss of character. The trimmed upper margin, also intended as an improvement, is equally to be discouraged. However, it is as well to be able to detect such work.

have come away, checking them carefully and swabbing away any residue before proceeding to dry them. Gum residue may be especially troublesome. Even a light deposit, almost invisible, will cause curling or cockling when the items are dried. (An additional hazard is the tendency of the remaining gum to stick the item to the blotting paper during the drying process.)

Some specimens positively refuse to be soaked off. In really obstinate cases a last resort is the attack from the rear. The wet item is placed face downwards on a suitable hard surface and the moist paper of the mount is gently peeled away, layer by layer, the paper being continually re-moistened during the process. The work may be aided by lightly abrading the surface with a blunt-edged scraper. This may also be used to remove the deposit of glue on the back of the item, now revealed by removal of the backing. The process requires patience and an even temper.

In some cases, where it is clear that a whole batch of material has been mounted with the same intractable adhesive, it may be wise to leave things un-floated, trimming the backing paper within a millimetre or so of the exhibit, and settling for that.

A prime concern of the archivist is the matter of deacidification. This, and provision of an acid-free environment for storage and display, has in recent years become a major talking point. In museums, archives and libraries (and certainly in the catalogues of archival materials companies) 'acid-free' and 'deacidification' are recurrent terms.

Acids in the atmosphere in our twentieth-century environment—not to mention those built into the manufacture of modern papers—present a serious threat to papers of all kinds. Discoloration and embrittlement are the chief symptoms of the trouble, and detection of their presence at an early stage is vital. The problem is properly one for the expert, but there are measures that the ordinary collector may take to be on the safe side.

A first requirement is the use of acid-free mounting, storage and repair materials. These are available through archival aids suppliers, as well as from better-class board, box and paper firms. A second requirement is a means of checking for the presence of acidity, in ephemera and mounting materials alike. There are various methods, but for the amateur the easiest method is the 'pencil detector', a refillable pencil used in conjunction with a drop of distilled water on the paper surface. A reading of alkalinity or acidity is registered in 15 seconds.

The process of deacidification may also be carried out in the home laboratory. This is done with an immersion solution or by aerosol spray. (Sources of these and other conservation products are given on page 219).

Repair materials, already noted as required to be reversible, must of course be acid-free too. Moisture-adhesive repair tapes are available in acid-free paper and in transparent self-adhesive tissue. Both are reversible. They may also be used for hinge-mounting, either in the manner of stamp hinges or as strip hinges in print framing.

An additional form of repair, often viewed as a last-ditch option, is lamination. For the extra-fragile item this offers a form of combined repair and conservation, wholly enclosing the exhibit in a transparent protective film. The material may be all-over heat sealed, all-over self-adhesive, or edge-sealed. (Edge-sealing is commonly known as 'encapsulation'.) Here too the repair materials are acid-free, though prior deacidification of the exhibit is usually recommended. The processes are also reversible (insofar as the contents are not too far gone to survive yet another operation). On the whole, lamination and encapsulation may best be left to experts, but with tenacity the enterprising amateur may well become an expert too.

As we move from the subject of repair to storage and display, we pause for a reminder of the 'Sherlock Holmes' factor, referred to in earlier pages. As we have noted, it is in the course of repair and preparation for display that risks of 'tidying up' arise. Nowhere is this more pointed than in the matter of a specimen's outer limits—the nature of its edges. These may originally have been trimmed square by guillotine, cut roughly with scissors, torn by hand or separated by perforation. The item may be wholly or partly 'deckle-edged' (untrimmed hand-made paper) or it may have become ragged through ordinary wear and tear. These characteristics are as much a part of the item as its surface content. Typical examples are the rough-and-ready turnpike tickets on pages 128–9, the showman's hand-made paper bill on page 130, and the corner-worn language cards on pages 194–5. In these cases, as with similar examples elsewhere, there has been no attempt to square the items up. (Nor, by the way, have marginal pencil notes been removed: Meredith's two-wheeler handbill (page 131) still bears its discount annotation, and Tomlinson's 'Winter Clothing' item (page 185) shows the pencilled price that someone paid for it at a 1970s ephemera fair; this too may be seen as part of the history of the item.

Storage and display of ephemera remains a field for personal exploration. Much depends on the range and nature of the material concerned, much also on the collector's budget. Generally speaking, the album is the standard answer to the problem, specimens being individually mounted on loose leaves or alternatively slipped into transparent plastic sleeves, loose or fixed.

The size of the album must of course depend on a long-term view of the possible development of the collection, enabling the largest potential specimen to be a candidate for inclusion. The album must also appear likely to remain available as a standard product for some years to come, so that an expanding collection may be housed in uniform style. Many such products are available, most of the slip-in variety offering a range of compartments—one, two, three or four to a page.

The slip-in plastic album allows easy insertion and re-arrangement of exhibits. It also admits inclusion of slender three-dimensional specimens—pin-papers, needle packets and similar items, together with their contents.

In the slip-in album the quality of the transparent plastic is all-important. The cheaper sleeves are made with a polymer plasticizer, a substance which gives flexibility to the sheet, but which may also endanger the specimen it holds. Items stored over-long in the material are found to leave an ominous image of themselves on the inner surface of the plastic on removal. This, the result of 'chemical migration', bodes ill for conservation. The same trouble, to one degree or another, besets most of the plastic films used as specimen sleeves. These are suitable not for long-term use, but only for temporary storage. They should be viewed with some suspicion.

Chief among the few acceptable plastic films is polyethylene pterephthalate, more humanely known as Melinex in Britain, Mylar in America. This, a much more expensive product, is also much more desirable. It is non-acidic, chemically and dimensionally inert, resistant to extremes of temperature and humidity, and remarkably durable. It is suitable for loose-leaf sleeves for albums and may also be welded ultrasonically for encapsulation. It comes in two or three thicknesses, and may also be had with built-in UV light filtration to protect exhibits from fading.

A similar material is used in some top-quality albums, among them the SAFE range, a series offering a variety of different compartment schemes and a choice of loose-paper and fixed-plastic black dividers. These too are expensive, but probably the best obtainable. Cheap albums should be viewed as temporary housing; those with tacky pages and film overlays should be ignored.

The alternative to the full-blown album is the ring binder, in which punch-holed leaves may be inserted, the exhibits hinged or photo-cornered as desired. The method has disadvantages: unless the exhibits are hinged top and bottom, they tend to flap about, tangling with each other on opposite pages; all except the smallest photo-cornered items may come adrift with the curving of the pages as they turn; exhibits are unprotected from admiring fingers; and layouts take a long time to

arrange and mount (as opposed to the slip-in page, which takes none to speak of).

Another approach altogether is the mount and storage box. Here the collection is mounted on standard-sized cards housed in standard-sized containers, known in America as 'museum' or 'portfolio' cases, and in Britain as 'solander boxes'.

The boxes are built of plywood, hardboard or other strong board, and are lined with acid-free paper, They generally have a dust-proof 'shouldered' closure and are fitted with hook-latches and metal title-card holders. In the system specified for the collection of the Foundation for Ephemera Studies the boxes have an inside measurement of 47.2 × 32.4 × 8.25 cm ($18\frac{5}{8} \times 12\frac{3}{4} \times 3\frac{1}{4}$ in), and the card mounts, known as 'panels', measure 46.7 × 31.45 cm ($18\frac{3}{8} \times 12\frac{3}{8}$ in). The cards are dark brown in colour, offsetting the generally lighter tone of the exhibits. The boxes are stored horizontally in open racks.

The panel-size accommodates all but the largest of general ephemera (though some oversize items are stored folded). Exhibits are tab-mounted with archival tapes, commonly at four points; double-sided items are hinge-mounted to allow access to the reverse. Fragile exhibits are protected by a Melinex overlay.

It must be said that the method is costly and time-consuming. The boxes, when full, are heavy and may have to be lifted by a slender research assistant from racking at ceiling height. Average capacity of the boxes is 70 panels, bearing in all some 150–200 items. Each panel is laid out individually to display exhibits to advantage.

The Collection of the Foundation f Ephemera Studies is housed in horizontally-racked solander boxes Specimens are hinge-mounted on standard-sized display cards. Exhibits themselves are untouched during inspection, the open box lying flat or resting at an angle on lectern (centre) or, as shown here, resting temporarily on a chair. To obviate wear and tear, as well as fc economy of materials, boxes are housed on runners rather than shelves. Filing is alphabetical. Box are numbered.

The process of arranging and mounting takes considerable time: a single-item panel will take a minute to complete, whereas a panel bearing some dozens of miniature labels may take an hour or more.

The system has drawbacks, but it also has distinct advantages. Its standard-sized panels prevent movement of the contents within the box; horizontal racking prevents material buckling and bending (which would be a problem in vertical storage); the system's semi-rigid panels allow the collection to be handled without actual contact with the exhibits themselves; the panels may be freely shifted from one location to another on the loose-leaf principle; and with the box opened out on a lectern, the contents may be flipped through for quick inspection without removal. Panels may be transferred to the lid portion of the box for further attention.

Another advantage is the facility for displaying the panels away from the boxes.

The lie-flat solander box allows ready access to the specimen cards nd easy transfer of the cards, in due sequence, to the lid portion during spection. The specimens themselves receive no direct handling and only a minimum of frictional contact.

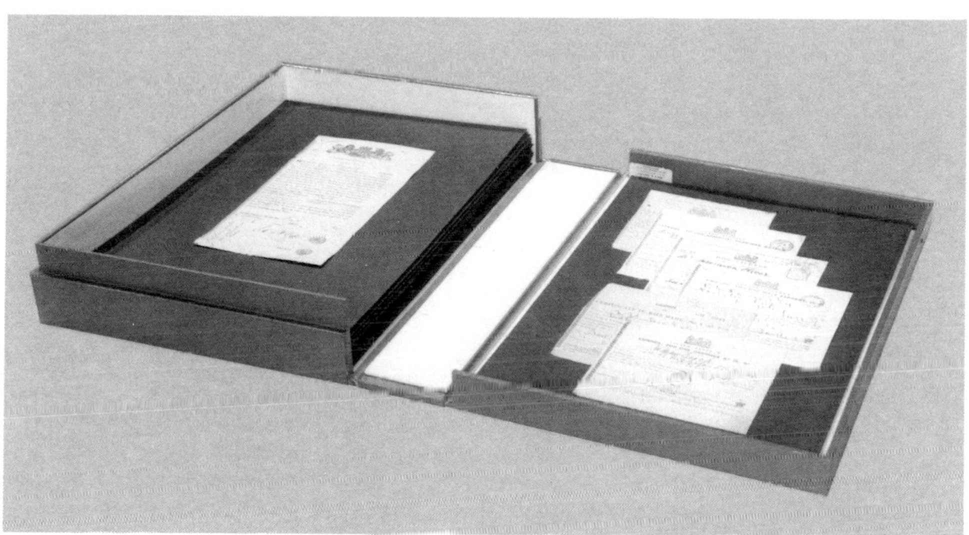

Using matching-format metal frames and perspex facings, the panels—ready laid out—may be used to form an in-house display or travelling exhibition.

It will be seen that ephemera, this relative newcomer to the world of evidential record, is still struggling to get itself organized. Unlike the book, which over centuries has been brought to a high state of manageability, the vagrant item of ephemera tends to resist control. For many of the world's librarians, accumulations of ephemera have been seen as cuckoos in the bookshelf nest. And yet, as we have seen, it is often to the library that ephemera tends to gravitate. It is perhaps small wonder then that in the most intractable of all ephemera problems—cataloguing—it has fallen to a bibliographer to take the first institutional step toward bringing it under electronic control.

Punched-card catalogues of ephemera had been in use privately in the 1960s and 70s, notably by William Helfand, whose Pharmaceutical History Collection went electronic in the late 1960s. But in 1976 Dr Robin Alston, Bibliographical Consultant to the British Library, successfully argued the case for including printed ephemera in the library's computerized catalogue of eighteenth-century publications. Thus for the first time ephemera was brought from its grey-area status to academic and electronic recognition. Alston's initiative means that today it is possible to search the Eighteenth-century Short-Title Catalogue (ESTC) and locate some 50,000 items of ephemera previously unrecorded.

The development has enormous implications for the future. If all goes well, the system will allow instant-access interrogation on a worldwide basis, linking libraries and ephemera collections on keyboards everywhere.

The vision goes farther than that. Before too long technology will bring not only computerized printed listings, but actual pictures of the material, gathered on the same basis. In a further refinement, the high-definition full-colour image may be 'peeled off' at the receiving end as a take-away print. The image-bank idea is applicable in countless areas of academic and commercial activity; in ephemera studies its potential is virtually limitless. The matter is among a number of research projects under review by the Foundation for Ephemera Studies.

In the meantime the average collector pursues an independent—mostly penny-pinching—course. The personal computer, increasingly accessible, is clearly part of the answer, and the time may come when everyone's keyboard is linked with Robin Alston's. But for finding our way about our own collections (for most of us, enough to be getting on with) we have to settle for today's home technology.

In the course of his speech of acceptance of the Ephemera Society's medal in 1986, Dr Helfand reflected on the relationship between private and institutional computers and computer methods at large:

> Individuals such as ourselves can use these methods, even if at the start we do so only in a primitive way. We progress as the usefulness of the systems progresses . . . We should not wait for the perfect solution. It is better to take advantage of equipment and programs that exist and adapt them to changing circumstances. It is not possible to solve all problems of access at once; rather they should be considered sequentially.
>
> Now that the British Library's Eighteenth-century Short-Title Catalogue as well as a computerized storage and retrieval system for images, is being developed, I will have to see how I can adapt these developments to my own needs and my own system. I am afraid it has to be 'my' personal need because, like most of us, I do not have an affiliation with a university or other institution that allows me working relationships with a library. It is important to know of the existence of ephemera collections, and where they are, but somehow this information has to be brought into my own system quickly and economically. Meanwhile, as the advances are awaited with great interest, I will do what I can with what I have.

One other aspect of collecting and curatorship, a problem still to be solved, is the matter of terminology. Though not yet a pressing matter for the individual collector, the question is a major thinking point in libraries and museums: *when and how will everyone agree on what to call things*?

At the heart of the concept of the catalogue lies common acceptance, not only of alphabetical order, but of nomenclature. Without agreement on these, all is chaos. The matter comes sharply into focus in computerized storage and retrieval of ephemera. Are we concerned with, say, a 'leaflet' or a 'handbill'? Or a 'flyer'? Should we call for 'posters' or 'notices'; 'announcements' or 'proclamations'? 'Broadsides' or 'broadsheets'? Should it be 'calling card' or 'visiting card'?

And should we write *trade card*, *trade-card* or *tradecard*? *Catalogue* or *catalog*? *Check* or *cheque*? Among ourselves, both locally and internationally, we must sort these matters out. The computer, more logical than we are, demands consistency.

These and a host of other issues need deciding *now*—long before Dr Alston's world circuit arrives. As someone said in a report on nomenclature to the Smithsonian Institution: 'We may almost envisage a re-run of the account of Adam, called on to name everything that was brought before him; whatever he called it "that was the name thereof".'

Collecting ephemera has lately come into its own; but it is still at an excitingly awkward age.

NO'

Specimens illustrate
the following pages
grouped very largely
scale with each oth
varying degrees of reduct
or enlargement
indicated by percent
figures at appropri
poi

Part Two

PRINTING PROCESSES, CATEGORIES, THEMES

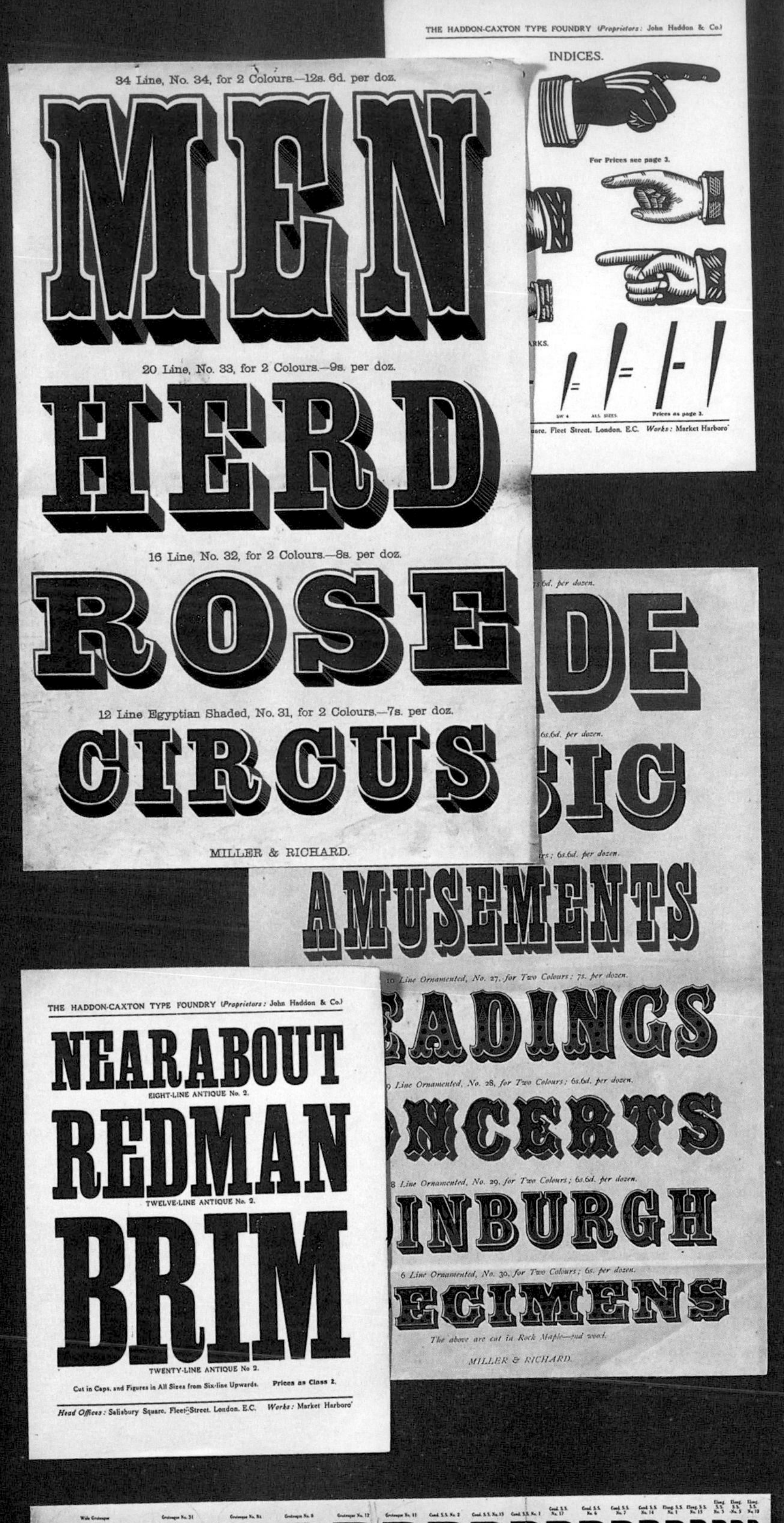

Letterpress

Also known as 'relief printing' (from the raised printing surface it employs) the letterpress process is best understood by reference to the ordinary office rubber stamp. The raised portions are inked, and pressed against paper, leaving an impression.

Much of the work of the general printer, from the time of Caxton to the middle of our own century, has employed the principle. Working with wood or metal type and blocks, the printer has produced in this period, not only books and journals, but a vast output of general ephemera.

When a second set of printing blocks, inked with a different colour, is added to the first impression, a two-colour effect is produced. The idea is epitomized in the so-called 'chromatic' wood letters of the latter part of the nineteenth century, widely used to liven up the music hall, circus and concert poster. Type sheets from the firm of Miller & Richard (left) and the CONCERT strip (right) show them in action.

Most of the time the letterpress printer's work was in a single colour—black—with just an occasional use of coloured paper by way of a change. Most things were printed in a hurry, and as cheaply as possible. The effect of this is seen in uneven inking, smudging, and over-heavy pressure. (In some cases the printing surface has punched deep into the paper, producing a raised impression on the reverse.)

The letterpress printer needed a big store of wood and metal raw material, and as type fashions changed the problem got worse. A specimen range of capital Rs, available in 18 different widths and as many depths, conveys the predicament.

Early years of the nineteenth century saw a revolution in type design. To meet the need for public-notice impact, big new chunky types were introduced. As the examples here show, printers made the most of them.

3rd MAY 1817.

Removal
OF
MUD or SOIL.

ANY Person or Persons who wish to Contract to remove MUD and SOIL from the lower part of the Town's Mills Pond, upon the Mud and Soil adjoining on the north part, are desired to meet the Bailiffs and Committee of the Corporation of Bridgnorth, at the Town's Mills, on Monday morning next, at Ten o'clock precisely; when the Particulars of the Work to be done, will be explained.

From the Printing Office of G. Gitton, Bridgnorth.

BOOTS

REPAIRED

...eam Conveyance
BETWEEN
Sunderland & London.

THE
...berdeen and London
Steam Navigation Company

...eg to intimate to the Public of Sunderland, Newcastle, North and ...outh Shields, Durham, and Neighbourhood, that they have made ...rrangements for their powerful and splendid Steam Vessels, the

...uke of Wellington
AND
Queen of Scotland,
Of 200 Horse-power each,

to call in Sunderland Roads weekly, on their passages to and from London; to take on board and land Passengers and light Goods at Sunderland.

The Du...

will call in the Roads o... o'Clock, afternoon. Pass... have to go on board a cle... attendance at Thornhill... to be conveyed to the R...

Sunderland, April 8th, 1835.

MAD DOGS having been seen in this Neighbourhood, the
OWNERS of DOGS,
within the PARISH OF BURSLEM, are required to keep them up until further Notice.
Any Dogs hereafter found at large will be Destroyed.
By Order of the Chief Constable,
W. HARDING,
J. P. HARDING,
Clerks to the Commissioners of the Burslem Police.
Dated, 21st July, 1834.
MARY BROUGHAM, PRINTER.

A
MEETING
Of the Inhabitants of the
BOROUGH OF BERKELEY,
WILL BE HELD AT THE
BERKELEY ARMS HOTEL,
On TUESDAY Evening Next,
At Six o'Clock,
To consider the propriety and possibility of Lighting the Town with
GAS.
WILLIAM GAISFORD,
MAYOR.
Berkeley 21st January, 1854.
POVEY, PRINTER, BERKELEY.

5000 Laborers,
300 Carpenters,
300 Stone Cutters,
200 Stone Masons,
WANTED
Immediately on the West Central Division
Ohio & Miss. Railroad.
THE HIGHEST WAGES
Paid, and constant employment given, until the completion of the work.
APPLY AT VINCENES TO
ALLEN, M'GRADY & CO.

From his racks and trays of miscellaneous type the letterpress printer compiled the wording of his work. The notices here show the apparently random nature of his choice of typeface. Many such items—not least the MAD DOGS *specimen—were scribbled down, put together and printed in a few hours.*

The CONCERT *slip, though none the worse for it, is badly out in the placing of its second colour. Instead of fitting in its proper place, the orange has slipped, producing a white gap at the foot of the letters and overlaps elsewhere. (Compare with the properly printed examples on the left.)*

Use of the woodcut title piece in the STEAM CONVEYANCE *poster was merely a convention. Selected from the printer's store-shelf, the image did not necessarily resemble either of the ships concerned.*

27%

The printer's store of type was augmented by a range of stock blocks. These, originally hand-cut in wood, were later produced in quantity by the process of stereotyping—taking metal casts from the original block. The Morgan Turk horse, as well as its border, was undoubtedly printed from stock stereos. Borders were available in put-together units, with corner pieces to match. Continuous rules (far right, below) were available to any desired length, also with matching corner pieces. Later came stereos in a range of sizes, enlarged or reduced photo-mechanically.

MORGAN TURK

Morgan Turk is a beautiful Chestnut, with silvery mane and tail, stands 15 3-4 hands high, and is 4 years old the 6th day of next June, and from the superior speed and strength which he exhibits, bids fair to head the list of Stock Horses in Western New York, both as a Draft and Trotting Stallion.

MORGAN TURK

Was sired by the Celebrated Horse Tecumseh, owned by Enoch Fobes, of Oakfield. His dam was a Bright Bay above the medium size, and has trotted her half mile in one and a half minutes, taken from the field without fit, and was from an Eclipse Mare and Durock Horse.

MORGAN TURK

will stand for Mares at the Stable of the Subscriber 1-4 mile East of Wheatville.

***TERMS.*—Six Dollars to insure a foal—Five Dollars by the Season—Three Dollars a leap.**

The Season to commence April 10th, and end on the 4th of July.

N. B.—All accidents at the risk of the owners of Mares.

G. KNAPP.

Wheatville, May 10th, 1858.

PRINTED AT THE HERALD & TIMES OFFICE, BATAVIA, GENESEE COUNTY N. Y.

Both pages 68%

COINS & VIGNETTES

v. et c. 559

v. et c. 81

v. 547 - c. 518

v. 1099 - c. 1228

v. et c. 317

v. 372 - c. 373

v. 79 - c. 78

v. et c. 179

No. 367,—21s.

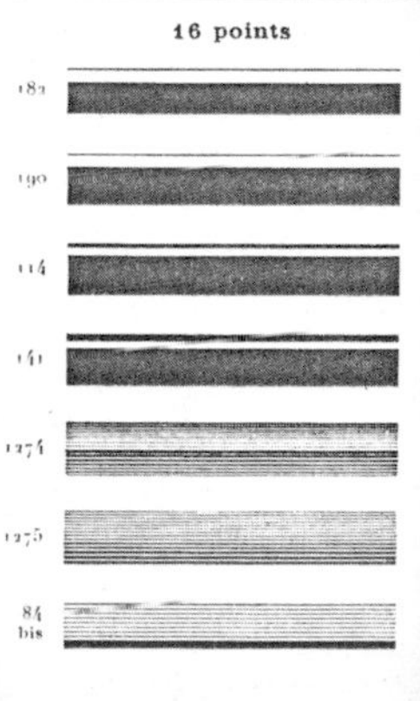

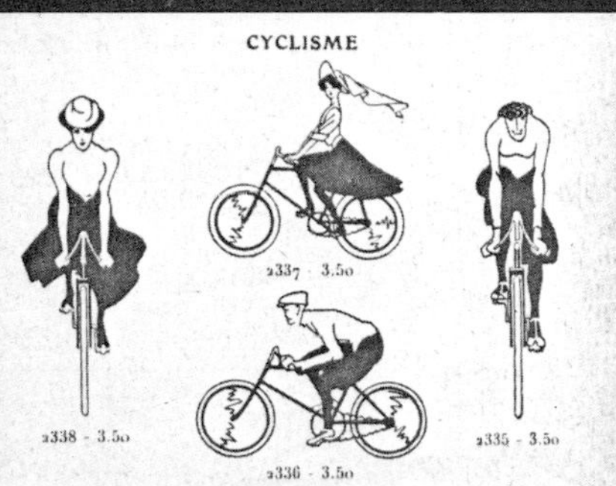

Engraving

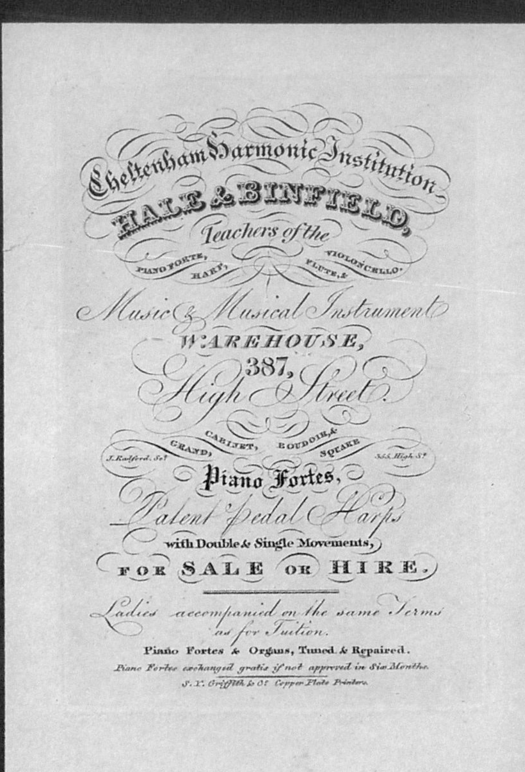

67%

Though it is also applied to the incised image in wood, the term 'engraving' is more generally taken to mean work in metal. It is used to refer both to the image inscribed in the plate and the one printed from it on paper.

The method differs from the relief (letterpress) process in that ink is held *below* the level of the printing surface, the plate being wiped clear before the impression is made. Under pressure, ink is lifted from the incisions to the paper. The method is also known as 'intaglio'.

In engraving, the whole of the image, including any wording, is rendered on the plate (in reverse). It is thus unsuitable for long texts. But for decorative and pictorial purposes, for title pages, bookplates, invitations, tradecards, certificates etc., the method allows a freedom that letterpress lacks.

The best-known form of metal engraving is 'copperplate', a term applying to a calligraphic style as well as to the method. Its script and flourishes have influenced the manuscript form it mimics, producing a handwriting style that itself came to be known as copperplate.

The engraving process came into its own in the nineteenth century, being widely adopted for 'social stationery' and for certificates, tax stamps etc., as well as billheads and tradecards. The general introduction in the 1820s of steel engraving—on much harder and more durable plates—allowed finer detail and longer printing runs, and the process became viable in mass production. Steel engraving had originally been developed for use in banknote printing, and many of the big security printers later did commercial work as a sideline.

Engraving technique relies essentially on the incision of a single line, but with cross-hatching, stipple and other methods, effects of shading are produced.

HEALTH WEALTH HONOR DISEASE POVERTY INFAMY

E.F.B. Del.t Eng.d by V. Balch

This CERTIFIES that
Selleck J St John
is a Member of the
AMERICAN
Young Men's Total Abstinence Society.
New York April 3rd A.D. 1841.
Lewis Hallock President
Olivr V. Bartles COR. SECR.Y

In their appeal to the nobility and gentry, nineteenth-century trades and professions made full use of copperplate elegance. The Hale & Binfield card (facing page) is typical of an idiom that was virtually universal in the period 1830–60.

Copper engraving was used over a wide spectrum of printing, from tax stamps to the local lending library's book labels. Tax-stamp plates, used for very long printing runs, rapidly wore out, and had to be re-engraved by the Stamp Office. Re-workings of this kind were signalled by a system of marked numerals, as seen in the hat tax example. The markings were changed at each re-working.

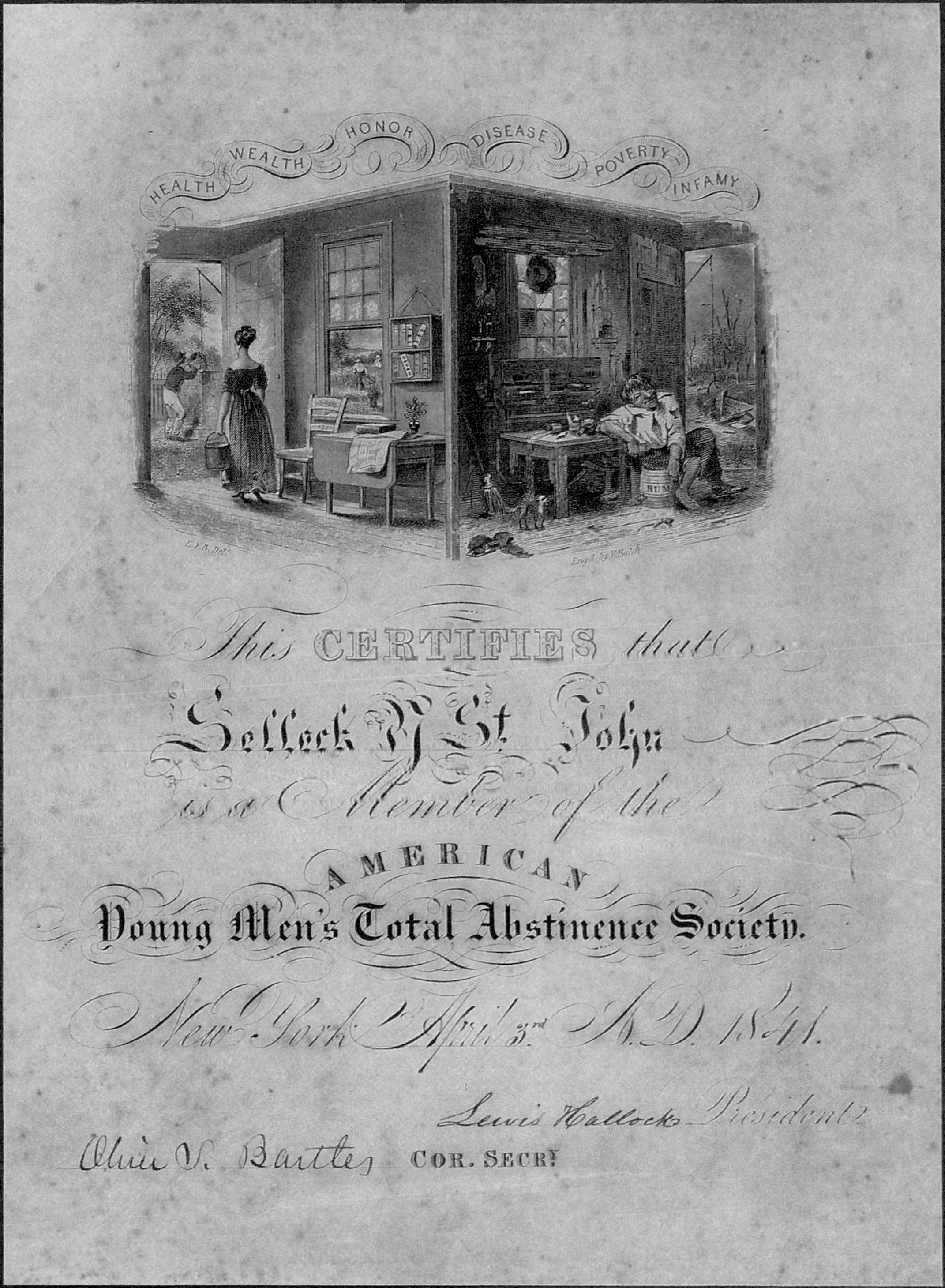

The 'ceremonial' style of the copperplate made it appropriate for use in awards, diplomas and certificates. It also allowed the inclusion of pictorial material, and engravers became adept at rendering images of the glorious and the ideal. The anti-drink certificate (this page) is unusual in its depiction of disaster. It is signed on the left (below the figure of the woman) by E.F.B., the original artist, and on the right by V. Balch, the engraver.

67%

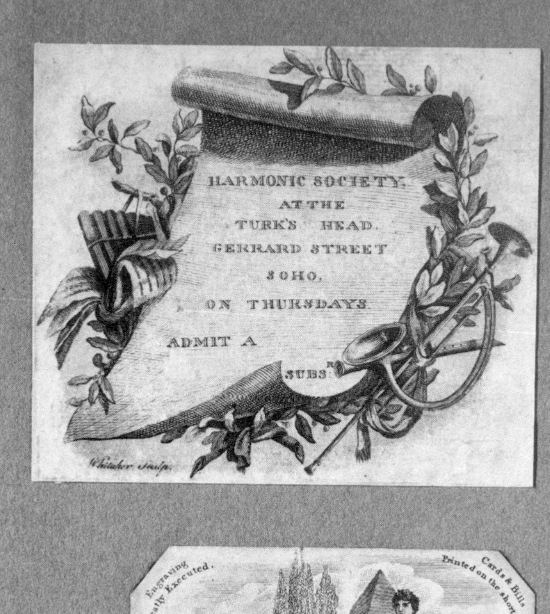

The pictorial element in copperplate and steel engraving gradually moved from the decorative to the representational. By the second half of the nineteenth century the romantic steel engraving (right) had become a popular collector's piece. Also much in demand was the view card (below), a new mass-market product, forerunner of the picture postcard.

The engraver's skills were dominant in security printing, where elaborate borders and classical figures lent not only dignity but complexity to share certificates and banknotes. Standard images, filed by number, could be pieced together as desired for new issues or denominations.

59%

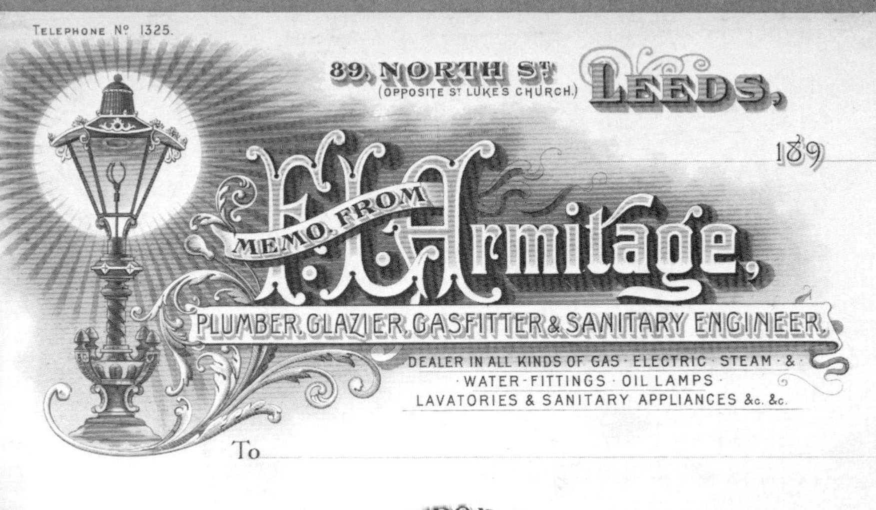

The commercial engraver, like his 'fine art' forebears, sometimes engraved his own original work, sometimes the work of others. The billhead and letterhead man was often his own designer, and his creations gave due rein to his expertise. In the F.L. Armitage design the engraver has pulled every trick. (The 'Invoice from' scroll is designed to paste in place of a 'Memo from' scroll for a variant version when the work is transferred to litho stone or metal.)

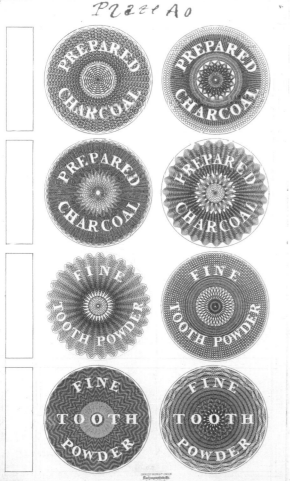

The patterned roundels designed as pot-lid labels, show examples of the work of the geometric lathe, a mechanical engraver. Originally devised for the production of anti-counterfeit patterns for banknotes, the 'machinagraphic' image became popular as an indicator of quality in commercial products.

At the other end of the scale of skills are the labels, coats of arms etc., of everyday stationery. In jobs of this kind the engraver commonly worked from visual materials supplied.

59%

PRINTING PROCESSES (3)

Lithography/ chromolitho

Today's full-colour printing uses only four impressions—red, yellow, blue and black—to convey the whole range of the rainbow. (Black is added as a final 'strengthener'.)

A century ago this remarkable trick neede at least double that number of printings—sometimes even four or five times as many. The system—chromolithography—require a fine degree of judgement in analysing the colouring of the original and manual skill in rendering each component separately on a printing stone. By printing each stone, exactly in register, one image upon the othe the original colour picture was reconstituted. (For a word on the general principle of lithography see overleaf.)

Commercial chromolithography burst upon the world like magic in the 1860s and 70s. It had been a world almost wholly devoid of colour printing; by contrast with the half-hearted efforts of the past, the 'chromo' was a riot.

The art of the chromo had been brought to the rest of the world from Central Europe by emigrant printers. It was the nearest to 'real art' that many had ever seen. Luxuriantl coloured (layered sometimes a dozen or so deep), and later surfaced with the apparent texture and varnish of an oil painting, the chromo flooded the market. First as pictures in their own right, and later as the heart and soul of advertising, chromo images were everyone's pleasure. For many enthusiasts in the 1980s, the magic still holds.

For technical reasons the printing processes of today cannot faithfully reproduce the unique chromolitho effect. It is up to the connoisseur to examine an actual chromolitho under a magnifier to see the distinctive colour stipple printed from the solid stone a hundred or more years ago.

56%

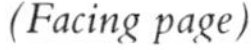

(Facing page)

'Chromos' made their American debut in the 1860s. (The term is said to have been coined by their chief pioneer, the US printer Louis Prang.) Portraying popular landscapes, and reproducing the works of European artists, they ranged in size from little more than a postcard to a large wall-poster.

The process generated many patriotic and commemorative items, as, for example, at the conclusion of the American Civil War. But the overwhelming weight of output was to be in the advertising tradecard.

The much-enlarged rose image, a latter-day item of ephemera, was published by the Ephemera Society in 1977 as part of a popular exposition of the chromolitho principle.

Commercial calendars were prominent among the printed matter triggered by the chromolitho process. The Cunard specimen represents the method near the end of its heyday. The four-colour system was but a few years away.

56%

The roots of the litho and the chromolitho process lie in the principle established by Senefelder in 1792. An image is drawn in a greasy crayon on a flat stone surface; the stone is dampened and the whole surface is rolled with oil-based printer's ink. The ink sticks only to the greasy image, not to the damp parts of the stone (oil and water do not mix). A sheet of paper, pressed on the surface, picks up the inked image. Further inking allows more prints to be taken.

This process was made famous by some of the great names of the nineteenth century, among them, notably Daumier and Gavarni in France. They drew directly on the stone, producing a large number of satirical drawings for the press. Daumier alone did nearly 5000.

(In the shop-window example a husband reflects on corset sizes. He has known them all in his time—the last, in the top right-hand corner, his wife ...)

ÉMOTIONS PARISIENNES

27.

Chez Bauger, R. du Croissant 16. Imp. d'Aubert & Cie

C'est unique! j'ai pris quatre tailles, juste comme celles là dans ma vie; Fifine ma première!
Cocotte, cette gueuse de Cocotte! la grande Mimi, et mon épouse là haut dans le coin:

68%

BOTHAM'S HOTEL, SALT HILL.

It is pleasantly situated, with extensive pleasure grounds, and well adapted for Families who do not wish to be far from London.
Commanding a beautiful View of Windsor Castle, distant only 1½ Miles and ¾ of a Mile from the Slough Station.

Black and white lithography had only limited applications in fields outside the fine arts and illustration. The Botham's Hotel item is an unusual tradecard example (c.1845); the billsticker item (1827) is from a scrap-album title page, captioned 'I want all the scraps I can collect', and the flower print (c.1860) is from a drawing book.

68%

Embossing

90%

The process of embossing uses a metal die, applied under great pressure, forcing an impression into the paper, and permanently altering its structure. The aim is to impress as deeply as possible short of actual penetration. Success depends on the speed and strength of impact and the thickness, texture, and moisture content of the paper.

Beneath the paper a secondary die presses into the cavities of the primary die. Between the two, the paper is squashed into shape.

Decorative embossing of paper has always been closely associated with Victorian social stationery, and more particularly with its pioneers, Dobbs, Kidd & Co. of London, who started business at the turn of the eighteenth century and remained active under various styles until the late 1890s.

Other names in the field were Mansell, Woods, Dobson, De La Rue and Windsor. In the United States, at first using dies imported from Britain, and later their own, the dominant name was Samuel Dickinson of Boston. (Makers' names are often to be found discreetly tucked away within the design.)

Embossing was widely applied to such materials as leather, textiles and wallpaper, but the Dobbs treatment of papers exploited a relatively cheap material in everyday use. The intricate relief effect was highly decorative, and Dobbs used any additional embellishment that came to hand. These included gold and silver printing inks, 'enamel' and metallic papers, lace-paper and cut-outs, and the affixing of chromolitho prints or scraps.

The technique was applied to virtually every sort of personal stationery, greeting cards, labels and so on, and in less garish form it was used on outsize invitation cards to royal and civic banquets.

Embossing is also found without a printed image ('blind' embossing), often as a border to a printed centre panel. In some cases the relief effect approaches that of plaster moulding.

Gold embossing, with the addition of chromolitho prints, was a standard success formula in the Victorian period. Decorative envelopes were produced to contain no less decorative greeting cards ('Joyful be thy days'), and gold embossed linen labels, and box lids brought glory to a host of everyday products. 'Spare parts' (far left) were also available for use by other manufacturers and for do-it-yourself gift and greetings enthusiasts.

90%

GENERAL BOOK AND JOB PRINTING ESTABLISHMENT.

Samuel N. Dickinson,

IS PREPARED TO EXECUTE ANY AND

All kinds of Printing

With which the Public may favor him,

IN ANY STYLE,

AND AT THE LOWEST CASH PRICES,

AT THE OFFICE OF THE ROTARY PRESS 52 Washington St.

BOSTON.

80%

105%

52%

No
ADMIT
To the Guildhall of the City of London,
On LORD MAYOR'S DAY,
9th November, 1837,
on the occasion of Her Majesty
QUEEN VICTORIA
Honoring the Corporation with her presence
AT DINNER.
TOWN CLERK

60%

Admit
To the opening of the
NEW ROYAL EXCHANGE.
No 516
James Barnes
No 516

78%

Blind-embossed cards with blank centre panels for overprinting were widely used for invitations, admission tickets and memorial cards (see page 175) as well as for quality tradecards.

The Walter Scott head (facing page), part blind-embossed, is one of a promotional series produced in the 1830s by Charles Whiting, apparently in association with Dobbs.

The medallion device, embossed on bronze paper, is from the die files of the De La Rue Company. Engraved by Leonard Wyon from a drawing by Daniel Maclise, the design was produced for the 1862 International Exhibition in London. It is thought to be a paper 'trial' from an actual medal die made in honour of the occasion.

Lace Paper

Lace paper may be said to be an accidental development of the embossing process. If carried too far, embossing will not merely press into the paper but will begin to break through it. The result is a sheet of paper at risk of falling apart — a stage not far short of lace.

Lace paper proper is said to have been created by Joseph Addenbrooke, an employee of the Dobbs company, in 1834. He is reported to have used a sandpaper rasp on paper impaled on cutting dies, converting the paper to a perforated filigree. (In a later development the practice was to use a light hammer to break the paper on the cutting edges of the die.)

Addenbrooke set up on his own in the lace paper business. He was the first of a number of specialists, among them George Meek (who supplied Rimmel's, the perfumed-valentine firm) and Dobbs themselves, who also became producers.

A number of French companies moved into the field, notably the Heste Company, Maison Carrière, and Pepin. A French speciality was decorative stationery; another was the first communion memento, either as a card or a valentine-like box.

In Germany too, lace paper was taken up, but largely for bouquet papers, cake papers and shelf ending.

In America lace paper was at first imported from Britain in the late 1840s, notably by Charles Whitney (from whom Esther Howland bought supplies). The first American lace paper appears to have come from Berlin & Jones in New York, whose lace was stamped 'Lang's Patent Process'. The firm was bought out by Whitney in 1869. Another US name is Taft, father and son, who were in the lace paper business in Worcester, Mass. in the period 1860–90.

For the British, as the examples on these pages indicate, the love affair with lace paper was deep and lasting.

Both pages 72%

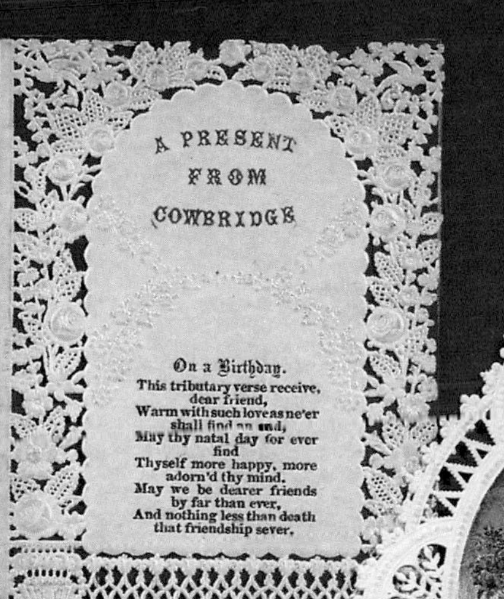

A PRESENT
FROM
COWBRIDGE
On a Birthday.
This tributary verse receive,
dear friend,
Warm with such love as ne'er
shall find an end,
May thy natal day for ever
find
Thyself more happy, more
adorn'd thy mind.
May we be dearer friends
by far than ever,
And nothing less than death
that friendship sever.

Truth
From one that loves you.

TO MY FATHER.
Dear Father, oft my thoughts recur
To early scenes and happy hours
And now I only live to prove,
Affection I can ne'er repay.

To Mrs Barrs
The senders quite hope
to see you at the "Family
Party," Friday January 5th
1877.
1
H.R.H. the Prince of Orange.
2
The Bank of England.
3
Valle-Crucis Abbey.
4
London.

Closely related to lace paper were two other products, 'lace relief' and perforated card. Lace relief, as in the Family Party invitation card, was more specifically a pierced embossing, presenting a sculptural rather than lacy appearance. The style is also seen in the two 'Forget me not' items (facing page), combined in these instances with the perforated card treatment. The invitation and the larger 'Forget me not' card are by Windsor; the smaller is by Wood.

70%

rforated cards were sed for silk or wool embroidery or adwork. They also ed as caption cards or scrap- and view- ms and as message name cards. Some, decorated with bossing or amateur twork, were pasted lbums in their own t. Perforated paper and card was in the 50s and 60s among standard products of manufacturing and ail stationery trade. ost of the specimens vn here are thought to be by the Dobbs, Kidd Company.

70%

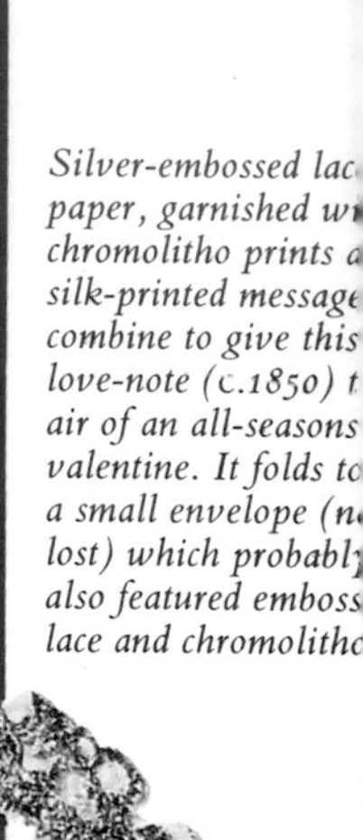

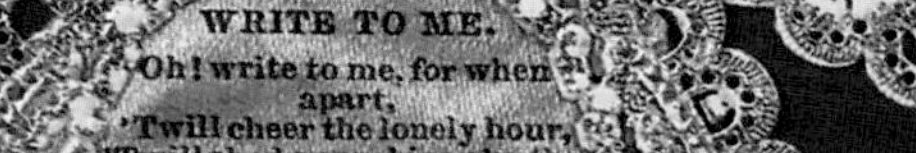

A PRESENT
FROM
THIRSK
OH!
WRITE TO ME.
Oh! write to me, for when apart,
'Twill cheer the lonely hour,
'Twill shed a sunshine o'er the heart,
Where haply, clouds would lower
Oh! write to me—thy cherished love
Will never fade away,
But, like the polar star above,
Will shine where'er I stray.

Silver-embossed lac paper, garnished wi chromolitho prints a silk-printed message combine to give this love-note (c.1850) t air of an all-seasons valentine. It folds to a small envelope (no lost) which probably also featured emboss lace and chromolitho

The 'Present from Thirsk' disc bears the embossed imprint 'Wood' (presumably J. T. Wood of Holywell Street, London).

Categories

Tradecards

The tradecard has its origins in the early seventeenth century. Apart from the tradesman's signboard, it is about the earliest generally recognized form of trade publicity.

However, it was only in the eighteenth and nineteenth centuries that it developed into an actual card. In its original form it was a paper, a general-purpose printed slip showing name, trade and location, and used as a customer's *aide-memoire*, invoice, receipt and jotting slip. The term tradecard may be seen as a misnomer, though it is universally applied to any printed single item showing the name and address of a tradesman (later, company or corporation).

The tradecard was commonly printed in black from a copper engraving, classically incorporating the sign of the proprietor's trade or premises.

Hanging signboards had been a major feature of street life in earlier times, and their proliferation, and the dangers they posed to passers-by, led to their enforced removal in the mid-1700s. The emblems they had borne were often transferred to tradecards. Thomas Heming's card (opposite page) is typical, showing the sign of the Hand and Hammer and giving the location in the manner generally used in the days before street numbering. Typically too, it bears a hand-written record, partly illegible, of the purchase of candlesticks in 1759 (just prior to the era of street numbers).

American tradecards for the period are scarce. Much prized in the collection of the American Antiquaries Society are unique examples by two famous names—Nathaniel Hurd and Paul Revere.

The tradesman's card was to become possibly the most prolific form of ephemera, produced by virtually every printing process on a wide variety of substances, including celluloid, cork, leather, silk, wood, foil and metal.

Both pages 100%

ROBERT FOSTER,
BLUE-MAKER;
At Darfield, *near* Barnſley:

MAKES and Sells all Sorts of Stone and Powder Blue, Wholeſale and Retail at the moſt reaſonable Rates.

Alſo Poland Starch, and fine Flour of Muſtard.

William M'Auley, jun.
MARBLE CUTTER,
ARLINGTON, VT.

☞ All orders thankfully received, and promptly executed.

1759. [illegible]

[illegible] 8.5.

Thomas Heming

GOLDSMITH & JEWELLER,

at y^e Hand & Hammer, opposite

y^e Black Bear Inn, in Piccadilly.

LONDON.

Makes, Mends & Sells, all sorts of Gold & Silver Plate, after y^e newest Fashion, at the Lowest Price.

Also gives most Money for Burnt Silver, Lace, Plate & Jewels, &c.

MOURNING RINGS IN THE NEWEST TASTE

Plate, Jewels, Watches, &c. Sold by Commission.

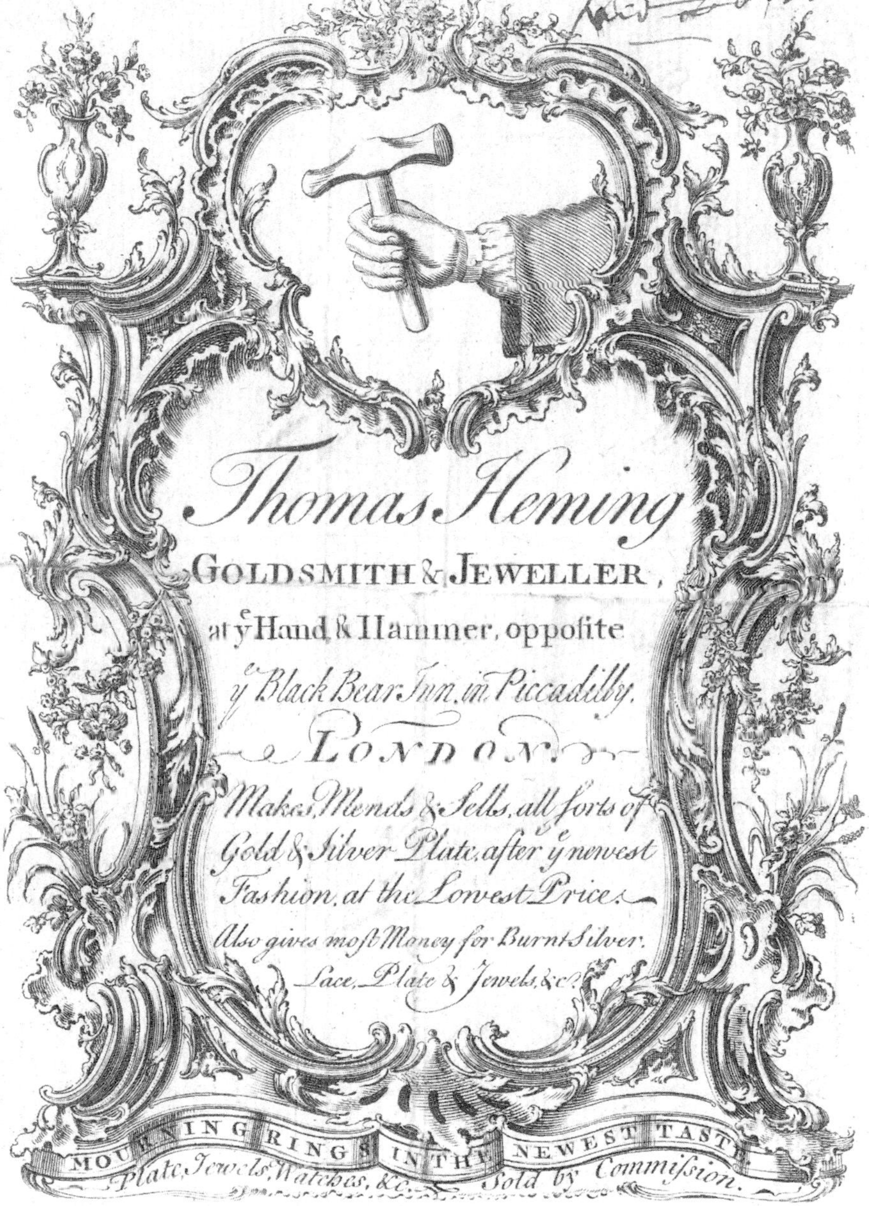

The Pelican Life Insurance card (c.1 is exceptionally la measuring 50 × 35 (20 × 14 in). Whi bears all the traditi marks of the tradec it was clearly used showcard or poster midway stage betw the tradecard and t mass advertising medium that it was become.

Prior to the com chromolitho (see 90, 91, 110, colou noticeably absent the tradecard. was some atten remedy this, as the use of colour- paper in the G and Edward C example (c.1845 Belgium at abou same time c iridescence appe This process metallic colour pow dusted on a glue- ink. Use of the m was abolished i 1860s, when it be clear that the me dust was harmful t health of pri Specimens are not to com

The Oakford's ca from the 1890s, a c two-printing compe of the multi-colo chromolitho

39%

CARRET AND EDWARD GREEN,

Have constantly on hand and for sale a large quantity of Pine & Hemlock Boards, Plank and Joist; Oak, Ash & Maple Boards, Plank and Joist; Chestnut Joist; Cot Joist, Whitewood Columns, Boards Plank & Joist; Cedar Boards; Southern Pitch Pine Boards & Plank; Pickets for Fencing, Pine and Cedar Shingles; Oak & Ceiling Lath; Locust, Cedar & Chestnut Posts, Basswood Boards, Cherry Boards & Plank; Indian Gutters, with a large assortment of Timber at their Lumber yard, Cor. of **West & Horatio St. N.Y.**
N.B. A large assortment of Cart & Waggon Timber.

New York

Late nineteenth- and early twentieth-century development of the tradecard brought increasing use of illustration, commonly of the firm's premises, sometimes, though less frequently, of the product. In the barber shop example a publicity man's flight of fancy settles on a fiction.

74%

In Britain the royal arms were always a popular feature, though they were not always legitimately borne. Mr R. Williams of Ludgate Hill may indeed have held the coveted Royal Appointment, but Mr Deacon, Cornhill shoemaker, was apparently only a patentee. Smith & Co, Sloane Street, clearly had royals among their clientele, but were not appointment holders. Coats of arms, royal or otherwise, were much favoured by advertisers large and small.

Some tradecard motifs served a double role. The hatter's card (top right-hand corner) undoubtedly did duty as a hat label, and others, like the Saunders, Southampton, design, might also appear on billheads or in the pages of local trade directories.

74%

Weir Stove Co.
Taunton Mass.
JOS. S. SMITH,
DEALER IN
Flour, Grain & Groceries.
Dry Goods & Yankee Notions.
Seabrook, N. H.
JOS. S. SMITH,
DEALER IN
Flour, Grain & Groceries.
Dry Goods & Yankee Notions.
Seabrook, N. H.
JOS. S. SMITH,
DEALER IN
Flour, Grain & Groceries.
Dry Goods & Yankee Notions.
Seabrook, N. H.
JOS. S. SMITH,
DEALER IN
Flour, Grain & Groceries.
Dry Goods & Yankee Notions.
Seabrook, N. H.
BACH
FORBES CO.
THE ESTEY PHONORIUM.

Colour came to the tradecard with the chromolithographic process. In America chromolitho had an enormous impact, many millions of cards being turned out by printers who had brought the technique as mid-nineteenth century emigrants from Central Europe.

Designs were produced to customers' own requirements, often incorporating their own wording and product illustrations (as in the Estey Phonorium design, far left, bottom), or merely as pretty designs over which the client's name and wording could be printed. They also appeared as 'sets' (as in the Joseph E. Smith series), also for overprinting

In Europe sets of cards were issued in millions, chiefly by the bigger food firms. Among them, notably, was Liebig, top right, the first of whose hundreds of sets appeared in 1872. (They finally ceased in 1974.)

Both pages 76%

The novelty cut-out tradecard appeared in America in the 1880s and 90s. Stamped from standard dies, the shapes were applicable to a varied range of trades and were printed in black or a single colour on white or colour-tinted card. Shape cards were also produced in highly coloured chromolitho, but the simpler cards illustrated here, produced with ease by any jobbing printer, are prized by collectors for their engaging naivety.

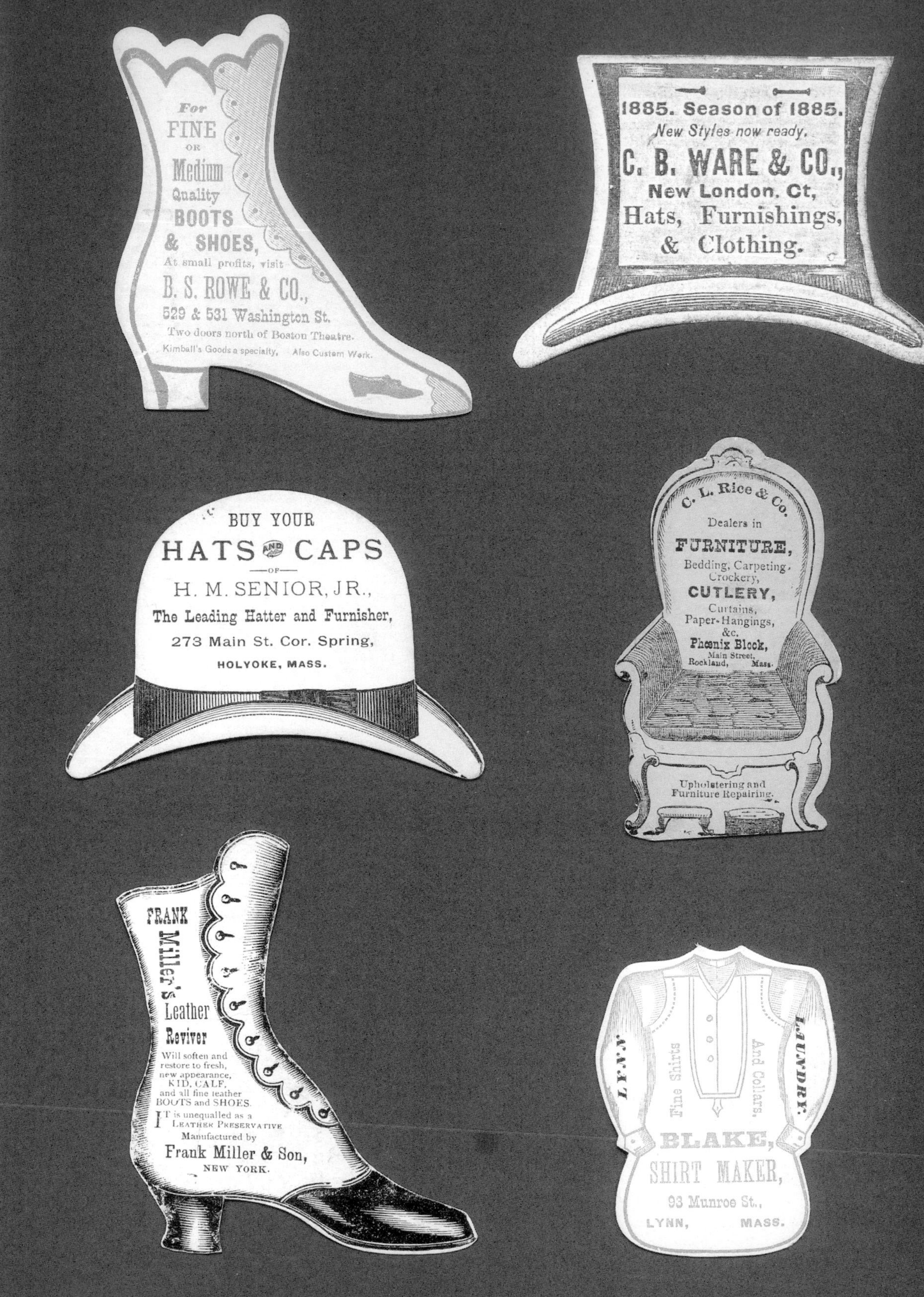

73%

Billheads and letterheads

A direct descendant of the tradecard (if not in fact a half-brother), the billhead has loomed large in everyday life for two or three centuries. Like the tradecard, it gives formal notice of the proprietor's existence; it is more than that however: it is a financial instrument—formal evidence of the recipient's debt.

The socio-historical evidence provided by bills can be revealing, not to say dramatic, and the connoisseur will often study them as much for their content as for the information in the heading alone.

The commodities and services supplied, their quality, quantity and incidence—above all, their prices—these may be elements more telling than the assertions of the printwork at the top.

Certainly in their timescale, many surviving specimens reflect the patience of those who penned them. Punctual payment was not the customer's first concern, and some bills, like the one on this page, may extend over many months or even years. Moore & Son, the Rochester butchers, supplied their customer every three or four days from July 1, 1879 to February 26, 1880. They rendered their account in August 1880 and were finally paid in November of that year. The bill, pasted together for the executors of the (by then) 'late' customer, extends to well over a metre in length. And it was not only death that delayed payment, as many other examples from long-suffering tailors, dressmakers and doctors testify.

In the selection that follows the focus is on the headings, redolent of the period that produced them. As with the tradecard, there is a thread of evolution. The billhead has become by the end of the century a letterhead, final flowering of the seventeenth-century, general-purpose shop-man's paper.

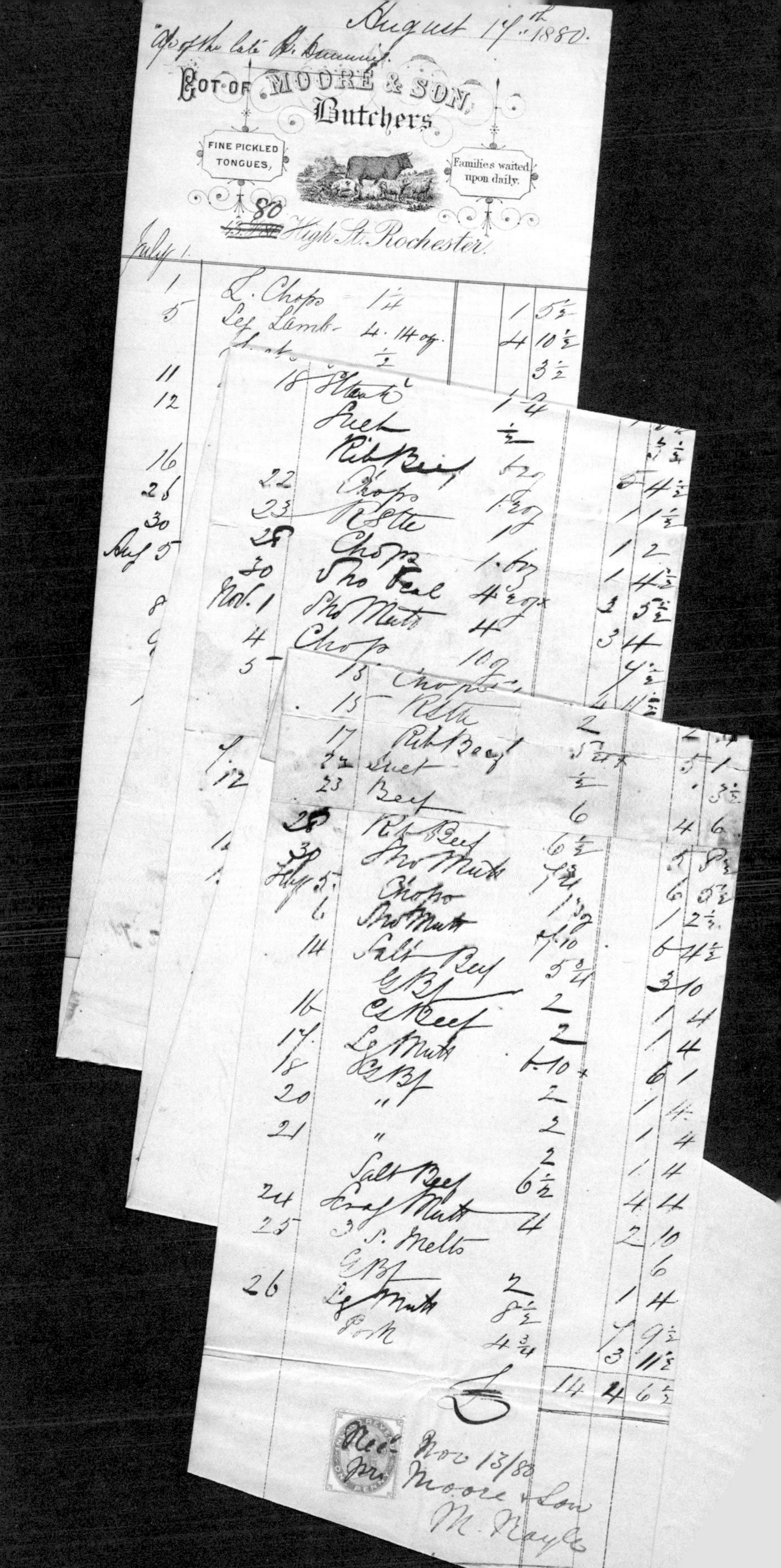
August 17th 1880.
Bot of MOORE & SON,
Butchers
FINE PICKLED TONGUES,
Families waited upon daily.
80 High St. Rochester.
Nov 13/80
Moore & Son

53%

Early billheads were little more than extended tradecards, distinguished chiefly by the provision of space for the name of the recipient, the date, and the words 'Bought of', 'To' or 'Purchased by'. As with the tradecard, colour was a long time coming, confined in the main to the use of colour-tinted papers.

Products and services provided by Spiers & Son of Oxford in the 1850s included toilet furniture, perfumery, haircutting and ornamental hair, as well as stationery, gloves, umbrellas, canes and whips, and hire of cutlery, china, lamps etc. As in the case of the supplier on the previous page, payment was unhurried: 'One year's credit is allowed, free of interest; after that time, interest is charged at five per cent per annum'.

Mrs Turnout

Bought of Peter Snee
(Successor to Collet Manhood)
DRUGGIST at the GOLDEN LYON & UNICORN,
over against the West end of the New Exchange in the Strand.

1759
May 25 2lb Finest Green Tea 16 £1„12

Recd: the same time the Contents in full for

M The Lord Chief Baron Pengelly Mar. 25 1727
Bought of Saml. Southouse Ironmonger
at the Cross Keys in Leadenhall Street.

The Revd. C. Gordon Ch: Ch:

To SPIERS AND SON, 102 & 103, HIGH STREET, OXFORD,
AND 45, CORN MARKET STREET.

LIST OF DEPARTMENTS.

STATIONERY OF EVERY DESCRIPTION.	CHINA AND EARTHENWARE GOODS.	TABLE CUTLERY AND FANCY CUTLERY.
DESKS AND DRESSING CASES.	GLASS OF EVERY DESCRIPTION	PLATED AND BRITANNIA METAL WARES.
TOILET FURNITURE AND PERFUMERY.	TABLE LAMPS, SUSPENDING DITTO, & OTHERS.	PAPIER MACHÉ MANUFACTURES.
HAIR CUTTING AND ORNAMENTAL HAIR.	CHINA, GLASS, PLATED GOODS, CUTLERY,	ORNAMENTAL GOODS SUITABLE FOR PRESENTS
GLOVES, UMBRELLAS, CANES, AND WHIPS.	LAMPS, ETC. LENT ON HIRE.	AND REMEMBRANCES OF OXFORD.

BILLS DELIVERED TWICE IN THE YEAR.—A DISCOUNT OF TEN PER CENT. ALLOWED FOR CASH, OR ON ACCOUNTS PAID QUARTERLY; OF FIVE PER CENT. ON ACCOUNTS PAID HALF YEARLY.

TERMS OF CREDIT;—ONE YEAR'S CREDIT ALLOWED; AFTER THAT TIME, INTEREST IS CHARGED AT FIVE PER CENT. PER ANNUM.

1856			
April 1	Hard water soap 1/6 Gas congreves 3	2	9
4	Head washing	1	6
	One years hair cutting	5	6
12	20 College envelopes color'd	1	3
19	Bottle of ink	.	6
May 20	50 Ch: Ch: envelopes	1	"
	50 Ditto carmine relief	3	4
31	Shaving & head washing	2	"
June 3	Pair of grey gloves	3	9
11	Buffalo horn dressing case	1	2
13	100 Cards & printing	2	6
	Carried forward £	1 5	3

HIGH STREET AND REGENT STREET,

Miss Baker

Of R. W. GIBBS,

AL DRAPER, SILK MERCER, & UNDERTAKER.

Served by Examined by

3	Hanks	10½	
3	Belting	8½	
	Gloves		
1	Collarette		
1	Bonnet		

CARPET WAREHOUSE.

55%

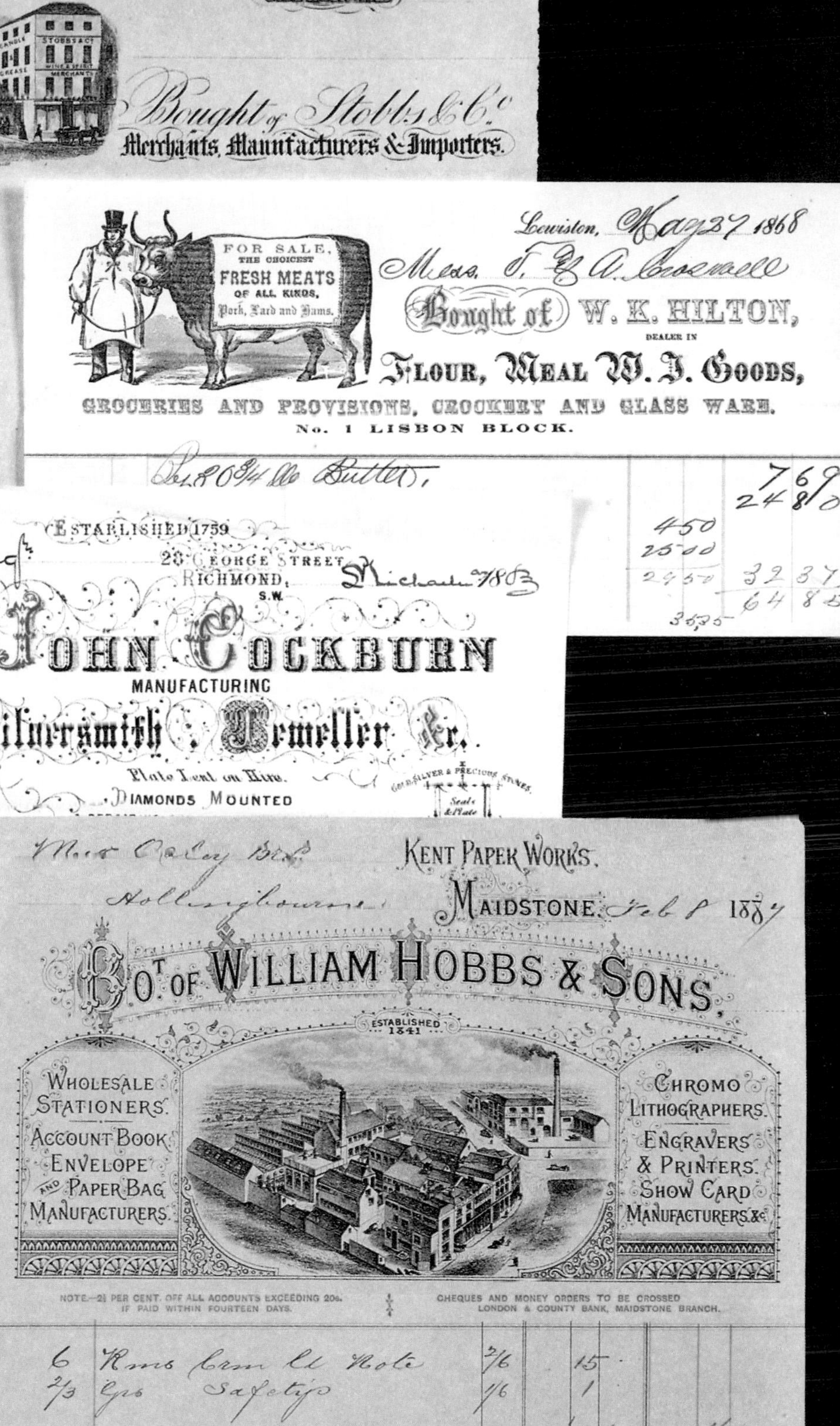

Moving from its early role as a document of accountancy, the billhead developed during the nineteenth century into a minor medium of publicity. Though many sought to 'beautify' their image, there was a concern with showing premises—shops, factories and, later, office blocks. Factory scenes, always well provided with smoking chimney stacks, became symbols of commercial success. (Some firms showed two views of their works, suggesting at first glance two separate factories.)

Scale and perspective were commonly much exaggerated, vehicles and passers-by often appearing lilliputian against the imposing mass of the premises.

55%

At the turn of the nineteenth century the billhead matured into the letterhead. The ruled columns and the words 'Bought of' gave way to a blank area for the tidal wave of correspondence that the new century—and the typewriter—would bring. (The specimens shown here have been folded for display purposes.)

It was at this period that there emerged a design idiom, now called 'gaslight style' which invaded not only letterheads but graphic design as a whole. Said to have derived from the play of lamps on three-dimensional street lettering, the style appears to have originated in Germany, spreading, through the influence of German printing skills, throughout the world.

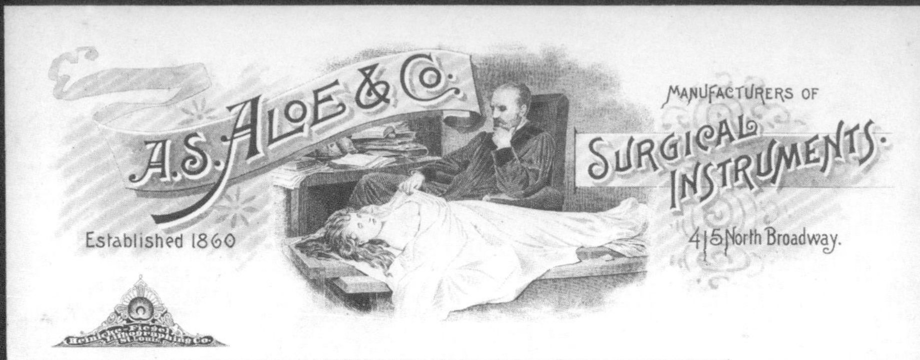

55%

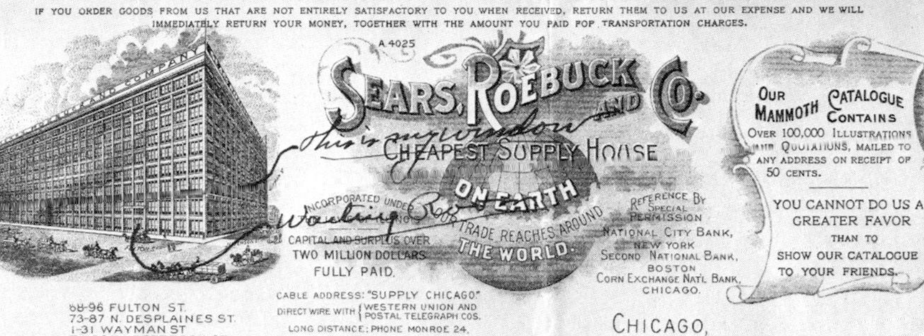

Preoccupation with pictures of buildings continued well into the 1930s, specially in the United States, where far-flung mail order customers needed the reassurance of size and unmistakable stability.

(Note, in the Sears, Roebuck specimen, someone's annotation: 'This is my window' and 'Waiting Room'.)

The 1920s and 30s brought the advent of the general graphic designer (as opposed to the commercial engraver) and the letterhead took its place as one of the recognized products of the publicity design studio. The 'Advertising Display Service' design is a typical hand-executed 'rough' of the late 1930s.

55%

Labels

In the long history of trade, the concept of the branded product is relatively recent. Prior to the age of industrialization the shopkeeper sold goods direct from shelves, bins and sacks, without much reference to where they came from. Delivered to his shop in bulk, unwrapped and unmarked, they reached the customer apparently from nowhere.

With the advent of the mass market in the 1850s and 60s, retail distribution, and above all, packaging, the buyer at last had a link with the source of the goods, and the label, pasted on the package, became a talisman. It also became attractive. By the last quarter of the nineteenth century it had become all-important, and the world's label printers vied with each other in beguiling the eye.

Packaging proper had not yet fully arrived. Plain bags, bottles and boxes were still the norm. But the label transformed them all.

Colour label printing became a major industry. Most designs, like the French linen-thread specimen ('*Aux souhaits*'), were custom-printed to the client firm's requirements. Others, like the bottled peach label, were straight from stock.

Output was prodigious. Even in the latter years of our own century supplies of unused labels survive in old store-rooms and warehouses—golden finds for the collector, curator and social historian.

In both style and content these items convey their turn-of-the-century atmosphere at a glance. As does the figure of Columbia with her pedestal phonograph and the hard-sell text: 'If it is a Columbia Record it is Good'. In another idiom was the 'wordless label', with an instantly recognizable motif that served to identify a branded product in markets where reading skills were low. As, for example, the label used by a Turkish fez maker, bearing an illustration of the Pennsylvania Railroad.

67%

The Pennsylvania Railroad fez label dates from November 1925, when the Turkish Government, in a number of sweeping changes, abolished the wearing of the fez, till then the national headgear. The fez industry, centred largely in Austria and Czechoslovakia, found itself with a major part of its market cut off overnight, and large quantities of labels designed in Turkish style became obsolete. As a result Turkish fez labels have survived in some numbers.

67%

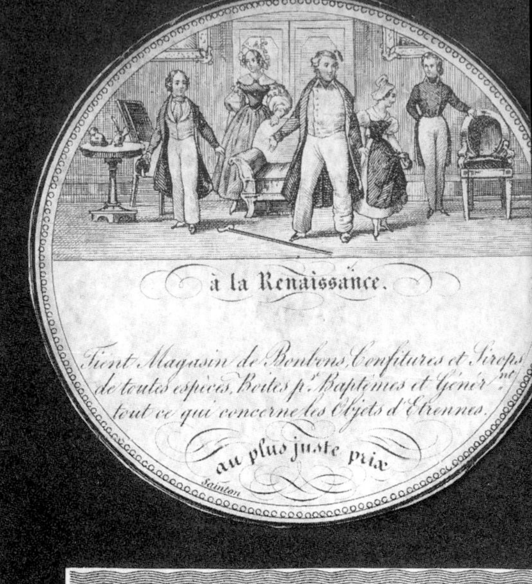

Early product labels were printed for the most part in a single colour, often from copper plates. Engraved by hand, many designs were executed as multiple images on a single plate so as to increase printing productivity. It later became possible to duplicate the engraved images by transfer, allowing vastly increased output.

The 'poignets' (cuffs) item was originally part of a multiple sheet showing other titles.

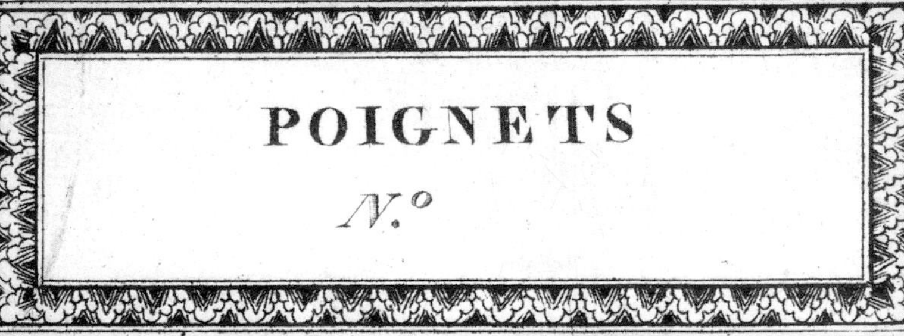

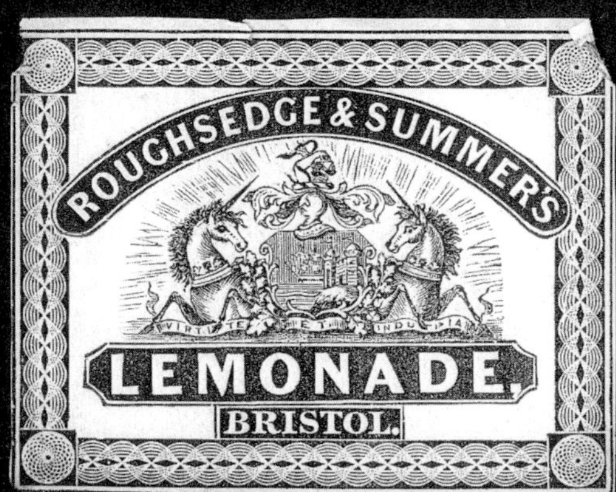

100%

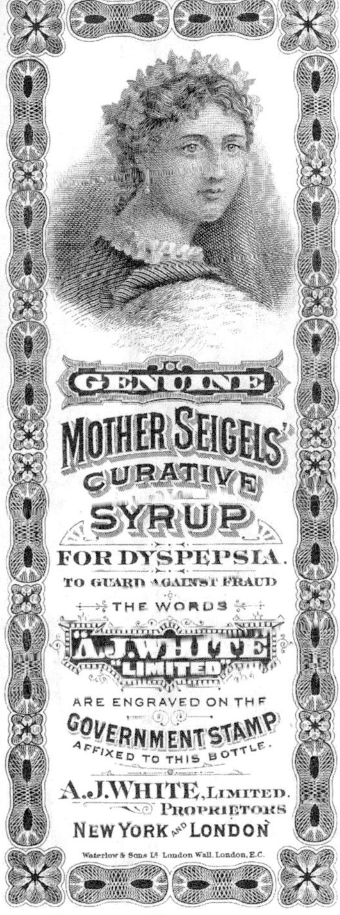

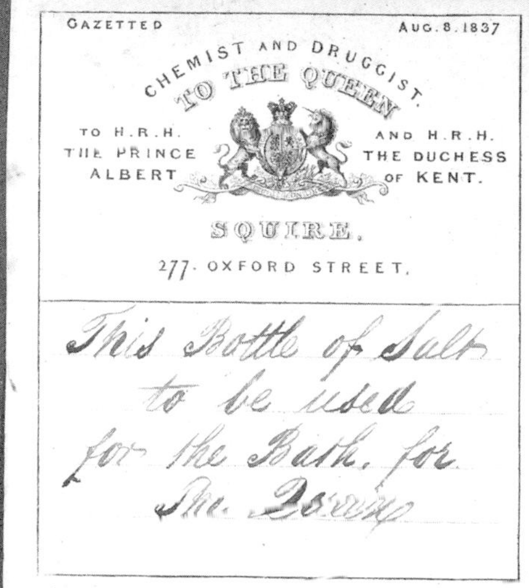

Included here are labels for ready cut quills (top), a seal engraver's box, and a halfpenny matchbox tax label, proposed by the British Government in 1871. In the event the proposal turned out to be so unpopular that it was abandoned. The labels were never issued, and are today exceedingly scarce.

The Mother Seigel's label shows a late nineteenth century application of security printing principles (geometric lathe patterns, etc.) to a purely commercial engraving—an unusually extravagant treatment for a dyspepsia syrup. However, counterfeit labels were by no means rare, as the text suggests, and the use of a top banknote printer may possibly have been justified.

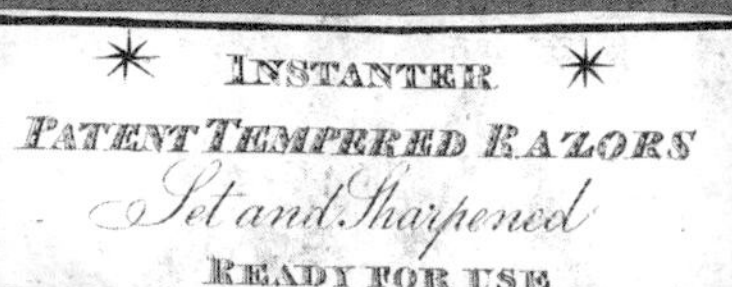

100%

The colour label achieved an elegance often far in advance of the levels of the consumer's daily life. It brought with it not only a product but a vision—as the 1890s ballroom candle label indicates. The buyer took home more than merely candles. A similar magic is to be found in the English fabric label (c.1860) and, in its own terms, in the American bourbon design (c.1880).

83%

Admission
·ickets

·part from its role as a minor security ·ocument the admission ticket has two ·dditional aspects. It serves as a record of the ·casion concerned, and expresses—however ·iefly—something of its flavour.

As the examples here show, each has a ·stinctive personality. Every one of them, in ·e matter of typography, decoration and ·yout, is individual.

In the matter of occasions, too, there is no ·ck of variety. From the gilded splendour of ·e Franklin firemen's ball to the four-square ·lemnity of St James's Hall; from Royal ·scot to Cremorne Gardens; from ice races at · Petersburg (second from top) to the ·merican Sunday School concert—here is a ·leidoscope of venues and events.

The admission ticket connoisseur may be · attracted by their minor mysteries as their ·imary information. How come the rugged ·anklin fire crew chose a card so ladylike? ·ow come winter races on the Neva? Ice ·chts? Sledges? Troikas? And the three-part ·remorne ticket; and the curious staining on ·e Dickens ticket?

The ice-race item reads: *Admission to the ·ommittee Room during the Winter Races on the ·eva during 185*[ ]. (The precise year was to · filled in by hand.) Details of the sport ·main unknown.

Still unfathomed is the reason for the ·ividing of the Cremorne ticket. It was ·und in pieces as shown. But a close look ·veals that it is not a single ticket cut up; the ·arts are from three separate tickets. A small ·atter, but all the same . . .

The Dickens ticket is less difficult. It comes ·om inside an upright piano. Piano ·ssemblers, it seems, used tickets to pack out ·ose frame-joints. Characteristically such ·ckets show fresher areas where they were ·amped, as this one does, horizontally across ·e middle.

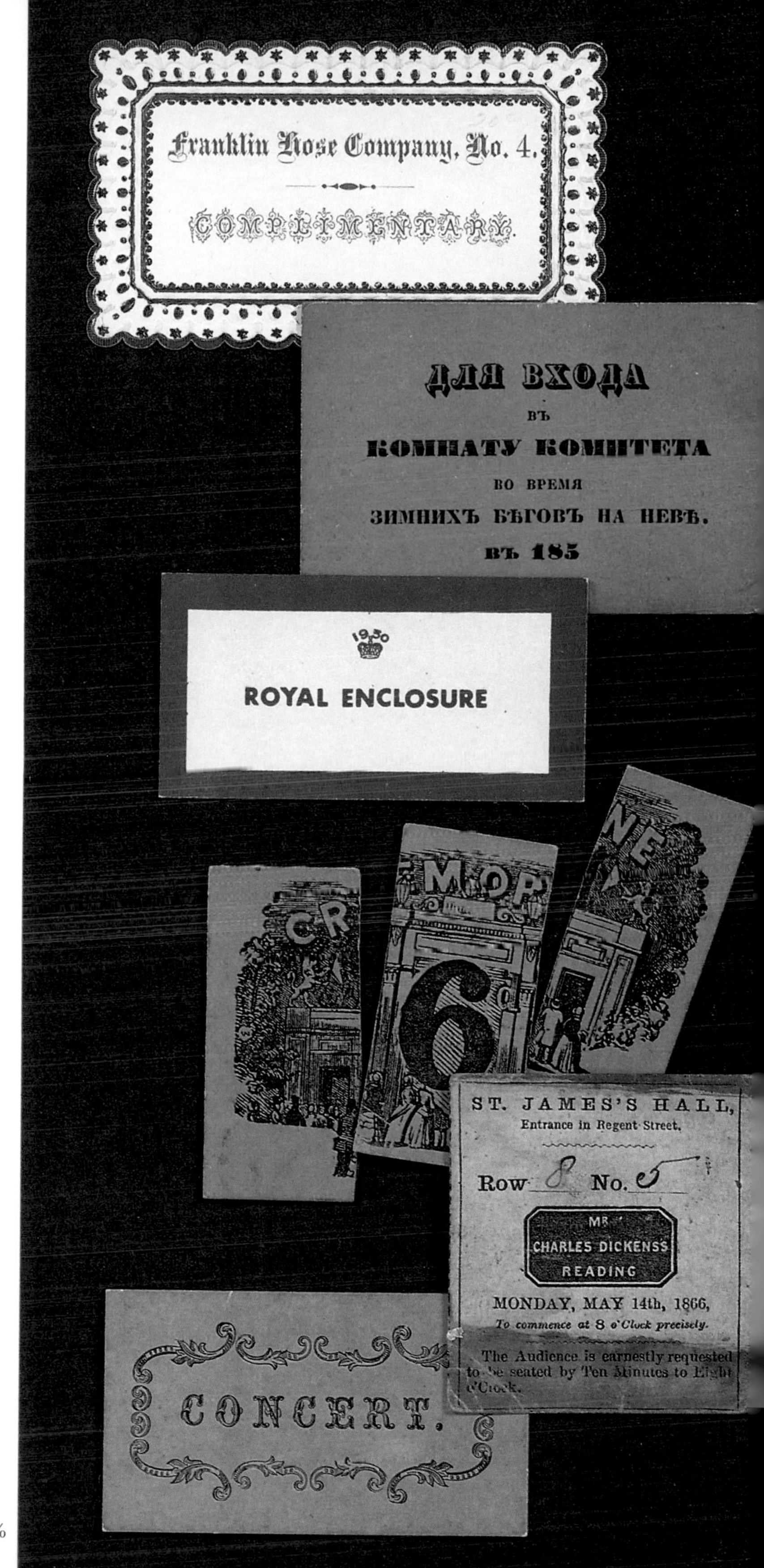

83%

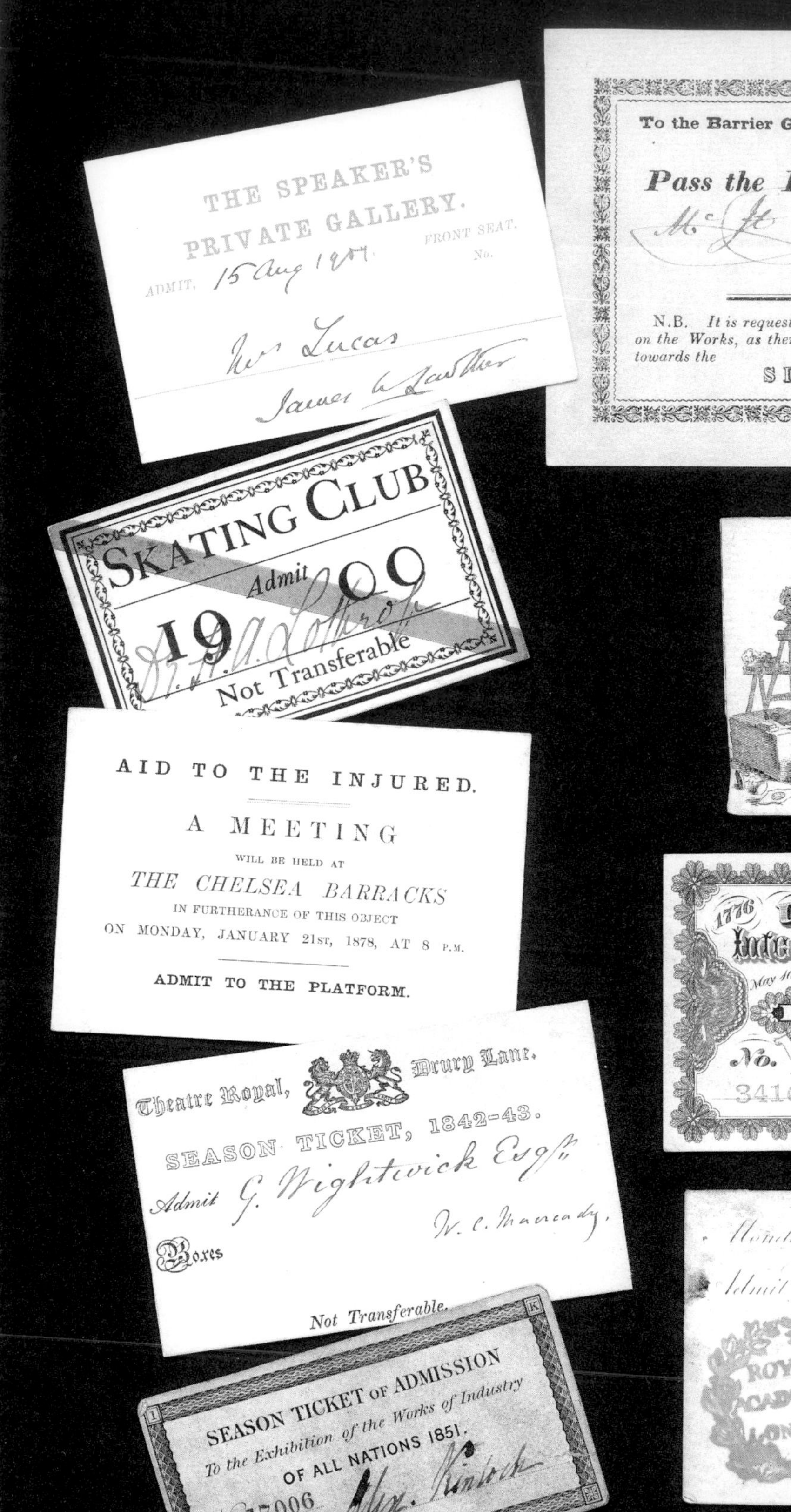

Tickets of admission gained currency in the early eighteenth century, and were commonly engraved or etched on copper plates. The 'Polite Arts' specimen (1763) is a miniature example of an idiom established, on a more ceremonial size and scale, by such artists as Hogarth, Bartolozzi and Cipriani.

Early methods of security included the use of seals, stamps and signatures. Among tickets on these pages are examples signed by Marc Brunel (Thames Tunnel 1842); William Macready (Theatre Royal 1842) and John Soane (Royal Academy 1819). Some admission tickets may owe their survival to such signatures, and 'celebrity tickets' are seen by some specialists as a collecting theme.

72%

The security factor in some cases led to the use of full-scale security printing. The Great Exhibition season ticket (1851, (facing page, bottom left), was printed with machine-engraved borders and 'philatelic' corner letters; and the US International Exhibition example (1876) has the classic lathe work of the banknote. The United States Senate Chamber ticket (1941) (this page) shows survival of the security treatment in more recent times.

The Jardin du Roi *Museum ticket (c.1825) shows the French convention for checking numbers in groups, the corners being cut off to leave three, two or one admission indications,*

72%

Flagday emblems

In America the term Flag Day refers to June 14, the day celebrating the adoption of the national flag, but in a European context the expression derives from World War I, when miniaturc flags of the Allies were sold in the streets in aid of war charities. The flags were at first of fabric, but later paper was used.

The idea had originally come from a Danish priest, who in the late nineteenth century sold roses from his garden in aid of orphans, and in San Francisco in 1908 there had been 'tag days', in which paper tags were sold for charities.

But it was in World War I that the idea made its mark. In August 1914 a Welsh housewife made up little flags in aid of the National Relief Fund. She sold them, making a total of £10.

A few weeks later Mrs Morrison of Glasgow set up Union Jack Day, under the slogan 'Support the colours by wearing the colours'. The revenue went to the Soldiers' and Sailors' USA Families Association. Mrs Morrison's initiative prompted other cities to take up the idea.

Britain's first national flagday was for Belgian relief on October 3, 1914, and this was quickly followed up with flagdays for each of the Allies. At first the flags were simple miniatures, but before long they also carried wording ('Bravo Belgium!'; 'Help Russia' etc.). Later, though the flag shape was retained, the emblems diversified. Days were allocated to special themes and causes: National Red Cross Committees ran collections under the title 'Our Day', and there were such titles as 'Hut Day' (for army hut hostels), 'Cup Day' for provision of Forces' coffee stalls, 'Splint and Bandage Day' and 'Crutch Day'.

Proliferation of flagdays led to increasingly stringent controls, including authorization cards and special emblems for collectors. These, together with associated sellers' trays, posters and display material, also form part of the flagday ephemera record.

69%

The flag motif moved in the course of World War I from the literal (facing page) to the nominal. Charity images featured children, nursing, animal welfare and war wounded. 'Hospital blue', the regulation uniform for military patients, was virtually an appeal symbol in itself. As specimens on this page show ('Our Day'; 'Cheer Oh!'; 'Thumbs Up'), the white lapelled blue suit and red tie were much in evidence

The large emblem opposite, 'Remember their Dependants' was put out by the Soldiers' and Sailors' Families Association, probably as identification for the flagseller.

69%

Toll/turnpike tickets

The appalling state of the roads in the eighteenth century led many authorities to set up turnpike trusts to repair and maintain them. The trusts, whose members paid for the right to do so, in turn charged road users for the right of passage.

Traffic was stopped at tollgate or turnpike (a swinging bar across the road) and drivers, riders and drovers were charged according to a scale shown on a board. The gatekeeper received the money and gave in exchange a ticket, which was to be shown at specified gates along the way and given up at the exit gate.

The tickets were commonly printed in sheets, to be cut out singly by the gatekeeper. Some had counterfoils, retained at the gate as a tally. Most bore the name of the trust and the issuing gate, and many listed the gates for which they were valid on the route. Some also listed types of user (wagon, carriage, gig etc.) and classes of animal, numbers and charges to be filled in by hand.

Certain tolls were charged by weight. Vehicles passed over weighing-machines at the gate and weights and charges were entered on the ticket.

To discourage re-use of tickets, some were printed on colour-tinted paper, changed from day to day. A small number bore the day of the week in print.

The system was open to much abuse—by trustees who failed to keep up the roads, gatekeepers who swindled trustees, and road-users who dodged the gatekeepers.

Tolls and turnpikes were used in America and elsewhere, but Britain was the great turnpike country. At the height of the nineteenth-century turnpike era the United Kingdom had some 8000 tollgates. Toll tickets, common as they were, were surrendered at the end of their use, and have thus become rarities.

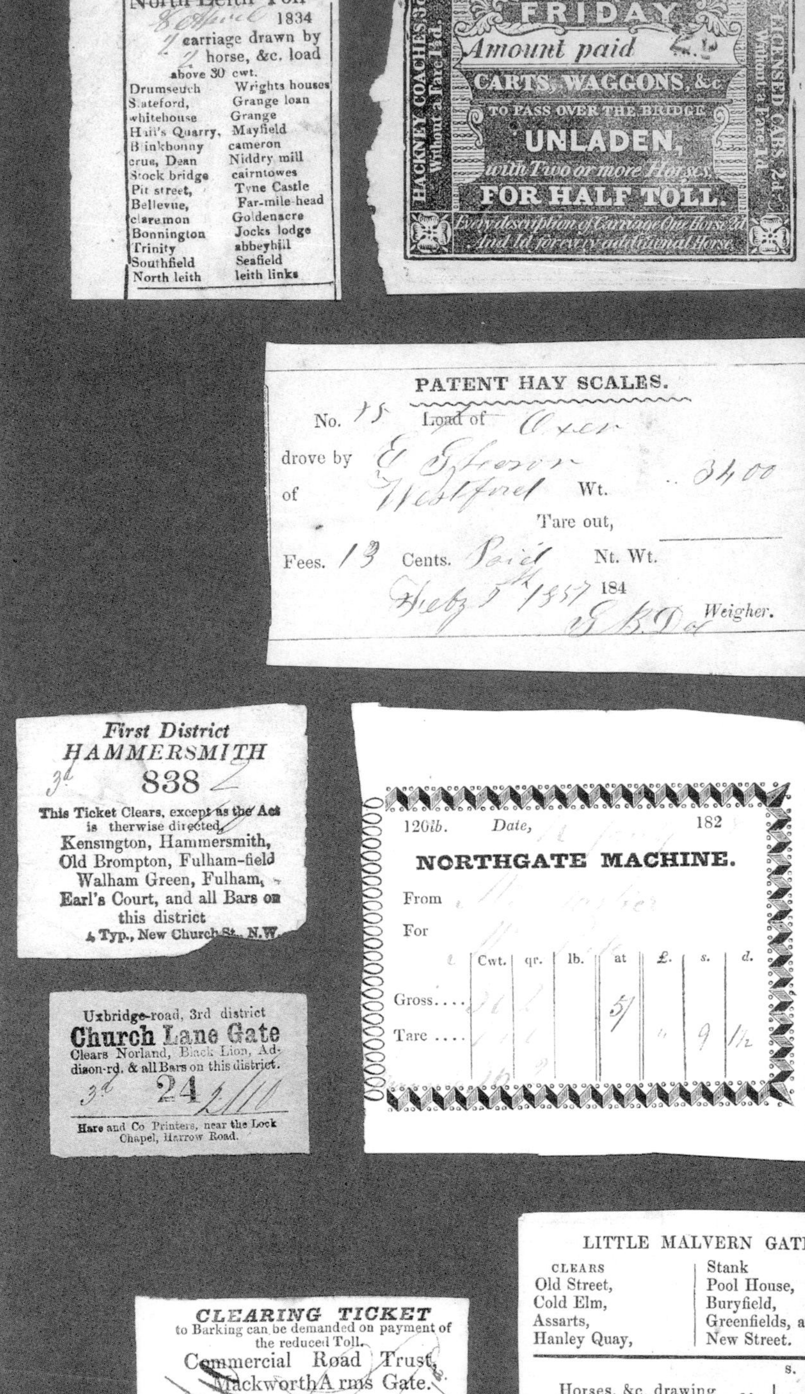
North Leith Toll
1834
carriage drawn by
horse, &c. load
above 30 cwt.

Drumseuch	Wrights houses
Slateford,	Grange loan
whitehouse	Grange
Hail's Quarry,	Mayfield
Blinkbonny	cameron
crue, Dean	Niddry mill
Stock bridge	cairntowes
Pit street,	Tyne Castle
Bellevue,	Far-mile-head
claremon	Goldenacre
Bonnington	Jocks lodge
Trinity	abbeyhill
Southfield	Seafield
North leith	leith links

HACKNEY COACHES 3d. Without a Fare 1d.
WATERLOO BRIDGE
FRIDAY
Amount paid
CARTS, WAGGONS, &c.
TO PASS OVER THE BRIDGE
UNLADEN,
with Two or more Horses,
FOR HALF TOLL.
Every description of Carriage One Horse 2d. And 1d. for every additional Horse.
LICENSED CABS 2d. Without a Fare 1d.

PATENT HAY SCALES.
No. Load of
drove by
of Wt.
Tare out,
Fees. Cents. Nt. Wt.
184
Weigher.

First District
HAMMERSMITH
838
This Ticket Clears, except as the Act is therwise directed,
Kensington, Hammersmith, Old Brompton, Fulham-field Walham Green, Fulham, Earl's Court, and all Bars on this district
Typ., New Church St., N.W.

120lb. Date, 182
NORTHGATE MACHINE.
From
For

	Cwt.	qr.	lb.	at	£.	s.	d.
Gross....							
Tare							

Uxbridge-road, 3rd district
Church Lane Gate
Clears Norland, Black Lion, Addison-rd. & all Bars on this district.
24
Hare and Co Printers, near the Lock Chapel, Harrow Road.

LITTLE MALVERN GATE
CLEARS

Old Street,	Stank
Cold Elm,	Pool House,
Assarts,	Buryfield,
Hanley Quay,	Greenfields, and
	New Street.

	s.
Horses, &c. drawing ..	
Horses, &c. not drawing	
Cows, or neat Cattle ..	
Calves, Swine, Sheep ..	

day of 18

CLEARING TICKET
to Barking can be demanded on payment of the reduced Toll.
Commercial Road Trust,
Mackworth Arms Gate.
M
This Ticket clears Tons. Cwt.
Mackworth Arms
Limehouse
Stepney — Poplar and
West India Docks Gate
And all Bars between Whitechapel and the West India Docks.
Except as the Act otherwise directs.
Vincent & Skeen, Printers, Great St. Helens.

70%

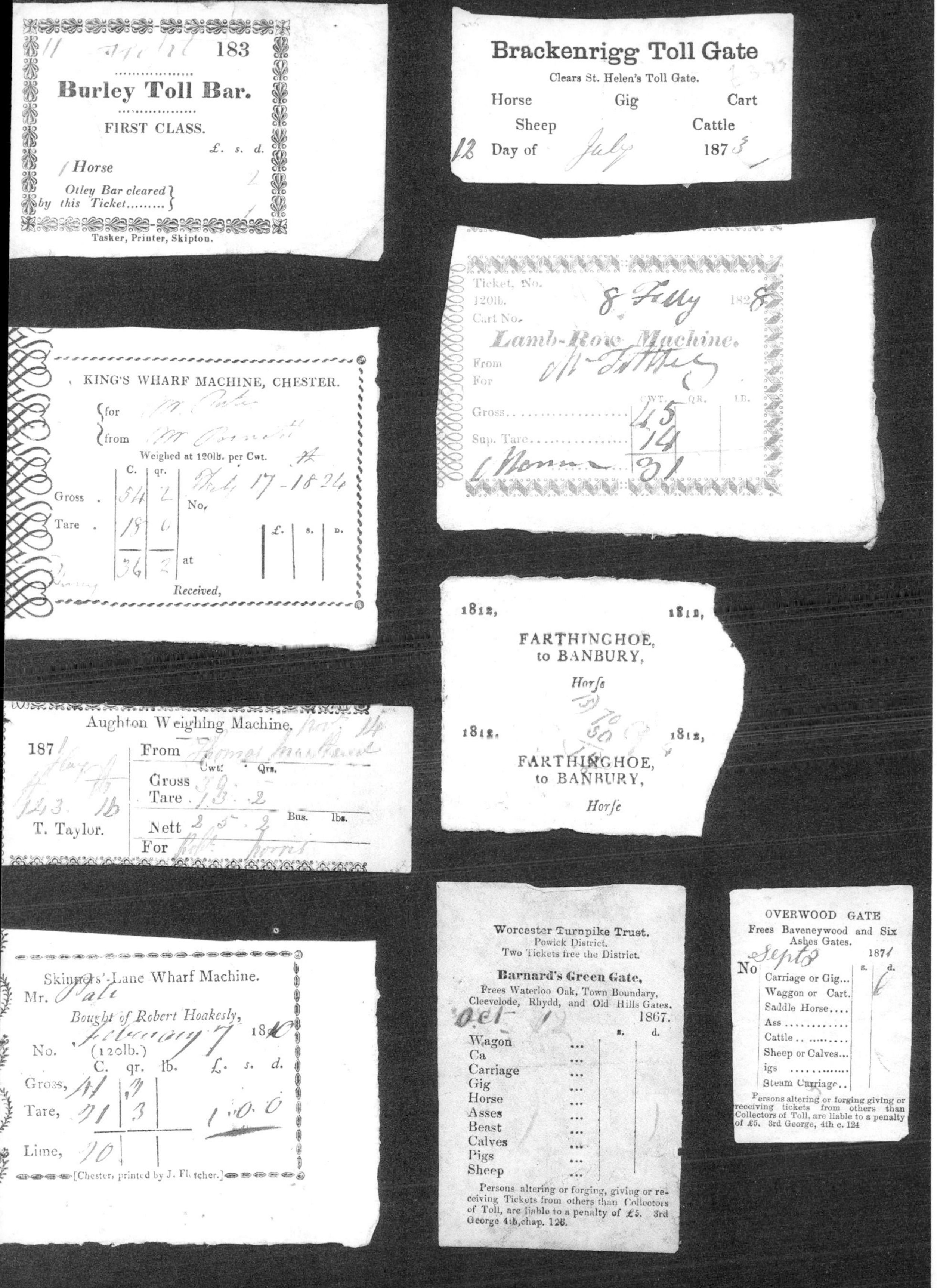

Burley Toll Bar.
183
FIRST CLASS.
£. s. d.
Horse
Otley Bar cleared by this Ticket........
Tasker, Printer, Skipton.

Brackenrigg Toll Gate
Clears St. Helen's Toll Gate.
Horse Gig Cart
Sheep Cattle
12 Day of July 1873

KING'S WHARF MACHINE, CHESTER.
for
from
Weighed at 120lb. per Cwt.
C. qr.
Gross 54 2 No.
Tare 18 0
36 2 at
£. s. D.
Received,

Ticket No.
120lb.
Cart No.
Lamb-Row Machine.
From
For
CWT. QR. LB.
Gross........
Sup. Tare........

1812, 1812,
FARTHINGHOE, to BANBURY,
Horſe
1812, 1812,
FARTHINGHOE, to BANBURY,
Horſe

Aughton Weighing Machine.
187
From
Cwt. Qrs.
Gross
Tare
Nett
Bus. lbs.
For
T. Taylor.

Skinners'-Lane Wharf Machine.
Mr.
Bought of Robert Hoakesly,
18
No. (120lb.)
C. qr. lb. £. s. d.
Gross,
Tare,
Lime,
[Chester, printed by J. Fletcher.]

Worcester Turnpike Trust.
Powick District.
Two Tickets free the District.
Barnard's Green Gate,
Frees Waterloo Oak, Town Boundary, Cleevelode, Rhydd, and Old Hills Gates.
1867.
s. d.
Wagon ...
Ca ...
Carriage ...
Gig ...
Horse ...
Asses ...
Beast ...
Calves ...
Pigs ...
Sheep ...
Persons altering or forging, giving or receiving Tickets from others than Collectors of Toll, are liable to a penalty of £5. 3rd George 4th, chap. 126.

OVERWOOD GATE
Frees Baveneywood and Six Ashes Gates.
No 187
s. d.
Carriage or Gig...
Waggon or Cart.
Saddle Horse....
Ass ....
Cattle ....
Sheep or Calves...
igs ....
Steam Carriage..
Persons altering or forging giving or receiving tickets from others than Collectors of Toll, are liable to a penalty of £5. 3rd George, 4th c. 124

The majority of toll tickets bore the name of their place of issue—the words 'turnpike', 'toll bar' and 'toll gate' being used more or less interchangeably. (In Britain 'bar' and 'gate' survive in a number of place names, as for example Potters Bar, and New Cross Gate.

Tickets were also issued at bridge approaches. The half-toll 'Friday' ticket for Waterloo Bridge (opposite page) is unusual in naming the day of the week and being printed from a hand-engraved wood block rather than printer's type. The half-toll rate is for an unladen vehicle.

Weighing-machine examples include one for an American 'patent hay scales', used in this case apparently for oxen.

70%

Handbills

Known variously as leaflet, flyer, throwaway—sometimes, in larger format, as a broadsheet—the handbill is one of the earliest and most enduring forms of printed publicity. The word makes its first appearance in the 1750s, but the thing itself must pre-date that by a century or more.

The heyday of the handbill was the period 1850 to 1890, when street distribution was so widespread as to be a public nuisance. They were given out by honest tradesmen, showmen, cheapjacks, quacks—and even ratcatchers. (*Mayhew's London* [1851] records Mr Jack Black's handbills, headed 'VR: Rat and Mole Destroyer to Her Majesty'.)

For the local printer the handbill was a paying proposition. It needed little in the way of expertise; layout, wording and general style emerged on the spur of the moment, and the life of the finished product was mercifully brief. What the customer wanted was speedy production. The style is epitomized by the printer's own handbill (this page, top).

Show business made wide use of the handbill, often using it as an *ad hoc* poster. In *Nicholas Nickleby* Dickens describes a typical operation: 'Extra bills were flung down areas . . . thrust under knockers . . . They were placarded on all the walls too . . .'

It was by its air of urgency that the handbill made its greatest impact; it was the ideal medium for local trade publicity.

Eighteenth-century examples are rare, but the two shown here are typical. Citizen Kaestner's showbiz item '*Par Permission*' (*c.*1765) offers 30 different animal acts, with a cannon-firing mountain stag, pistol shots and fireworks. James Sharp's Rolling Waggon leaflet (*c.*1780) combines information, public relations and hard sell.

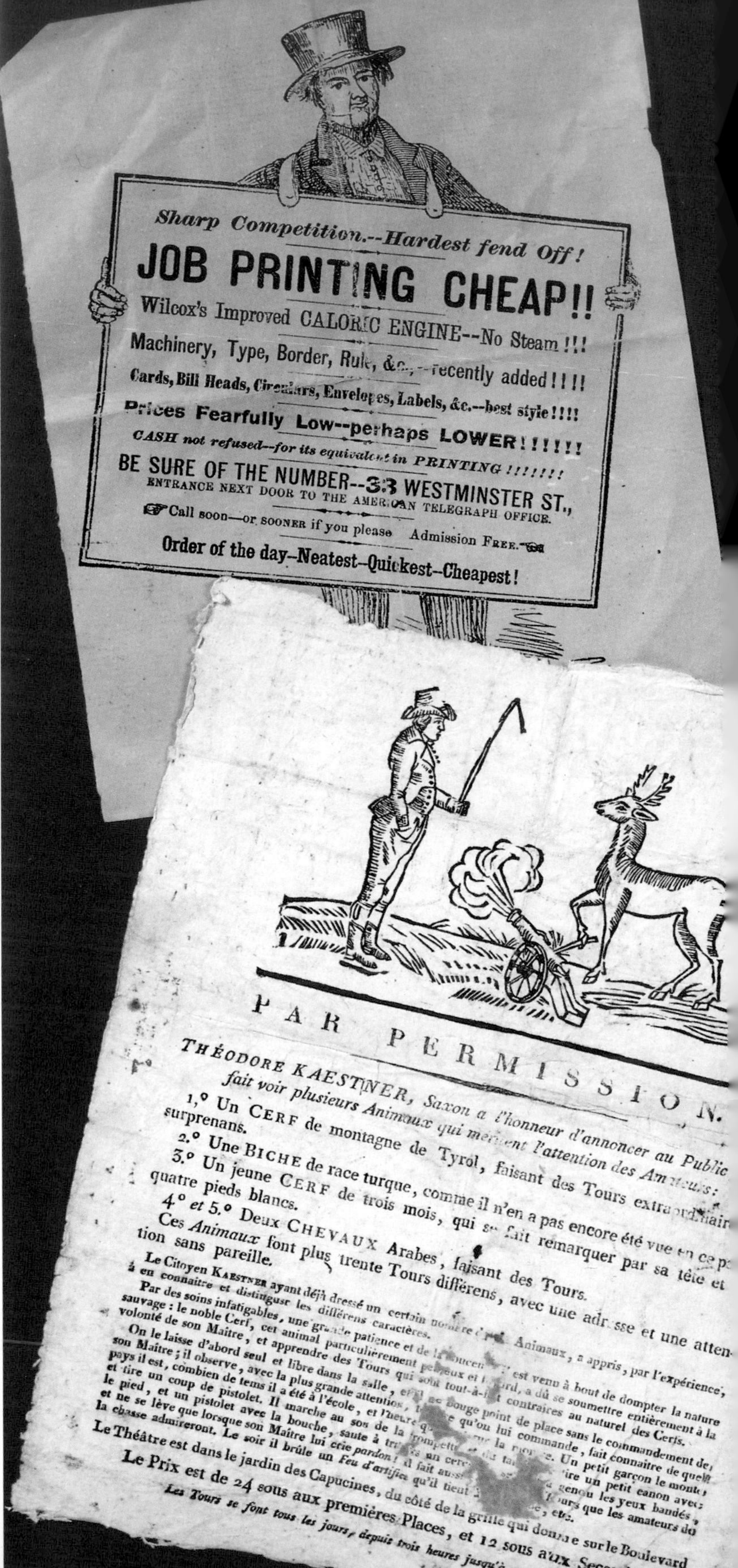

General Directions for the Driver of the Rolling Waggon.

LET the Waggon be greaſed as often as you conveniently can, whilſt it is new.

Be careful that you replace all the Rings or Waſhers, and examine the Boxes often (as they may be liable to get looſe at firſt) and wedge them up tight.

Hook up the Back Bands of the Thiller Horſes very ſhort,* that the Cattle may draw upwards as much as poſſible, and let the Body Horſes (or the Pair next the Thillers) have Pads or Saddles on their Backs, to ſuſtain the Preſſure occaſioned by the Leaders.

Load the Waggon forward, and leave the hind Part as light as poſſible.

Theſe Precautions obſerved, every Owner will find his Account in ſuch Carriages, from the very firſt; for no Road or Country can prevent their being uſed with Advantage.

* *Note*, It is abſolutely neceſſary that this ſhould be ſtrictly obſerved, for if it is not, the Thill and Body Horſes will ſoon be gall'd upon the Top of the Neck, by the too great Preſſure of the Collars, which will be entirely taken off when the back Bands are hook'd up ſhort.

N. B. Great Variety of Rolling Carriages, according to Act of Parliament, and alſo Garden and Land Rollers of a new Conſtruction, are ready for Inſpection; and are built by JAMES SHARP, No. 15, *Leadenhall-ſtreet, London.*

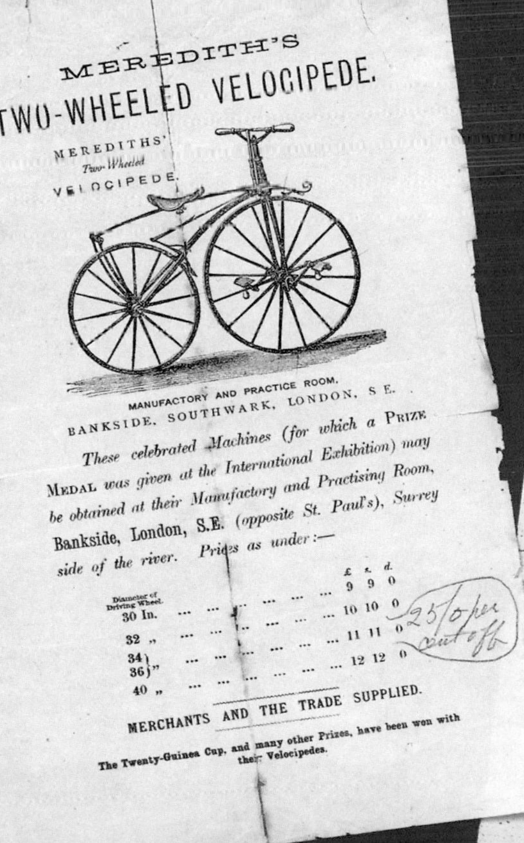

MEREDITH'S

TWO-WHEELED VELOCIPEDE.

MANUFACTORY AND PRACTICE ROOM,

BANKSIDE, SOUTHWARK, LONDON, S.E.

These celebrated Machines (for which a PRIZE MEDAL *was given at the International Exhibition) may be obtained at their Manufactory and Practising Room,* Bankside, London, S.E. *(opposite St. Paul's), Surrey side of the river. Prices as under:—*

Diameter of Driving Wheel.	£	s.	d.
30 In.	9	9	0
32 „	10	10	0
34 } 36 }"	11	11	0
40 „	12	12	0

25/0 per cent off

MERCHANTS AND THE TRADE SUPPLIED.

The Twenty-Guinea Cup, and many other Prizes, have been won with their Velocipedes.

BEWARE!

We hereby caution everybody not to deal with the so-called American Supply Co. or Albany Supply Co., of Albany, N. Y., as they are Frauds, having copied both our "Silent Assistant" and "Soap" Circulars.

H. C. ROWELL & CO.,
RUTLAND, VT.

Not least of the uses of the handbill was in the public expression of private anger. The Rowell Company's charge of plagiarism may well have been only the first shot in a succession of claim and counter-claim. It was not unusual for one handbill to provoke another—sometimes, it is said, produced by the same printer.

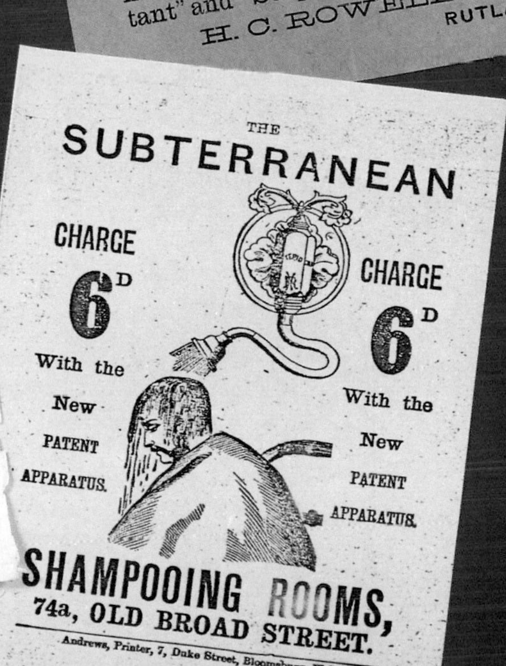

THE

SUBTERRANEAN

CHARGE 6^{D} With the New PATENT APPARATUS.

CHARGE 6^{D} With the New PATENT APPARATUS.

SHAMPOOING ROOMS,

74a, OLD BROAD STREET.

Andrews, Printer, 7, Duke Street, Bloomsbury, W.C.

55%

The 'Fatal Hour' newspaper item (1841) dates from the formation of Robert Peel's new Conservative ministry after the defeat and resignation of Lord Melbourne.

Newspapers of the period were frequent users of the handbill as a promotion medium, though few had reached this level of sensationalism.

Westminster Central Mart,

CORNER OF SOUTHAMPTON-STREET, STRAND,

Is Open Daily, from 9 to 5 o'Clock, for the Purpose of

Hiring Servants

OF ALL DENOMINATIONS,

For Noblemen and Tradesmen's Families; and also for providing Situations for Servants of every Class and Description, who are furnished with proper Recommendations suitable to their Capacities.

From the system laid down and pursued in this concern, for the purposes above alluded to, it must. from its very nature, produce the most beneficial effects to every individual. The New Plans which the Proprietors of this Establishment have adopted, by having a daily Register of upwards of FIVE HUNDRED APPLICANTS for Servants of every kind and denomination, will remove those inconveniences, particularly to Servants, which always attend Newspaper Advertisements.

Families from abroad, or from the Country, can be immediately furnished with suitable Servants of unquestionable character. And Servants wanting Places will be sent to Employers immediately.

THE

FATAL HOUR

HAS

ARRIVED.

THE QUEEN

Can now be considered in no better situation than that of a

STATE PRISONER.

She has been delivered over by her New Parliament to the tender mercies of her worst enemies. The dreadful crisis has arrived, and the

FACTIOUS PROCEEDINGS

of those who have produced it will be

Unflinchingly Exposed

BY THE

SUNDAY TIMES

On Sunday next, the 29th August.

The men who are about to take office care as little for the Queen as they do for the country. Distress will henceforth abound from one end of the kingdom to the other, and the people, who are on the

VERGE of STARVATION,

Continue the victims of accumulating privation.

Orders Received by all Newsvenders.

[Printed at the Steam Press of Chapman and Elcoate, Peterborough-court, Fleet-street.

SIGNOR BERTOLOTTO

HAS RE-OPENE[D]

HIS CELEBRATED AND EXTRAOR[DINARY]

EXHIBITION,

Patronised by the Royal Families of England, France, &c. &c. &c.

THE INDUSTRIOUS

FLEAS

209, REGENT STREET

With a variety of new and surprising feats, among which a Gigantic and Herculean Flea will move a weight of 5000 times its own, being a representation of the Liverpool and Manchester Railway, near the Warrington Branch, a first train with the Mail consisting of the Steam Engine, the Coal Waggon, and 16 Carriages, the whole drawn by a *Single Flea.*

THE CELEBRATED

Perpetual Motion.

Invented and executed by Mons. Charles Chevalier, Ingineur du Roi, never Exhibited in England, representing an elegant Jeu de Bague, which continually revolves by Magnetic and Electrical Power, and will last as long as the diamond on which it turns. This has been attempted for ages, and considered an impossibility.

The above is only an addition to the usual Exhibition which has deserved and obtained such unparalleled celebrity.

The Industrious Fleas

will continue their surprising feats, such as Dancing a Waltz, Playing on Musical Instruments, drawing a Coach, a Gig, the Great Mogul on his State Elephant, a complete Man-of-War, 120 Guns, Pull a Bucket from a Well, Fight a Duel with real Steel Swords, Play at Whist, Flirt, &c. Also the Three Heroes of Waterloo, Riding on as many well caparisoned Fleas, and a variety of other feats too long to detail. The objects are all new and of exquisite workmanship.

Those Persons who doubt the veracity of the above, need not pay for admittance till they are convinced that there is no deception

Open from 10 till Dusk. Admittance 1s

E. & J. Thomas, Printers, 6, Exeter Street, Strand, London.

63%

Notice is hereby
riven! that on Wednesday, the
8th Day of THIS MONTH, (Oc-
ober) Six Prizes of £30.000, and
ll other Prizes will be decided, being the very Last Drawing and the
very Last Lottery that can ever take
place in this Kingdom.

BY ORDER
OF THE
Lords of the Treasury.

6 £30.000
ALL TO BE DRAWN IN ONE DAY,
18th THIS MONTH,
(OCTOBER) WHEN ALL
Lotteries End for Ever!

T FAIL
SEE THE
-HEADED
LADY
E BLUE AND WHITE STRIPED TENT.

NEW PHOTOGRAPH & AMBROTYPE ROOMS,
FIFTY RODS FROM THE GARDINER HOTEL,
ON CAUSEWAY STREET,
(Next house to the residence of the late F. Allen, Esq.)

MRS. M. E. HAMLIN

Has built and fitted up nice and convenient rooms on the first floor, thereby avoiding the necessity of climbing one to three flights of stairs, which, as everyone knows, makes the "heart go pit-a-pat, and the brains go whirl-a-gig," where she again hopes to meet her former liberal patronage. Thankful for past favors, she hopes, by attention and courtesy in business, to merit a continuance of the same. Pictures can be obtained at as reasonable a rate as at any place on the River, and perfect satisfaction warranted. Particular attention to

COPYING PICTURES,
TAKING PICTURES OF CHILDREN,
AND TAKING PICTURES OF THE DEAD.

OVAL FRAMES,
Of every Size and Quality, Constantly on Hand, and for sale at her Rooms.

Daniel R. Variell's Rooms, over Palmer's Bookstore, and Ezra Kimball's Rooms, over the Express Office, having suspended operations and closed up, renders it more favorable for an opening with me, and I hope to have a full attendance. DON'T FORGET THE PLACE,

Over the Causeway, toward Augusta.

You will see the sign if you seek it, "and there shall no other sign be given," except the one now on the building, four feet by two.

All are Invited to
Call & Examine Specimens Gratis.

GARDINER, JAN. 20, 1866.
MRS. M. E. HAMLIN.

N. C. HILL,
SURGEON DENTIST,

Respectfully informs the citizens of this place, that he has taken rooms at
where he will be in readiness at all times to wait on those who may be in want of his professional services, as a Practical Dentist. It gives him pleasure to say, that all that can be done for the benefit of the Teeth, such as Cleaning, Filling, Setting and Extracting, he will do for those who favor him with their patronage, and on reasonable terms.

Families will be waited upon at their residences without any additional charge.

He has constantly on hand, for sale, Tooth Powder, and Tooth Brushes, of the best quality.

In Britain the royal coat of arms had a mesmeric power of attraction. The public lottery handbill, at first glance an official notice, soon discloses its true function as a lottery 'puff'. The impending abolition of lotteries (1826) meant a final fling—not only for the public but for the organisers.

For the itinerant dentist the leaflet did double duty—as a street handout and as a public notice. Staying in each place only as long as demand required, he filled in his address as appropriate. Some practitioners worked to a planned itinerary, sending on announcements ahead of arrival.

63%

Poster stamps

Appearing first in Central Europe at the turn of the nineteenth century, the poster stamp was used as a promotional sticker on correspondence. Its immediate fore-runners were the official letter-seal, widely used by bureaucrats to complete the closure of envelopes, and the mock postage stamp, affixed as a commemorative or promotional item to the front of the envelope.

The poster stamp took its inspiration from the full-scale advertising poster. Some, but not all, reproduced actual posters; most were merely 'posteresque'—designed in the poster idiom.

In Germany, heartland of the cult, the medium attracted the attention of major poster artists, and by 1914 the country's leading poster journal *Das Plakat* was able to publish an extended feature on the subject, showing the miniature work of 40 top designers.

In Britain reactions were slower, though the idea had been imported under the allegedly non-commercial aegis of the Society of Poster Art, founded in London in 1913. The London *Evening News* ran a competition for designs for the medium, as did others.

America responded with the formation of three or four specialist printing firms, and a lively promotional drive in industry and among state publicity commissions. One poster artist, Edward E. Williams, designed a poster stamp advertising his own prowess as a poster stamp designer.

British designers were distinctly cool on this new-fangled medium, though a few found themselves in miniature more or less by accident when their big posters were reproduced as correspondence stickers. The same thing happened to some of the country's resort poster men. They too, as a Southern Railways afterthought, were brought down a size or two (as in the Lyme Regis example). The reproduction quality, all were agreed, was not very good.

100%

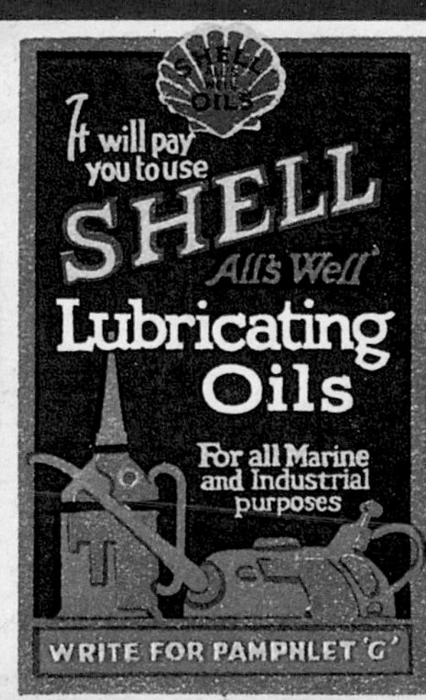

Of the poster-stamp designs on these pages, only seven are known to have been derived from actual posters. They are: Curacao Extra Dry; Daily Mail Ideal Home Exhibition; Wiener Messe (Vienna Fair); Building Exhibition Olympia; Wiener Schuh und Ledermesse (Vienna Shoe and Leather Fair); Ostdeutsche Austellung fur Industrie Gewerbe und Landwirtschaft, Posen (East German Trade, Industry and Agriculture Exhibition, Poznan); and Lyme Regis.

In the 1920s and 30s the European poster stamp became a cult object. Special albums appeared for storing them, and in many cases the stamps were produced in sets to encourage collecting. The British resort series ran to some dozens; El Verso cigars to ten.

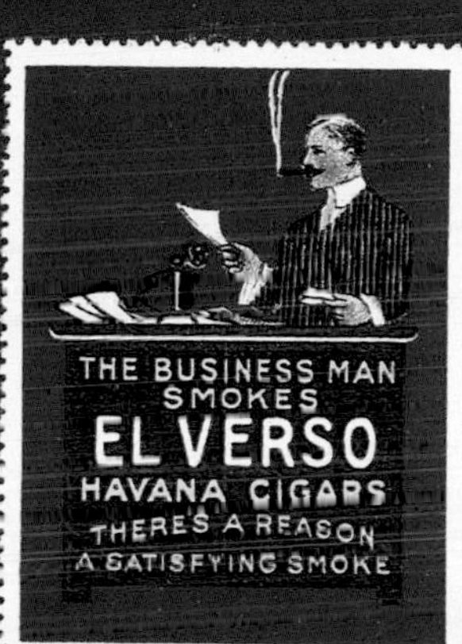

TO BUILDERS, JOINERS, &c.

TO BE

Sold by Auction,

BY MR. WALKER,

At the CASTLE OF YORK,

On TUESDAY, the 10th of AUGUST, 1830,

AT TEN O'CLOCK IN THE FORENOON,

All the Materials of the

HUSTINGS

AND

BOOTHS,

Erected for the COUNTY ELECTION, and now Standing in the CASTLE YARD, which will be put up in Lots, as follows:—

No. 1.—The Hustings, up to and including the Planks of the First Floor, with the whole of the Stairs, Carriages, Handrails, &c.

No. 2.—The Upper-Part of the Hustings, including the Sheriff's Box.

No. 3.—The Barriers and Doors.

No. 4, to 14.—The Booths, as Numbered.

☞ The above may be Viewed any time previous to the Sale, and for further Particulars, apply to the AUCTIONEER, No. 10, Davygate.

York, 7th August, 1830.

Printed by THOMAS STONES, Courant-Office, Coneystreet, York.

Administrator's

SALE OF

SLAVES.

The undersigned, administrator of the estate of ROBERT E. DOWNING, dec'd., will on *WEDNESDAY*, the 4th day of January next, at *Bell Air*, in Cooper county, Mo., sell publicly to the highest bidder, six negres belonging to said estate, to wit: One negro boy about 20 years old; one negro girl about 16 years old, and one young negro woman, with three children. A credit of six months will be given, the purchaser giving bond and approved security.

JAMES L. BELL, Admr.

December 9th, 1853.

Sale notices

Sales by auction cover a wide variety of properties, and the auction notice, with or without a detailed listing of the items concerned, provides an informative sideligh on human affairs.

Among the many thousands of occasions thus recorded are sales not only of houses, horses and cattle, domestic goods and personal effects, but less conventional properties. If the Coldstream street manure sale reflects an unusual degree of civic enterprise, no less does another sale at the same period reported from North Berwick, when roup lots included a year's rights in th customs, shore dues and anchorages, the steelyard, the seaweed, the sand, and herring stances at harbour. (The term 'roup' is Scots for auction.)

The slave sale notice from Bell Air, Missouri, viewed in the context of paddle steamers and street manure, may come as a shock. But as with all the others, it is a document of its time.

Among other surviving sale notices are those featuring turnpike rights, ecclesiastical advowsons (rights in the appointing of a clergyman to a benefice), post-horse hiring licences and, in Ireland, rights to cut turf (peat).

Sales for distraint of rent are also thus recorded. These (in the United States under the heading of Sheriff's Sales) set out the lots as handwritten entries on a pre-printed form

Larger notices, up to 60 × 40 cm (24 × 16 in), listed every lot in the sale, providing a full domestic inventory from back kitchen, through each room to cellar, yard and garden.

In another category were notices for majo sales—the heavyweights of auction history. Among these in the nineteenth century are such properties as the *Great Eastern*, 'the celebrated and magnificent Iron Paddle and Screw Steamship', sold on 28 October 1885 for £26,200.

STREET MANURE FOR SALE.

A Large Quantity of **STREET MANURE**, collected upon the **STREETS** of **COLDSTREAM**,

WILL BE SOLD BY PUBLIC ROUP,

AT THE

MANURE DEPOT,

DUNSE ROAD, COLDSTREAM,

ON

THURSDAY, 26th October 1865.

As a great portion of the Manure has lain for a considerable period in the Depot, it will be found in excellent condition for immediate use. The Manure will be put up in Lots to suit intending Purchasers.

Further particulars will be learned on application to GEORGE BROWN, Writer, Coldstream, Clerk to the Commissioners of Police, in whose hands are the Articles of Roup.

SALE TO COMMENCE AT THREE O'CLOCK AFTERNOON.

FAIRBAIRN & PENNY, Auctioneers.

COLDSTREAM, 14th October 1865.

PRINTED AT THE "MAIL" OFFICE, KELSO.

Street manure was one of the most noticeable features of increasingly congested nineteenth-century towns, and its disposal was a serious problem. In some cities it became big business. New York, even in the early years of this century, still had its Manhattan Horse Manure Company, 'Gatherers, Dealers and Shippers of Manure'.

The hustings, wooden platforms from which elections were then conducted, formed a disposable asset; at the sale in York in 1830 a prudent local authority (as at Coldstream) gets the last penny out of civic goings on.

The slave sale notice is a single item from a large body of slavery ephemera—inventories, invoices, receipts and all the minor records of day-to-day business dealings.

67%

Playing-card stationery

When paper was less readily available than it is today, the disused or defective pack of cards was a handy substitute for a notepad. Of more or less standard shape and size and, at least until the 1860s, unprinted on the back, the playing card was used in a wide range of improvisations. These, apart from playing-card history as such, are the subject of study in their own right.

The playing card was used not only for manuscript additions, but as a substitute for printer's stock, serving as a vehicle for invitations, birth, death and marriage announcements, admission tickets, trade- and visiting cards and other such items. Most of the examples surviving today are from the continent of Europe; few are from Britain; scarcely any are from America.

Earliest specimens date from the mid-eighteenth century. They include hand-written memoranda and messages, poetry, musical scores, shopping lists, receipts, IOUs, cheques, lottery tickets, delivery notes, and library catalogue entries. Edward Gibbon, author of *The History of the Decline and Fall of the Roman Empire*, used playing cards for bibliographical references, one thousand of which are now housed in the British Museum. Gibbon also used playing cards in written acknowledgement of gambling debts.

Playing cards have also served as emergency currency in time of coin shortage, notably in seventeenth- and eighteenth-century Canada, when the French authorities introduced them for the payment of troops pending arrival of money supplies from France.

They were similarly used after the French Revolution, when private individuals gave them as 'small change' for high-value *assignats*, and they also appeared as substitute money in Germany in the 1920s.

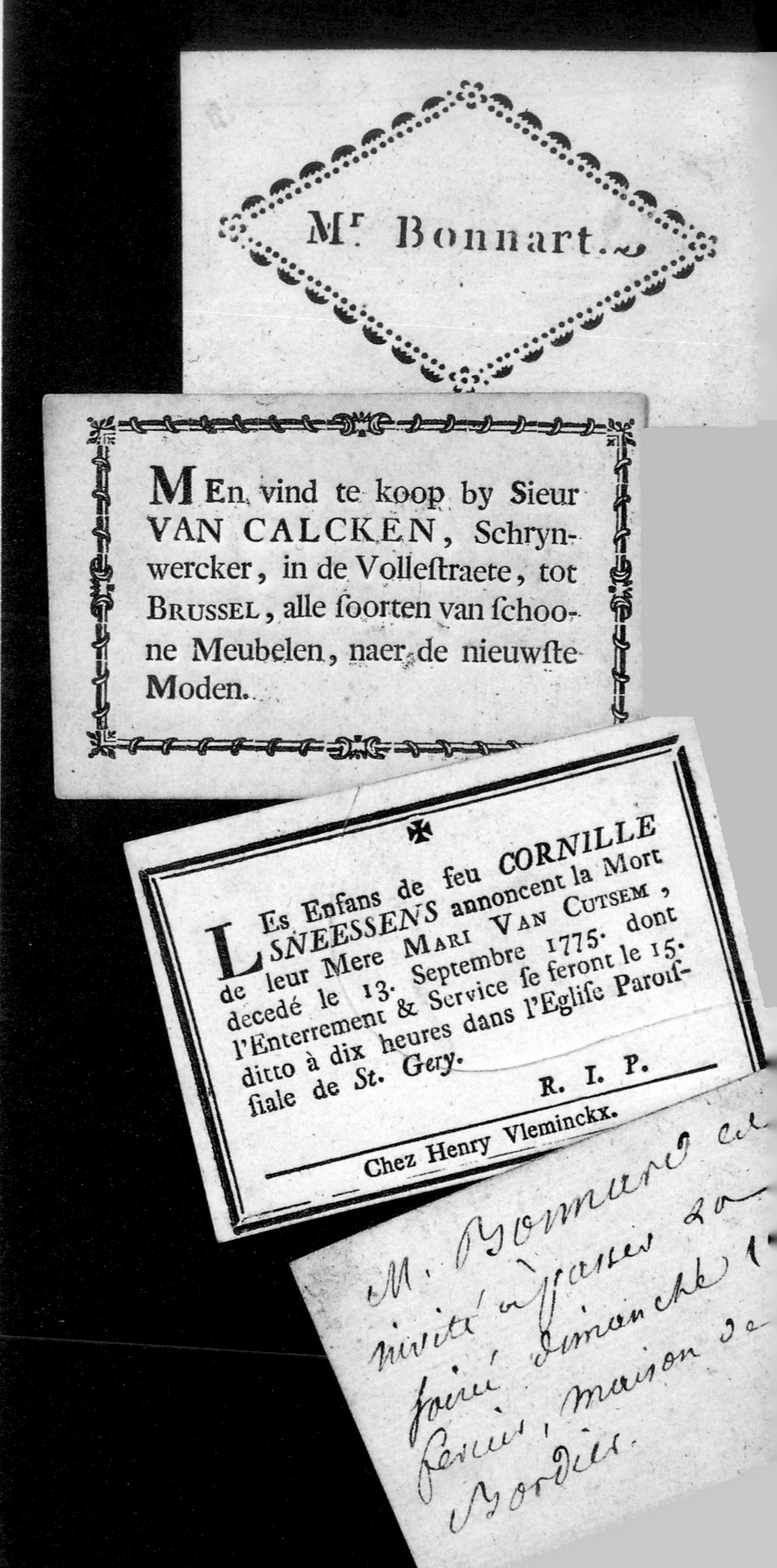

Mr. Bonnart.

MEn vind te koop by Sieur VAN CALCKEN, Schrynwercker, in de Vollestraete, tot BRUSSEL, alle soorten van schoone Meubelen, naer de nieuwste Moden.

LEs Enfans de feu CORNILLE SNEESSENS annoncent la Mort de leur Mere MARI VAN CUTSEM, decedé le 13. Septembre 1775. dont l'Enterrement & Service se feront le 15. ditto à dix heures dans l'Eglise Paroissiale de St. Gery.

R. I. P.

Chez Henry Vleminckx.

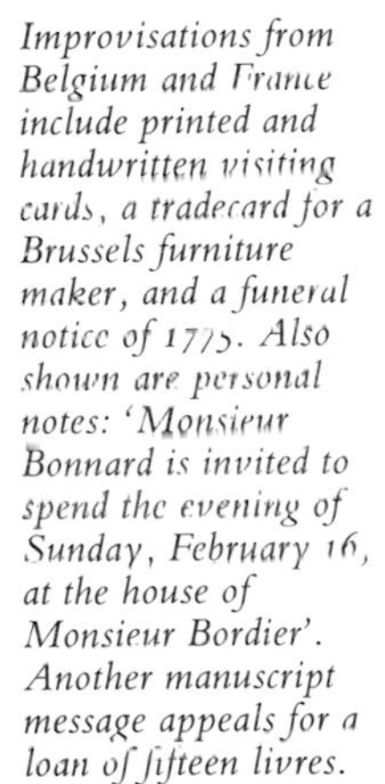

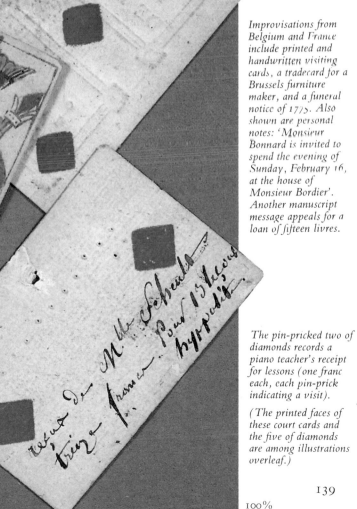

Improvisations from Belgium and France include printed and handwritten visiting cards, a tradecard for a Brussels furniture maker, and a funeral notice of 1775. Also shown are personal notes: 'Monsieur Bonnard is invited to spend the evening of Sunday, February 16, at the house of Monsieur Bordier'. Another manuscript message appeals for a loan of fifteen livres.

The pin-pricked two of diamonds records a piano teacher's receipt for lessons (one franc each, each pin-prick indicating a visit).

(The printed faces of these court cards and the five of diamonds are among illustrations overleaf.)

100%

chap. . 326.

palladii episcopi helenopoli-
-tani de vita S. J. chrysostomi
dialogus, homilia S. J.
chrysost. in laudem diodori,
acta tarachi, probi et andronici,
passio bonifacii romani,
evagrius de octo cogitationibus,
nilus de octo vitiis.
graecè et latinè. Studio
emerici bigotii. lutetiae
ed. martin 1680. in 4o.
veau
paris. d'artois

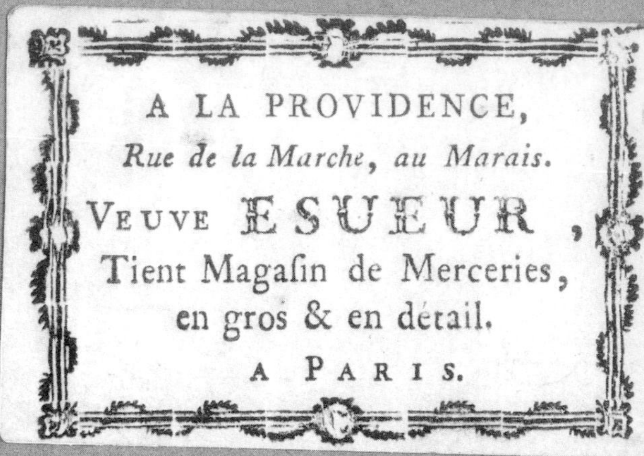
A LA PROVIDENCE,
Rue de la Marche, au Marais.
VEUVE ESUEUR,
Tient Magasin de Merceries,
en gros & en détail.
A PARIS.

AU TÉLESCOPE,
Au Palais Royal, sur le Jardin, No 244.
TROCHON, OPTICIEN,
Fabricant d'Instrumens d'Optique, Physique, Lunettes fines pour conserver la vue, Lunettes de Spectacle, Microscopes, Chambres noires, Instrumens de Mathématiques, Barometres, Thermometres, & autres Marchandises.
Demeure à sa Fabrique, Quai de l'Horloge du Palais, vis-à-vis le Méridien. A PARIS

BERGER,
MAITRE CORDONNIER
POUR LES DAMES,
Demeure rue Montorgueil, chez le Potier-d'Etain, vis-à-vis le Passage du Saumon, au troisieme sur le devant.
A PARIS.

A manuscript library card (top left) records details of a book published in Paris ('Quarto, calf') in 1680.

Playing-card tradecards, all from Paris, advertise (top) a retail and wholesale draper, (centre) a scientific instrument maker, (bottom) a ladies' shoemaker.

The three of spades is a pin-prick receipt for 36 francs in payment for 60 grammar lessons, November 15, 1820.

100%

A quelle heure aux Tuileries me voulez-vous,

Je passerais a sept heures
M°

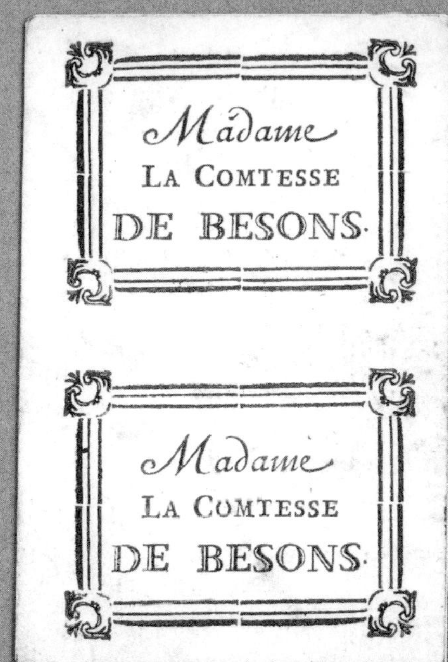

Loterie d'un très beau Schal de Madras blanc façon cachemire a gagner sur le premier numero qui sortira au 1er tirage de mars loterie de Paris. No 10 a 36 toute la bille

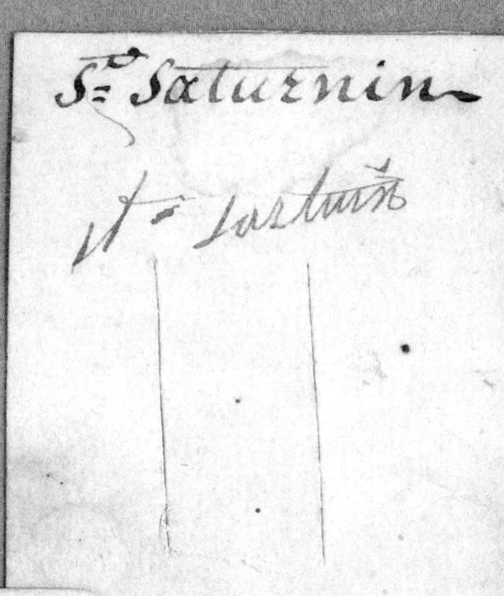

Thanksgiving Ball
The Company of Miss Mercy Clark is requested at Dr Cutler's Hall on the 6 Dec at 4 O-Clock P.M. — — Dec 6 1800
J. Hall } managers { J Clark
J Gould } { O Lovell

A manuscript note (top left) records an assignation c1820: 'At what time would you like me at the Tuileries?' 'I will call at 7 o'clock'.

A handwritten lottery ticket (centre) offers a first prize of a fine shawl, and a rare American item (bottom) invites a Miss Clark to a Thanksgiving ball on December 6, 1800.

Above, right, is a two-in-one calling card, designed for cutting into two miniature cards. Below it is a makeshift bookmark, apparently made from a library card.

100%

Playing cards were used as emergency money in the town of Steyregg, Austria, during the severe inflation of the 1920s. Shown here are the front and back of the 'Hungarian' deck, much used in Austria at the time, the back bearing a value overprint (20 heller) and the official stamp of the local council.

The two tradecards are from Belgium. They are printed, c.1920, on surplus playing-card stock.

100%

Watchpapers

These paper roundels were inserted within the hinged flap of the early pocketwatch. Introduced in the later years of the eighteenth century, they served as watchmakers' advertisements, as packing for loose-fitting watch cases, and sometimes as personal souvenirs or love-notes. They remained in general use until the early 1920s, when the pocket watch began to be superseded by the wristwatch.

In its earliest form the watchpaper was engraved with a decorative rendering of the maker's or repairer's name and address, often with classical figures, images of Father Time and other references to time and transience. Later details were added—sometimes fairly extensive—of the watchmaker's other activities ('Money lent on plate, watches, rings etc.'; 'Rings made to order')

The paper was commonly used as a record of repair and servicing, dates and details being entered by hand on the back. In many cases successive repairs are recorded in a number of papers in the same watch. The increasing thickness of the pad of papers had the effect of compensating for progressive loosening of the cover hinge, restoring the snap closure to its former satisfactory 'clunk'.

Personalized watchpapers, hand produced by admirers, fulfilled the same role as the locket memento—a private pledge of attachment and commitment. These are found as elaborate paper cuts, embroidery and micro-manuscripts. Microscopic renderings of the Lord's Prayer were also popular, as were other religious texts and moral aphorisms.

Also found are perpetual calendars in various forms, date adjustments being effected by shifting cut-out strips, discs, or other movable cut-outs. And more down-to-earth items are found too—roundels cut from scrap paper, old playing cards, or newspaper—simply to serve as packing.

Major collections are held by the Guildhall Library, London, and by the American Antiquarian Society, Worcester, Mass.

100%

Centred on this page is a watchpaper from Massachusetts with a photocopy of the reverse, inscribed with details of work on the watch. It records that a new mainspring was fitted in December 1855 at a cost of one dollar, and in August 1863 a new centrate wheel pinion and cleaning cost two dollars.

Other specimens include a typeset timetable (Isle of Man, 1880s), an improvised watchpaper cut from an eighteenth-century newspaper, and a hand-written poem of mourning.

100%

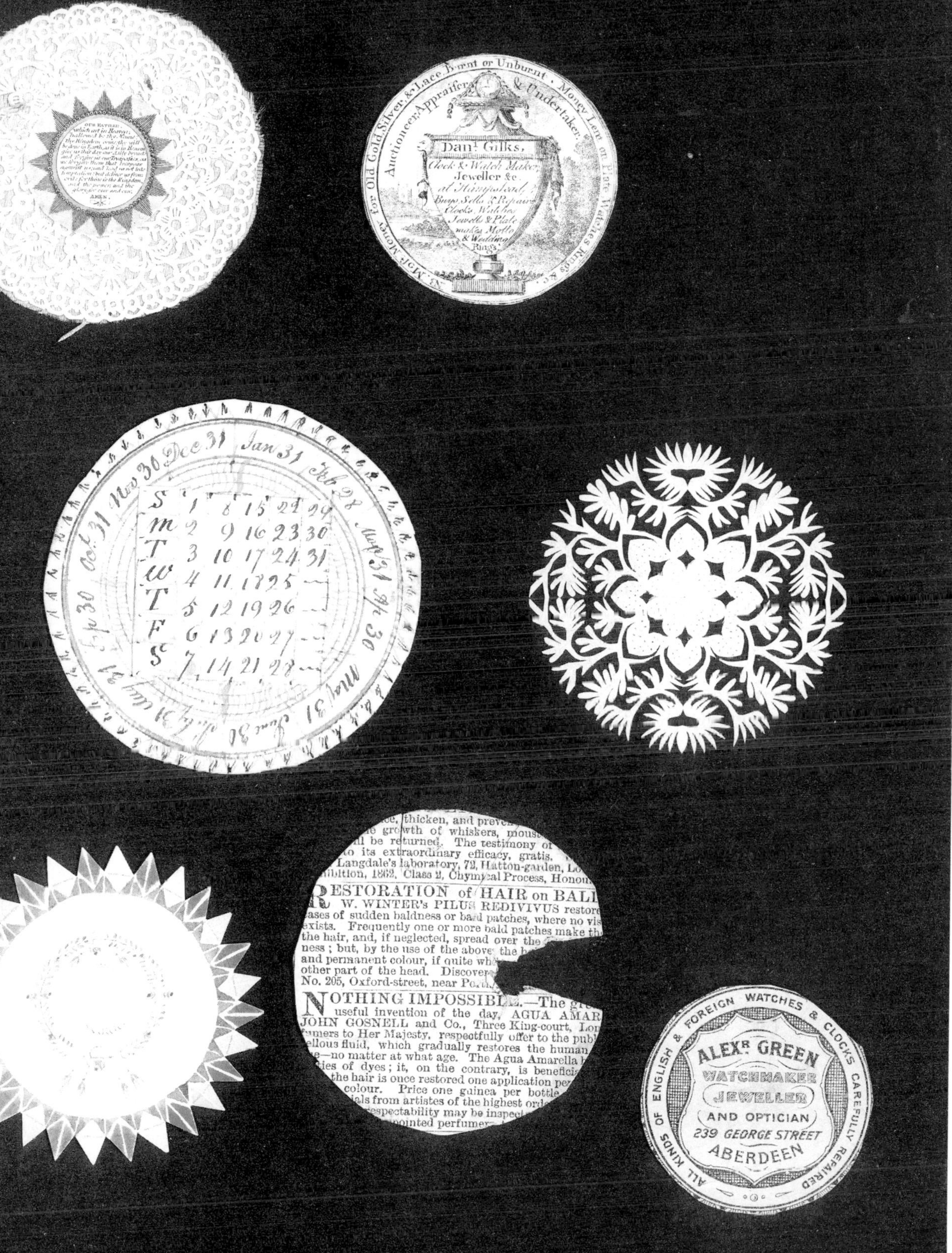

This selection includes a micro-engraving of the Lord's Prayer (top left), a hand-executed permanent calendar with movable strip, and a hand-drawn star design, also with the Lord's Prayer (now very faint) as centre-piece.

'Star' motifs, as well as cuts around the periphery of papers, were designed to allow papers to conform to the concavity of the watch case.

The paper-cut specimen is typical of the work of the Pennsylvania Dutch, seventeenth- and eighteenth-century immigrants to America from Germany and Switzerland.

100%

Dance programmes

An essential feature of the formal ballroom, the dance programme was used by nineteenth-century ladies to note their engagements in the evening's dancing.

The programmes usually took the form of a folded card, small enough to be carried in an evening bag, and often supplied with a tasselled pencil and cord. A printed running order on the inside listed the dances. Partners' names were to be pencilled in the blanks provided. Some cards were single-sided, dance numbers and names being written on a plain back. Others had running order and name spaces on the face of the card.

The cards were generally supplied from printers' stock, for overprinting with details of date and occasion—or not—as the customer desired. Only in special cases was the programme designed wholly to the client's requirements.

The majority of dance programmes were highly decorative. In Britain such printers as De La Rue and Goodall vied with each other in luxury and printing virtuosity. The chromolitho process, with its extravagant use of colour from lithographic stones, brought luxury to this staple of 'social stationery'. It was the fashion in the 1880s and 90s for the programme to be worn suspended from a wristlet clip—ostensibly for ease of reference, but in fact as an added feminine grace.

The programmes today provide a running record of dance fashions, from the schottisches, lancers, galops and quadrilles of the 1850s to the two-steps and fox-trots of the 1920s and 30s.

Surviving cards may come unused from the files of printers and stationers or from among mementoes of dancers themselves. The latter, in their pencilled entries, crossings out and cryptic notes, poignantly evoke their time and place.

89%

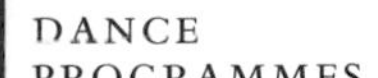

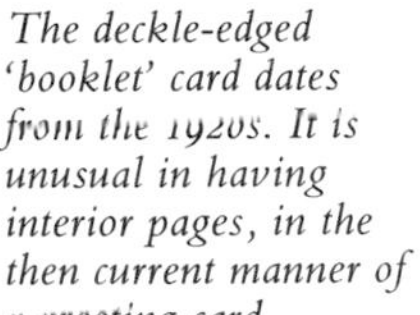

The deckle-edged 'booklet' card dates from the 1920s. It is unusual in having interior pages, in the then current manner of a greeting card.

The twentieth-century programme of the Domestic Servants Benevolent Institution lists 29 dances (as against the traditional 20 or 22), but retains the cotillions, polkas, schottisches and quadrilles of former times.

89%

The American fire-fighter's social impact was clearly as dramatic as his calling. Though replete with galops and quadrilles, his dance card leaves the ladies in no doubt as to the debt they owe their heroes. This card, like the 1920s specimen on the previous page, adopts the unusual greeting-card format.

86%

The butterfly card was designed and printed by Parkins & Gotto, the former Oxford Street stationers, and sold by the 'Army & Navy Cooperative Society'. The cut-out card was an expensive novelty. The address and date of the ball (22, Lyndhurst Road, January 14, 1875) are incorporated in the patterning on the other side of the butterfly's wings.

86%

Scraps/diecuts

The Victorian 'scrap' or die-cut was one of the major outlets for the work of the chromolitho printer.

Produced at first only in Germany, these cut-out reliefs brought German chromolithography a stage beyond the flat picture. Combining chromo printing with the die-cutting process, and then—a master stroke—embossed relief, gave chromolitho an irresistible appeal. Children everywhere, not to mention parents, took to them as one.

The scraps were sold separately or in sheets, each image linked to the next by a narrow tab which was cut off in separation. The tab commonly bore the name of the distributor or printer. Other tabs, also designed to be cut away, might carry names or captions, as in the examples, top left.

For the printers who produced them, scraps remained only a sideline. Their major work was in the production of large-scale chromos and advertising material. But in the 1860s and 70s the scrap industry flourished in its own right, and the cult of the scrap album, which had formerly been fashionable in polite drawing rooms, received new impetus. The scraps for which the albums had been devised were random oddments cut from newspapers and magazines, feathers, dried flowers etc., but with the advent of the German *Oblaten* or *Glanzbilder* ('wafers' or 'gloss pictures') the word 'scrap' took on a new meaning.

Prominent printers were Zoecke & Mittmeyer, and Mamelok & Soehne in Germany, and Louis Prang in America. The great name in Britain was Raphael Tuck, who began by importing huge quantities of scraps, and at a later stage themselves manufactured them.

Scraps are not infrequently found that look like fakes. These, in less brilliant colours, and lacking full relief, are merely latter-day 'revivals', clearly inferior to the real thing. As such they should rightly be cheaper.

55%

Scraps were used as decorative additions to Christmas cards, valentines and a wide range of other such items, but in the Victorian home a popular use was in embellishing the three- or four-fold screens that draughty living rooms required. Fire screens were also thus decorated. Scraps were pasted in profusion, much in the manner of the montage shown here, with overlaps and juxtapositions at the whim of the paster.

The world of the relief scrap was a never-never land of hearts and flowers and peaches-and-cream complexions. But the mixture was relieved by touches of near-reality, like the steam train and the Oxford Circus bus. (Note the manufacturer's realistic use of the bus-side advertising space.)

55%

NO.

THIS BOOK

WAS GIVEN BY

TO THE

Parochial Library

AT THE PARSONAGE OF

PRINCES RISBOROUGH,

IN THE COUNTY OF BUCKS,

And Diocese of Lincoln.

FOUNDED BY THE ASSOCIATES OF THE LATE

REV. THOMAS BRAY, D. D. and

REV. RICHARD MEADE,

Minister of the Parish.

1816.

MARSHALL'S

CIRCULATING LIBRARY,

160, NEWINGTON BUTTS.

TERMS FOR READING.

One Penny per volume for three days for old works.
If kept longer, One Halfpenny each day over.
To prevent confusion, each volume to be paid for when returned.
If a set of Books are taken out at one time and kept over three days,
One Halfpenny per volume for each day until returned.
Deposit required according to the value of the Books taken out.

Dealer in first-class Cigars and Tobacco.

RICHARD NICHOLS,
BOOKSELLER,
STATIONER & BINDER,
Silver Street,
WAKEFIELD.

Book labels

Broadly speaking, the term 'book label' applies to virtually any label pasted in or on any book, whether it is an armorial bookplate, a simple nameplate, a mark of private ownership or donation, a library identification, a school prize, or a miniature tradecard from a bookseller, stationer, binder or printer.

The purist may favour more specific terms, and many would question the inclusion of any of these items under the heading 'ephemera'. Are these not pasted firmly in place, as permanent as the book itself? For all that, they are often found loose, or still pasted to the boards of some discarded binding. The ephemerist does not throw them away.

The book label may be said to have its origin in Cambridge University, where it was the custom in the late 1500s to record gifts of books, not only in the general register, but in the volumes themselves.

The simple nameplate is said to have stemmed from the printer's traditional 'keepsake', personal labels set up and printed in the presence of visiting VIPs, as souvenirs of the occasion. The memento, to which the recipient often added the words 'his book', found its way into private libraries. The fashion spread, other bookmen having their own name labels printed for their own books. It was thus that from the two cities of Cambridge—in England and Massachusetts—the book label came into the world. (The first dated American book label is that of Samuel Phillips. It was printed on the first press in New England in 1650.)

The bookplate, as distinct from the book label, firstly and principally served only those entitled to bear arms. It is commonly an engraved heraldic design, whereas the book label is set from type.

Both forms have their ultimate origins in inscriptions on fly leaves or title pages, but some early book labels were printed as a separate sheet to be bound in with the pages of the book.

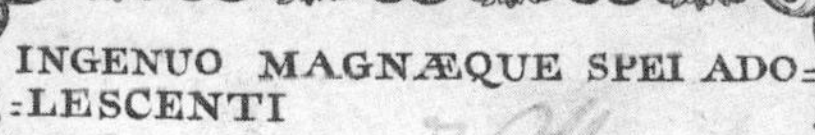

INGENUO MAGNÆQUE SPEI ADO=
=LESCENTI

PROPTER INSIGNES IN ARTIBUS
PROGRESSUS. In CLASSE

Præmium hoc Literarium dederunt *Præpositus* & *Socii Seniores* Collegii Sacrosanctæ & Indivi=
=duæ Trinitatis juxta *DUBLIN*.

Examinatione habita initio Termini
An. Dom. 17

Quod Testor,

This BOOK belongs to the
Circulating Library
OF
T. Skelton,
In High Street, *Southampton*;
Where NEW BOOKS, on every entertaining subject, are purchased, as soon as published, for the Library.
A choice Collection of MAPS & PRINTS.
PERIODICAL PUBLICATIONS will be regularly delivered to Subscribers as soon as published, at the London Prices.
New MUSIC, and MUSICAL INSTRUMENTS, sold or let out.
All the EVENING PAPERS regularly delivered to Subscribers at their own Houses.
STATIONERY & PERFUMERY of all Sorts, in the best Condition.
Also genuine PATENT MEDICINES.
☞ BOOKS bound in plain and elegant Bindings, on reasonable Terms.
PRINTING in general, correct and neat.
The NEW SOUTHAMPTON GUIDE, with many useful Additions. Price 1s.

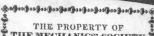

THE PROPERTY OF
THE MECHANICS' SOCIETY
OF LANCASTER.
APPRENTICES' LIBRARY.
No. 460

W. Houghton,
Twelve Years with & Successor to
Mr. Wrangham,
STATIONER &c.
161 New Bond St.

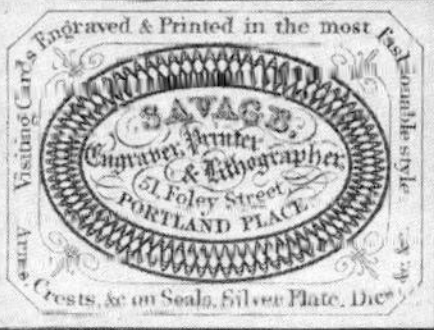

HALIFAX, OCTOBER 26, 1767.
GEORGE POLLARD's
BOOK.

BOOKS BOUND
by
Callender & Wills
Corner of South
& Market Streets
BALTIMORE.

EMBERLIN & HAROLD,
PRINTERS,
Booksellers & Binders,
MARLBRO'

POCOCK,
Bookseller,
BATH.

A. J. Barker,
BOOKSELLER,
Taunton, Mass.

The parochial library, pioneered in the late eighteenth century by Thomas Bray (opposite page) led the way to the popular mechanics' libraries, reading rooms and lending libraries of the nineteenth century. Many of their labels proclaim rules and conditions of loan. In the later trade-library labels, details of other goods and services appear (facing page, Marshall's) 'Dealer in first-class cigars and tobacco'; (this page, Hookham's) 'Visiting tickets . . . bookplates etc. neatly engraved and printed'.

Latin was the idiom of early academic labels. The book-prize specimen records the progress of Henry Watts in his second form examination at Trinity College, Dublin, anno domini 1765.

79%

Valentines

The valentine industry dates in Britain fron the start of the Uniform Penny Post in 184 when for the first time all classes of the pub were enabled to send messages to each othe at moderate cost. In America the idea caug on in the 1850s and 60s, when imports of la paper frivolities began to catch the public e

Popularized by the firm of Dobbs Kidd i London, the introduction of lace paper was big contributory factor in the growth of th valentine fad. For many, the valentine was become identified solely with lace paper, an it became progressively more elaborate and frilly as the century unfolded.

Using multi-layer effects, in which lace papers were 'sprung' one above the other o paper hinges, the girls who assembled the valentines produced not just a greeting card but something akin to a paper sculpture.

Though grossly underpaid, the girls nevertheless appeared to enjoy the work, an small assembly firms sprang up in back stre to cash in on everyone's good nature.

The girls used lace paper as a base, with silken pads, printed poems, scraps, artificial flowers, mirror glass etc. as added embellishment. They put the material together to a set pattern or, if they showed aptitude, to their own fancy. Many of their more elaborate creations were sold for the equivalent of one girl's wages for six month These were marketed in substantial cartons.

Extravagance ran riot. In the more exclusive making-up rooms in the latter par of the century components included jewellery, confectionery, perfume and, in some cases, musical box movements, playin as the box opened.

The stationery industry, impressed by the success of the lacy valentine, introduced lace paper into Christmas cards as well, substituting 'Christmas Greetings' for 'I am thine'. The principle was extended to Easter greetings too.

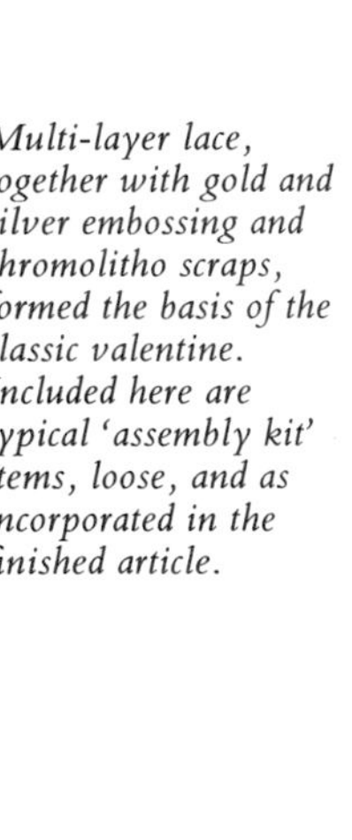

Multi-layer lace, together with gold and silver embossing and chromolitho scraps, formed the basis of the classic valentine. Included here are typical 'assembly kit' items, loose, and as incorporated in the finished article.

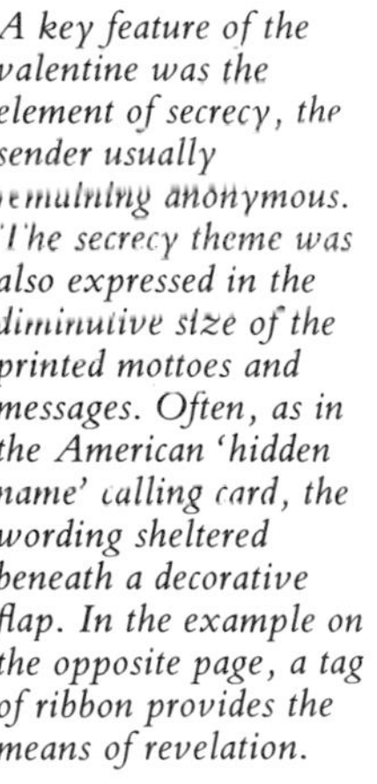

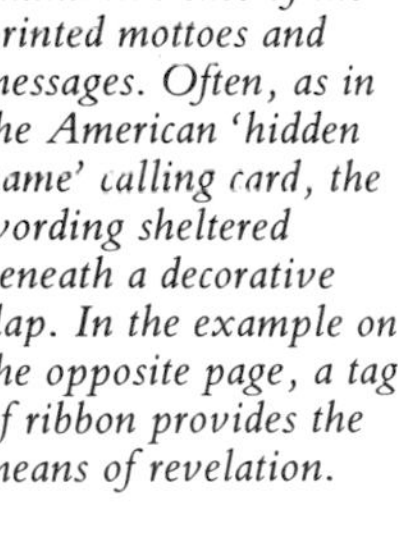

A key feature of the valentine was the element of secrecy, the sender usually remaining anonymous. The secrecy theme was also expressed in the diminutive size of the printed mottoes and messages. Often, as in the American 'hidden name' calling card, the wording sheltered beneath a decorative flap. In the example on the opposite page, a tag of ribbon provides the means of revelation.

88%

Shattering the image of the Victorians as over-sentimental, these graphic insults show another aspect of the valentine. Like the more orthodox kind, they were sent under cover of anonymity (from women to men, too, as these examples show), and they carried sometimes deeply wounding sentiments. Cheaply produced, they were available in a wide range of designs and doggerel, and were lively sellers.

FROM A LADY TO A RAKE.

Think not, gay Deceiver,
I'm a fond believer;
Your promises are air:
Oh, long did I discover
You're a general lover,
Attach'd to any fair.

Let whatever belle come,
You will make her welcome,—
Soft nonsense you've by heart:
Let her though be wary,
Or your strange vagary
May cause a lasting smart.

Both pages 89%

You'd like to be a Swell, I see,
But really it won't do;
The right is what you wish to be,
The left, my love, is you!

No. 30.

Rewards of merit

These cards were a notable feature of junior school life in America for the greater part of the nineteenth century. As a general rule they were signed and inscribed by the teacher to a named pupil. They recorded diligence and good behaviour, or more specifically 'neatness in writing' or 'correct deportment'.

The cards appeared in Britain too, but not under the title 'reward of merit' and not as a personal bestowal by the teacher. They were given almost exclusively for punctuality and regular attendance and, if signed at all, appeared as recognition by the school as an institution, rather than any individual teacher.

The American Reward of Merit became a national institution. Always attractively illustrated, at first in black only, and in the 1860s in colour, the cards were seen not as educational aids but simply as attractive gifts. In some cases the designs were based on the concept of currency notes or share certificates—sometimes both at once (opposite page, top right) and the recipient was encouraged to increase his or her holdings by further effort. 'God offers reward—my teacher also—they both encourage me', says the stockholder's motto.

The reward of merit became a useful sideline for the greeting card industry, and a certain cross-fertilization is apparent. As with the interchange of Christmas cards and valentine designs (previous pages) a simple modification turned a reward of merit design into a general greeting, and conversely. Such may have been the case with the reward fan, with its curiously ill-matched wording (or could this be an after-schooldays love note?)

There can be no doubt that many cards were teachers' tokens of personal affection. One handwritten example describes the pupil as 'a fine little boy'.

68%

The reward of merit began as a handwritten personal commendation from the teacher, but as the idea spread it was taken up by commercial engravers and jobbing printers. It was still, in the early part of the century, largely confined to a single printing—usually black. The top three examples on the facing page are from this period. After about 1850, colour became virtually mandatory. The angel head in the 'Fifty Merits' item uses the then novel chromolitho, a process borrowed from the greetings industry.

In a continuing search for novelty, publishers explored every variation of the 'gift from teacher' theme. The bookmark design, complete with its chromo centre-piece, is not only decorative but useful.

68%

Britain's reward cards are less inventive and more candidly instructive than the American cards. Only the anthropomorphic beach boy strikes a lighter—if irrelevant—note.

In some British schools (chiefly in Sunday schools) 'merit medals' were given. The one shown here bears the maxim 'Diligence conquers all' and on the reverse, 'For regularity, diligence and good conduct'.

As British suppliers were quick to point out, the importance of the 'attendance card' lay in the fact that educational grants were commonly geared to numbers. Effectively, the teacher's job—and the survival of the school itself—depended on keeping attendance high. The cards may be seen as an educational species of 'premium' or 'giveaway' aimed at retaining customer loyalty.

69%

Themes

Travel and transport

Travel and transport have generated ephemera in large quantities. At every period, organized transportation has required tickets, itineraries, timetables, waybills, bills of lading etc.—as well as the promotional trimmings that whet the traveller's appetite.

Most of the earlier material is in black and white, much of it devoid of illustration. The pictorial element, such as it is, shows standard images—stock blocks of wagons, coaches, ships and steam trains—more as ideograph than illustration. These well-worn woodcuts did for everything, waybill to broadside, ticket to billhead.

In the matter of illustration, the ephemera record shows three main surges of interest. The first marked the coming of the tourist trade at the turn of the nineteenth century, when Thomas Cook got going; the second was the cruising cult of the 1920s and 30s, when everyone took to deck quoits, and the last was the 1950s, when everyone took to the air.

Certainly it is the middle surge, the cruise age, that stands out most strikingly. Though limited to the upper middle class and their social superiors, the cruise appeal was expressed in a barrage of brochures, folders and other items, all in full colour, all bearing images of funnels and far-away places.

In its wake came the trappings of the adventure itself, the baggage tags and stickers, the ship-board menus, passenger lists and tour itineraries—also colourful, and for the most part illustrated. These, the spontaneous joys of the moment, are a favoured field for today's collector.

So are the productions of the air age (pages 166/7)—again a multi-coloured avalanche—with the addition of boarding cards, in-flight magazines and flight routes. And here, as technology speeds ahead, the public image changes from propeller to jet in scarcely more than a decade.

52%

Still not quite vanished from the attics and cupboards of today, the cruise items of the 1920s and 30s have yet to rank as sale-room antiques. But for the ephemerist of the 1980s and 90s they offer a graphic glimpse of a colourful era that seems only yesterday.

As the selection here conveys, the customer enjoyed not only the splendour of the ship and the thrill of ports of call, but the status symbol of baggage tag and sticker.

The ephemera of the luxury liner age is wide-ranging. Other items include ships' newspapers, concert programmes, radio messages, deck plans, library bookmarks and daily mileage charts.

Among early transport ephemera are items of promotion, such as the 'Twice a-week to Carlisle' handbill (1781) and the Boston 'Perseverance' notice (1813) opposite. Other items on this page are a carrier's bill for a load to Hastings (1836), a Stockton-to-Darlington coach-train timetable (1835), an engraved post horse tax ticket (c.1780) and an engraved tide table (c.1750) showing high and low water for Beaumaris Ferry 'where marks are Sett from Penmaenmaure to the Ferry side for ye Safety of Travellers'.

Twice a-week to CARLISLE.

BROUNS and HARKNESS, the CARLISLE-CARRIERS, depart from this City every Wednefday and Saturday, at four o'clock in the evening, and arrive at Carliſle on Monday and Thurſday the week following. The Moffat-Road, being nearly compleated, enables them to forward goods to London with more certainty, and is well known to be the ſhorteſt and cheapeſt conveyance. It has been the cuſtom to ſend goods directed to Briſtol, Exeter, Saliſbury, and places adjacent, by way of London.

All goods for the above places, and places adjacent, directed to the care of JOHN HARGREAVES in Kendal, will be forwarded by him in ſhorter time, and at much leſs expence than going by London, which muſt be a conſiderable ſaving upon goods to and from that quarter.

GLASGOW, Auguſt 30th, 1781.

JAMES and THOMAS BROUN.
WILLIAM HARKNESS.
JOHN HARGREAVES.

ROBT. SHEPHERD & Co.
Hastings and Battle Carriers.

HASTINGS,
ST. LEONARDS & BATTLE
Royal Blue Vans on Springs,
Lighted and Guarded, through
Robertsbridge, Lamberhurst, Tonbridge and Seven Oaks,—leave
Shepherd's Blue Office, 35, Camomile Street, City,
Every Day at 3 o'clock.

Mr. Luard, 17 Sep 1836

Carriage of Articles
Cartage ditto
Warehouse ditto
Charges paid out

William Byfield }
William Nash } Porters

A Tide Table for Bewmares F…
where mark's are Sett from Penmae…
to the Ferry side for ye Safety of Tra…

Highwater Morning Hours:min	Lowwater Morning Ho:min	The ☽'s Age	Highwater Evening Ho:min	Lowwater Evening Ho:min
10 - 30	4 - 18			
11 - 18	5 - 06			
12 - 06	5 - 54	1 - 16	10 - 30	4 - 1…
12 - 54	6 - 42	2 - 17	11 - 18	5 - 0…
1 - 42	7 - 30	3 - 18	12 - 06	5 - 54
2 - 30	8 - 18	4 - 19	12 - 54	6 - 42
3 - 18	9 - 06	5 - 20	1 - 42	7 - 30
4 - 06	9 - 54	6 - 21	2 - 30	8 - 18
4 - 54	10 - 42	7 - 22	3 - 18	9 - 06
5 - 42	11 - 30	8 - 23	4 - 06	9 - 54
6 - 30	12 - 18	9 - 24	4 - 54	10 - 42
7 - 18	1 - 06	10 - 25	5 - 42	11 - 30
8 - 06	1 - 54	11 - 26	6 - 30	12 - 18
8 - 54	2 - 42	12 - 27	7 - 18	1 - 06
9 - 42	3 - 30	13 - 28	8 - 06	1 - 54
		14 - 29	8 - 54	2 - 42
		15 - 30	9 - 42	3 - 30

STAMP OFFICE.
GR
No. 8.
EXCHANGE TICKET.
LANCASHIRE.
Received Day Ticket
From
HORSE I

STOCKTON AND DARLINGTON RAILWAY.

COACH TRAINS.

TABLE SHEWING THE TIMES OF RUNNING, CHARGE FOR FARES, &c.

DARLINGTON AND SHILDON TRAIN.

FARES: Inside, 1s., Outside, 9d., each way.

STATIONS.	TIME OF STARTING.	STATIONS.	TIME OF STARTING.
From the LANDS, at - - -	Quarter past 6 o'clock.	From DARLINGTON, at - -	Half past 8 o'clock.
St. HELEN'S AUCKLAND -	Quarter bef. 7 "	Do. - - - -	Half past 1 "
SHILDON - - -	Quarter past 7 "	Do. - - - -	5 "
SHILDON - - -	Half past 11 "		
SHILDON - - -	4 "		

Every MONDAY, the Train will leave Shildon at 11 o'clock (instead of half past), and Darlington at 2 o'clock (instead of half past 1).

DARLINGTON AND STOCKTON TRAIN.

FARES: Inside, 1s. 6d., Outside, 1s., each way.

STATIONS.	TIME OF STARTING.	STATIONS.	TIME OF STARTING.
From STOCKTON, at - - -	7 o'clock.	From DARLINGTON (during Summer) at	Quarter past 6 o'clock.
Do. - - - -	Half past 11 "	Do. - - - -	Half past 8 "
Do. - - - -	4 "	Do. - - - -	Half past 1 "
Do. (during Summer) - -	Half past 6 "	Do. - - - -	Half past 5 "

Every MONDAY, the Train will leave Stockton at 11 o'clock (instead of half past), and Darlington at 2 o'clock (instead of half past 1).

STOCKTON AND MIDDLESBROUGH TRAIN.

FARES: Inside, 6d., Outside, 4d., each way.

STATIONS.	TIME OF STARTING.	STATIONS.	TIME OF STARTING.
From MIDDLESBROUGH, at - -	Half past 6 o'clock.	From STOCKTON, at - - -	Half past 7 o'clock.
Do. - - - -	Half past 8 "	Do. - - - -	Half past 9 "
Do. - - - -	11 "	Do. - - - -	Half past 11 "
Do. - - - -	Half past 12 "	Do. - - - -	Half past 1 "
Do. - - - -	2 "	Do. - - - -	Half past 2 "
Do. - - - -	Half past 3 "	Do. - - - -	Half past 4 "
Do. - - - -	6 "	Do. - - - -	Half past 6 "
Do. - - - -	7 "	Do. - - - -	8 "

Every MONDAY, the Train will leave Middlesbrough at half past 10 o'clock (instead of 11).

All PARCELS are requested to be left with Mr. JOHN POTTER, at the Coach Office, King's Head Inn, Darlington, and at the MAJESTIC OFFICE, High Street, Stockton; and to insure punctual delivery, it is recommended that each Parcel be marked at the outside WITH THE HOUR OF THE TRAIN STARTING by which it is intended to be sent; and any complaints of want of attention in the Railway Company's Servants not delivering Parcels in due time after the arrival of each Train at its destination, are earnestly requested to be made at the Railway Office, Darlington.

Railway Carriage Waggons daily, at the times above specified, for the conveyance of GOODS and PARCELS, in immediate connection with the Stage Coaches and Carriers' Waggons to every part of the Kingdom.

April 14th, 1835.

COATES AND FARMER, PRINTERS, DARLINGTON.

PERSEVERANCE
BOSTON
New Post Coach.

To carry four Insides only.

THE Proprietors of the Boston new Coach return thanks for the liberal support already received, and beg to say their Coach in future will leave the KING'S HEAD, Old Change, every other Day at One o'Clock, through Cheshunt, Ware, Royston, Huntingdon, Peterborough, and Spalding, and arrive at Boston at One o'Clock the following Day; will likewise leave the RED LION INN, Boston, every other day, at six o'Clock in the morning, and arrive in London at six o'Clock the next morning.

FARE TO LONDON, INSIDE, £2. 5s. OUTSIDE, £1. 3s.

Parcels at and above 20lbs. three halfpence per pound.

Places and Parcels booked at the Red Lion Inn, Boston, at the King's Head, Old Change, at 99, Lower Thames Street, and at Waldegrave's Hotel Bishopsgate Street, London.

⁂ The Proprietors will not be answerable for any Parcel above the value of Five Pounds, unless entered and paid for accordingly.

Performed by the Public's humble Servant[s]

July 19, 1813. **MANNING AND**

NOBLE, Printer, Market-place, Boston.

ANTELOPE INN, DORCHESTER.

JAMES STENT

Respectfully announces to the Nobility, Gentry, Commercial Gentlemen, his Friends, and the Public in general, he has taken possession of the above established Inn, (which will speedily undergo considerable improvements) and he hopes, by an unremitting attention to their comforts, to merit a continuance of that patronage so liberally bestowed on his predecessor, Mr. Scott. He has laid in a stock of Wines and Spirits of the first quality. It will be his constant care to keep Post-horses and Carriages of the best description, with attentive and civil Drivers; and he assures those friends who may be pleased to honor him with their support, that no exertions nor expence shall be spared to render the accommodation at the Antelope Inn worthy the patronage of the Public.— COACHES daily to London, Bath, Bristol, Weymouth, Sidmouth, Exeter, &c.

N. B. MOURNING COACHES, HEARSE, &c.

Dorchester, Oct. 24, 1820.

CRISWICK

13, Bath
JERSEY
82
Received of
Carriage
Paid out
Insurance
Booking and Delivery

Parcel post agent for all parts of the world

Sutton & Co., Carriers. S. E. Angel, Agent.

...LINET,
...-vis le portail
... REIMS.

... prie le public ... ais bruits que ... font répandre ... ent pour leur ..., et annoncer ... Messieurs les ... ours chez lui tous les avantages désirables ; ils seront servis comme à l'ordinaire par des domestiques zélés, attentifs, et logés comme le permet la maison, qui est connue pour la plus belle de la ville et très-bien située à tous égards.

Nota. Il part tous les deux jours dudit hôtel une diligence pour Paris, dont le bureau, à Paris, est *rue du Jour, n°.* 4.

MOULINET HOTEL,
Post horses office, in face the gate of the Cathedrale, AT REIMS.

M. DESMARETZ prays travellers not to believe the falze teports that some of his partners scatter by post-boys (that the pay) in design of bringing foreigners to their house, in annoncing that he keeps no more his hotel. Strangers shall always find in his hotel all the advantages that a traveller could desire, they will be servee as by the past, by zealous et intent servants, et lodged as the house which is renowned for the finest et best situated of the town can permit it.

Nota. A flying coach departs wery two days for Paris where the office is, *rue du Jour*, N°. 4.

The Jersey carrier's bill (below left) dates from the 1860s; it promises a worldwide delivery service.

James Stent, keeper of the Antelope Inn at Dorchester (1820), advises that it will be his 'constant care to keep Post horses and Carriages of the best description, with attentive and civil Drivers', adding that he also has mourning coaches and a hearse.

In a bilingual card (c.1810) Monsieur Desmaretz 'prays travellers not to believe the falze reports ... that he keeps no more his hotel.'

66%

Early promotion items, tickets, folders and baggage labels convey the coming of the airways. The Air Union passenger booklet, dating from the mid-1920s, offers London-Paris return at £12.00 (30 lbs luggage free: excess three pence per lb), with free conveyance to and from aerodromes in private cars.

In the early years of flying the aviation meeting was a popular attraction. The postcard souvenir of the 1924 Lausanne event, sent by internal air mail to mark the occasion, is typical of many such mementoes, much sought after by today's collectors.

Tickets for five-minute joy-rides were also kept as souvenirs. Of the three shown here, those for Air-Trips Ltd and Edward A. Jones make a point of disclaiming responsibility for the customer's safety. Mr Jones does so in the small print on the back of the ticket, but he comes straight to the point in defence of the fabric of his aircraft's wing.

56%

AMERICAN AIRLINES
INTERNATIONAL
System Map
AMERICAN AIRLINES, INC.
AMERICAN OVERSEAS AIRLINES, INC.
AMERICAN AIRLINES DE MEXICO, S. A.

Internationalization of the air brought a new recognition of the existence of foreigners—and new claims for their custom. Route maps and passenger phrase books, as well as promotional baggage labels, competed for attention. The give away novelty flourished. An early example is the Air France bookmark, a souvenir from the flying-boat era of the late 1930s.

The air-line baggage label expresses the successive phases of commercial flight, with propeller giving way to jet and one airline replacing or incorporating another. The labels were produced in huge quantities. America's airline label collector's society (Aeronautica & Air Label Collectors Club) catalogues many thousands of issues.

STEAM FROM LIVERPOOL TO AUSTRALIA,

FORMING PART OF

THE LIVERPOOL "EAGLE LINE" OF PACKETS.

A Steamboat will leave the Old Seacombe Slip Prince's Dock, on Saturday Morning, 21st August, at 10 a.m., and 12 noon, taking off Passengers and their hat-boxes and carpet-bags only.

None but Passengers having tickets, will be allowed on board the "GREAT BRITAIN" on 21st Aug.

THE GREAT BRITAIN

IRON SCREW STEAMER, 3,500 TONS, & 500 HORSE POWER,

B. R. MATHEWS, COMMANDER,

WILL BE

DESPATCHED FROM THE RIVER MERSEY FOR

MELBOURNE, PORT PHILIP; AND SYDNEY, NEW SOUTH WALES,

CALLING AT THE CAPE OF GOOD HOPE FOR COALS, WATER, AND FRESH PROVSIONS.

On SATURDAY, August the 21st, at One o'Clock, p.m.

THE VESSEL WILL LEAVE THE DOCK THE PREVIOUS DAY.

This magnificent Ship, fitted up with every possible convenience, has just performed her Trial Voyage to New York in the most satisfactory manner, and with remarkable rapidity. Fully equipped for sailing, she combines all the advantages of a Clipper-ship with those of a powerful Steamer, adapting her in a peculiar manner for a long voyage, and securing its being made in the shortest possible time.

FARES:

To MELBOURNE:

After-Saloon,...70—72—73—80 Guineas, { *Including Provisions, Live Stock, Luxuries and Delicacies.*

Fore-Saloon,....40—41—42—50 „ { *Including all articles of food of the best quality necessary to provide a plain substantial table, and attendance.*

Second Cabin,...........30—35 „ { *Including food of the best quality, as per Scale, and attendance.*

To SYDNEY, 5 Guineas extra will be charged.

To the CAPE OF GOOD HOPE,—After Saloon 50 Guineas.

CHILDREN, FROM 1 TO 14, HALF-PRICE.

Including Stewards' Fees, the attendance of an experienced Surgeon, and all Provisions of the best quality, except Wines, Spirits, and Malt Liquors, which will be supplied at very moderate prices on board.

In the After and Fore-Saloon State Rooms every requisite will be provided, including Beds, Berths, Plate, Bedding, Linen.

In the Second Cabin the Passengers will have to supply themselves with Bed, Bedding, and Linen, which may be purchased at Silver & Co.'s St. George's Crescent, Liverpool. The berths are 6 feet by 20 inches.

The AFTER-SALOON is fitted with Ladies' Boudoirs, Music, and Smoking Rooms, Baths, &c.

DECK.—The Poop aft is appropriated to the After Saloon Passengers alone. The Spar deck amidships to the After and Fore-Saloon Passengers, and forward to the Second Cabin Passengers.

No Passenger can be accommodated in a State Room by himself, so long as he can be placed with other Passengers, unless the State-Room is specially arranged for; and Berths may be changed before sailing, if necessary, unless a whole State-Room is secured.

Forerunner of the 1930s cruise brochure, this prospectus for the Great Britain*'s trip to Australia offered 'All the advantages of a Clipper-ship with those of a powerful Steamer'. A cabin in the after saloon cost 70–80 guineas (including provisions, livestock, luxuries and delicacies); in the second cabin however, the trip cost 30–35 guineas, but the travellers had to supply themselves with their own bed, bedding and linen. On the morning of departure ticket-holding passengers would be taken out to the ship on a steamboat, together with 'their hat boxes and carpet bags only'.*

65%

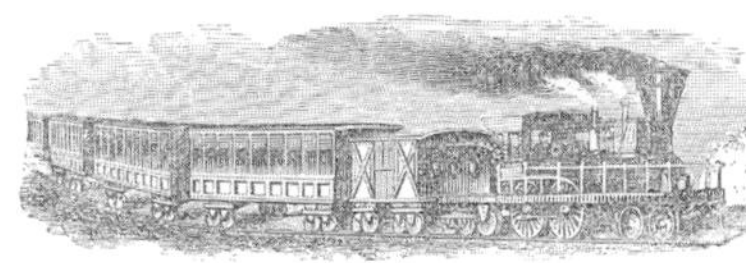

PORTLAND AND ROCHESTER

RAILROAD CORPORATION.

Gorham, Mch 1 187*7*

H. L. Davis, Stationer, Portland.

Marks and Numbers. *Received from Stephen Hinkley & Co.* WEIGHT.

Messrs Hopkins
Gardiner
Me

10 Bags Hair 2000

For the Corporation.

Steam-Packet Indiana.

STEERAGE PASSAGE.

From Buf *to* Sandy

Amt. pd., $ 3/00 Trip No. 23

No Pass. 1 I. T. PHEATT.

Steerage Passengers are not allowed to enter the Gentlemen's Cabin, except at Meals. Meals can be had at the second ringing of the Bell, for 25 cents.

This Ticket to be returned when called for.

No. 1.

Published with the Sanction of the Company.

REID'S MONTHLY TIME TABLE

AND ADVERTISER,

OF THE

York, Newcastle, & Berwick Railway,

APRIL, 1849.

PUBLISHED EXPRESSLY FOR THE COUNTIES OF NORTHUMBERLAND, DURHAM, CUMBERLAND, AND THE NORTH PART OF YORKSHIRE.

**Price One Penny, or Post-free Twopence.
Delivered in Town at 1s. per Annum.
Forwarded (Post-free) at 2s. per Annum.**

PAYABLE IN ADVANCE.

Newcastle upon Tyne:
PRINTED AND PUBLISHED BY ANDREW REID, 117, PILGRIM STREET;
And sold by all Booksellers, News Agents, and at the Stations.

THE TRAVELLER's GUIDE,

FROM

LONDON TO THE NORTH.

Roads.	Inns.	Innkeepers' Names.	Miles.
To Barnet - -	*Red Lion* - -	NEWTON -	12
Hatfield - -	*Salisbury Arms*	BRYANT -	9
Stevenage - -	*Swan* - -	CASS - -	12
Bigglesfwade -	*Sun* - - -	KNIGHT -	14
Bugden - -	*George* - -	SCARBRO -	16
Stilton - - -	*Bell* - - -	GIBBS -	14
Stamford - -	*George* - -	FAWCIT -	14
Witham Common	*Bull* - -	STURTLE -	11
Grantham - -	*Angel* - - -	DUNHILL -	10
Newark - -	*Kingston Arms*	LAWTON -	14
Scarthing Moor	*Black Lion* -	OSTLIFF -	12
Barnby Moor -	*Bell* . - -	CLARK -	12
Doncafter - -	*Angel* - -	DAY - -	14
Ferrybridge - -	*Swan* - - -	HALL -	15
Weatherby - -	*Angel* . . .	CLEMINGSHAW	17
Boroughbridge -	*Crown* - -	FRETWELL	12
Northallerton -	*Golden Lion* -	HURST -	19
Darlington - -	*Poft-houfe* -	THOMPSON	16
Durham - -	*Wheat Sheaf* -	SHOTTON -	18
Newcaftle - -	*Queen's Head*	TURNER -	15

The Great Britain *woodcut (opposite) was a fair representation of the actual ship, but the rail images on this page were only nominal. A useful feature of railage printing was the multi-unit block, allowing trains of any convenient length to be made up by the printer. The images became more or less standardized; the larger version, from a printer's proof, is American; the English version (Reid's monthly Time Table) is virtually the same train.*

Steerage ticket for the steam packet Indiana *advises that the bearer is not allowed to enter the Gentlemen's Cabin except at meals.*

The London to Newcastle Traveller's Guide (c.1815) gives not only towns and distances, but inns and innkeepers' names.

65%

Therapy

Apart from food and sex, few subjects command such devoted attention as the quest for relief from illness. At two levels—orthodox and quack—the matter is ceaselessly explored, and the ephemera record is full of it.

To the casual eye it might seem that level two comes first. Fringe medicine, with its cures and potions, its elixirs and head-and-stomach pills, makes an unmistakable mark. In folders, tradecards, magazine insets, labels and a host of other media, the nineteenth century offered health unbounded.

Most of the material seeks to impress. The image of authority shines through: the 'doctor-manager' image, as in the Bovril item; Established Tradition (Steedman's Powders); the Wisdom of the Ancients (Elixir China), or Mother Nature herself, bubbling forth in the springs of the Cure Establishment in Bohemia.

Pills were a major industry (as was the production of labels to go on the boxes). Many were for ailments as unspecific as the pills' ingredients: Bilious and Liver Pills, Indigestion and Wind Pills; 'Pills of Health' ('for purifying the blood, diseases of the liver, kidneys, stomach, chest, head, drowsiness, wind, indigestion, bile, habitual costiveness, piles etc.'); and Blood Capsules ('Cure falling out and prematurely grey hair')—all manifestly of use to almost everybody.

Foot Paste was clearly more specialized. So were Female Corrective Pills ('to remove obstructions to which females are subject') and Opium (just 'Poison'). The Italian Elixir confined itself to being 'prepared by a special method'.

So great was the demand, many printers set themselves up as 'pharmaceutical printers', often producing work for a score or so of clients on the same sheet, cutting them up in their thousands for separate delivery.

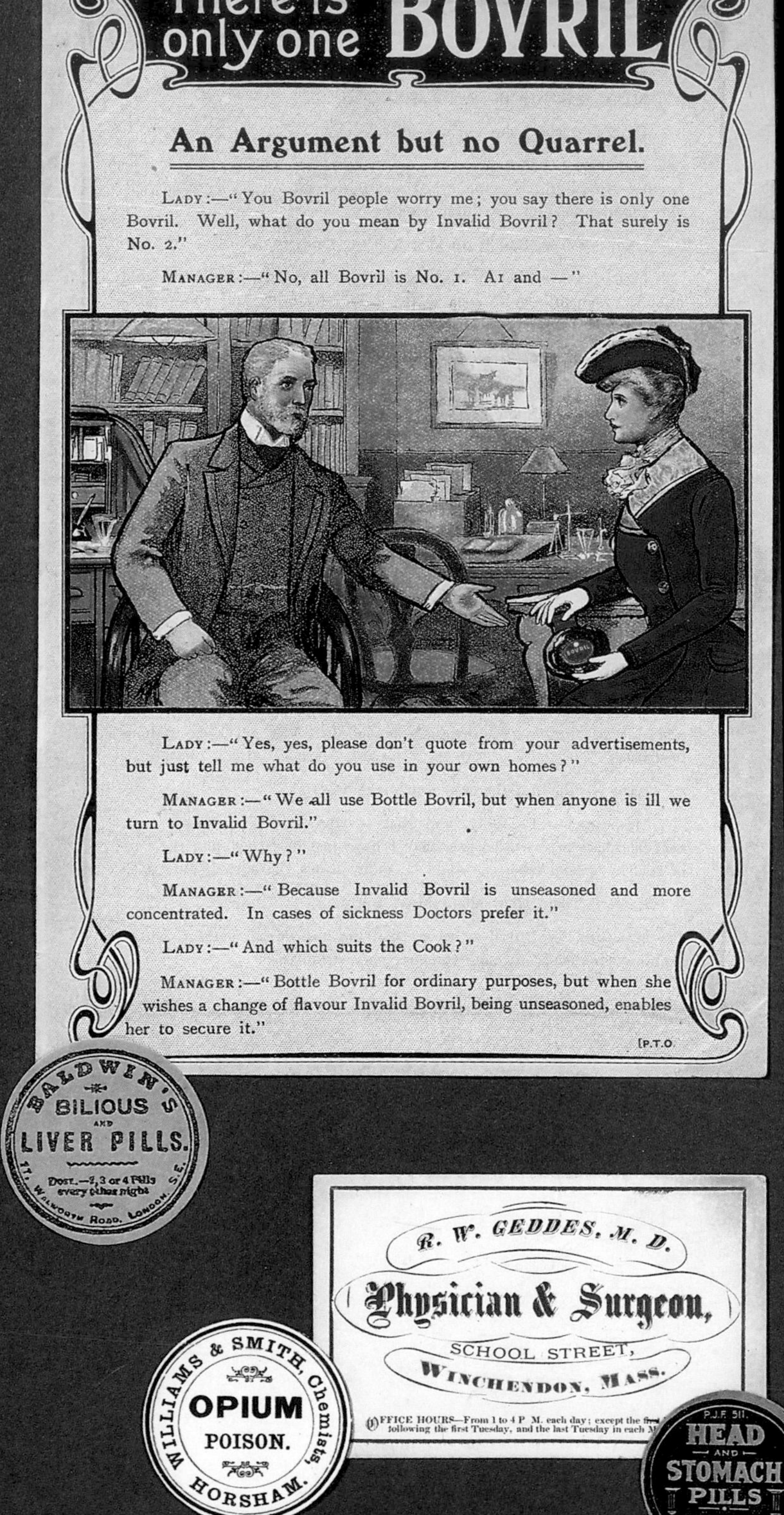

Both pages 68%

Natural
SPRING OF BILIN
Renowned medicinal spring
Bilin digestive tablets

Joseph-Spring
The Direction of the Springs
·BILIN·BOHEMIA·
Sole Agents for the U.S. of A.
EISNER & MENDELSON Co.
NEW-YORK N.Y. Barclay Street 6
Walkingway of the Cure-Establishment

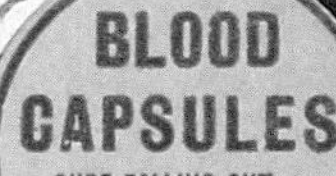

BLOOD CAPSULES.
CURE FALLING OUT AND PREMATURELY GREY HAIR.
Take two three times a day before meals.
BALDWIN'S HERBAL PILLS OF HEALTH

FOOT PASTE
Apply on lint and keep in position by adhesive plaster.
J. B. WILSON, Chemist, 95 North Street GOSPORT
For Sluggish Liver & Constipation.
Also for Stomach Troubles, Indigestion, Wind, Dizziness, Sallow Complexion.
BILE PILLS
FOR BILIOUSNESS.
F.T. WILBY, Chemist
FEMALE CORRECTIVE PILLS
1s. 1½d. and 2s. 9d.
T. G. BATTING & Co., Dispensing Chemists,
INDIGESTION AND WIND PILLS
DOSE—One Pill after meals
FINE HEALTHY LEECHES.
FROM
J. BATEMAN, Chemist and Druggist, STROUD.
ELIXIR CHINA
CALISAIA
Preparato con metodo speciale
DALLA
FARMACIA CHIMICA ROASENDA
CAVOUR

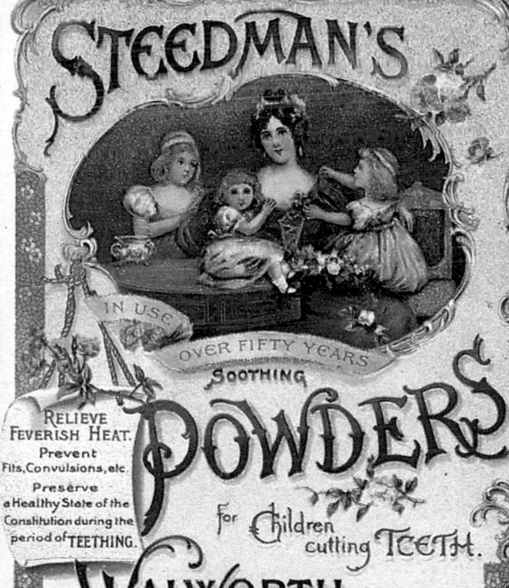

STEEDMAN'S
IN USE OVER FIFTY YEARS
SOOTHING POWDERS
RELIEVE FEVERISH HEAT.
Prevent Fits, Convulsions, etc.
Preserve a Healthy State of the Constitution during the period of TEETHING.
for Children cutting TEETH.
WALWORTH, Surrey.
MOTHER SEIGEL'S OPERATING PILLS

Whatever its shortcomings, orthodox therapy was specific in its documentation. Among its standard instruments was the so-called 'hospital letter', a part-printed form to be filled in by subscribers to the hospital as a charity. Use of the form avoided handing cash to the potential patient, who might not be trusted to spend it on the object desired. (Filled-in forms were in any case often used by recipients as an aid to begging. Specimens are to be found bearing the over-print: 'Not to be used for begging'.) This example is signed by the Duke of Wellington, whose home at No 1, Piccadilly was across the street from St George's Hospital.

The LETTER to recommend IN and OUT-PATIENTS.

GENTLEMEN,

I recommend the bearer Charles Brook residing at Lewisham Kent for an In Patient if the Board shall consider him a proper object of the Charity.

26th day of June 1844

Your humble Servant, Wellington

To the GOVERNORS of St. GEORGE'S HOSPITAL, *near Hyde Park Corner.*

CONTRIBUTORS are desired to observe the following ARTICLES: *viz.*

I. RECOMMENDATIONS are to be delivered every *Wednesday* morning by half-past Eleven of the clock, and *none* will be received *after* that time.

II. When there is not room in the House for all the Patients recommended at one time to be received, *those* only are admitted, who, the Board is of opinion, will most effectually answer the ends of the Charity; and the rest, if proper objects, are admitted Out-Patients till there is a vacancy in the House.

III. No person labouring under any infectious distemper, deemed incurable, or whose case is consumptive or asthmatic, or having old ulcerated legs, more proper for a workhouse, is to be received into the House.

IV. On account of the number of Contributors each Governor can have but *one* In-patient at a time, Subscribers of *three* guineas are allowed to recommend *three* In-patients every year; and no Governor can have more than *two* Out-patients on the books at one time.

V. Each Patient, if able, to bring two shirts or shifts.

VI. No security is required, should a Patient die, for the charges of burial.

☞ *The Contributors are requested to send their money to this Hospital upon any* Wednesday, *from Ten till Three.*

*** The large number of surgery Patients requiring a great quantity of Lint and Cloth for rollers, &c. if Ladies please to send in some old linen, it will be a valuable present to the Charity.

Printed by the Philanthropic Society, St. George's Fields,

As Mr George Wilson's appeal indicates, many hospital posts were filled by ballot.

To solicit the favor of your VOTE and INTEREST

FOR

MR. GEORGE WILSON,

FOR

ASSISTANT SURGEON

TO THE

LONDON HOSPITAL.

100%

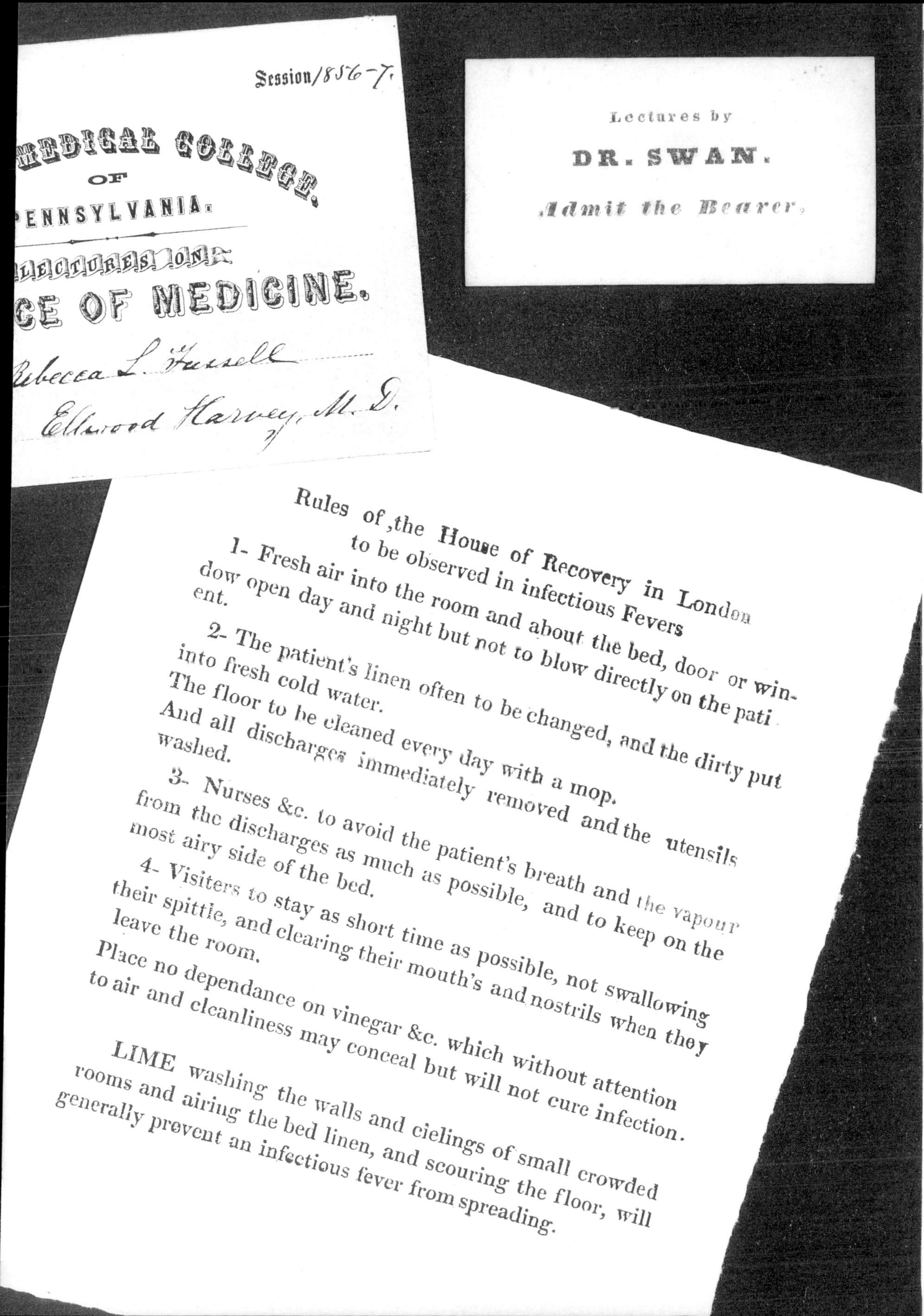

Session/1856-7.

MEDICAL COLLEGE
OF
PENNSYLVANIA.
LECTURES ON
...CE OF MEDICINE.
...ebecca L. Fussell
Ellwood Harvey, M.D.

Lectures by
DR. SWAN.
Admit the Bearer.

Lecture admission cards were a common feature of teaching hospitals in the nineteenth century. The Dr Swan item is unusual in having no provision for an authorising signature.

Rules of the House of Recovery in London
to be observed in infectious Fevers

1- Fresh air into the room and about the bed, door or window open day and night but not to blow directly on the patient.

2- The patient's linen often to be changed, and the dirty put into fresh cold water.
The floor to be cleaned every day with a mop.
And all discharges immediately removed and the utensils washed.

3- Nurses &c. to avoid the patient's breath and the vapour from the discharges as much as possible, and to keep on the most airy side of the bed.

4- Visiters to stay as short time as possible, not swallowing their spittle, and clearing their mouth's and nostrils when they leave the room.

Place no dependance on vinegar &c. which without attention to air and cleanliness may conceal but will not cure infection.

LIME washing the walls and cielings of small crowded rooms and airing the bed linen, and scouring the floor, will generally prevent an infectious fever from spreading.

Rules of the House of Recovery (1810) convey the evolving pattern of medical knowledge. (Today's medical opinion commends the general tenor of these rules. In the context of their time they are, it seems, eminently sensible.) The warning as to vinegar reflects its continued popular use as a disinfectant, still prevalent since plague times.

100%

Mrs Taylor.

SMALL & WILSON,
UNDERTAKERS,
GOFFSTOWN, N. H.

CALL AND EXAMINE OUR STOCK AND PRICES.

Having Refurnished our Rooms, We are prepared to furnish the public at short notice in all styles and sizes, from a cloth covered Casket, down to a pine Coffin. Also Robes of all kinds and sizes.

ALL ORDERS FILLED WITH PROMPTNESS

A MEETING
will be held
on Monday March, 1st. 1852. at Black
Horse Petticoat Lane.
to pay the Funeral expences of Michal Collins
Chairman T. Leonard
Deputy M. Donovan
Music provided

73%

Funeralia

The very high survival rate of Victorian funeralia is due to two factors. In the first place there was a lot of it: though much may have disappeared, much remains. Secondly, unlike most ephemera, memorial material is specifically designed to be kept.

In Britain, by far the most popular item was the embossed memorial card, 80 × 120 mm ($3\frac{1}{8} \times 4\frac{3}{4}$ in), black-edged and printed black on white or beige. The design blind embossed, and sometimes pierced as well, commonly featured a central panel for overprinting and angels or other attendant figures in attitudes of mourning.

The cards, bearing the embossed imprint of Wood, Mansell or Windsor (less commonly Sanders and Marcus Ward) were produced in some scores of variant designs, and may be found used, with overprinted or inscribed names and dates; or blank, as supplied by the manufacturer. The formula also appeared as a larger frame, embossed and pierced, with a central panel to take the printed memorial card.

In America the memorial card was generally vertical in format, about the size of a postcard and with rounded corners. Printed in silver or bronze on black ('White for a child or a young lady'), the manufacturers offered a choice of two dozen verses to go with the name.

Other items of funeral ephemera include promotional material from undertakers and mourning suppliers, black-edged stationery, funeral announcements and, in Britain, invitations to 'musical meetings'. These last were held as entertainments—generally in public houses—to raise money for defrayal of funeral expenses.

The ephemera of mourning is extensive. Mourning cards were produced not only for relations but for horses and domestic animals. They also appeared on public sale in memory of victims of fire disasters, shipwrecks etc., often with home-made poetry to match.

In Loving Memory
of
OUR JIM,
SEMPER
FIDELIS.
WHO DEPARTED THIS LIFE,
October 14th, 1898.
"Gone but not forgotten."

The OUR JIM item is a rarity, not only in its unusual subject matter but in the use of two colours in addition to black. (Colour in mourning items was extremely rare—even, as in the Jay's item opposite, for the eye-catching trade advertisement.) The item is also unusual in combining the products of two periods. Our Jim died at the turn of the century, whereas the elaborate outer frame dates from the 1850s or 60s. Someone, it seems, had saved the earlier item for sorrows to come.

73%

Two people, two continents, and a span of nearly 30 years are encompassed in the Linton memorial card. Though embossed and pierced, the card is backed with black paper, thus negating the 'see-through' effect of conventional piercing.

Also shown here are an itemized funeral specification from a London undertaker, c.1860; a monumental mason's sketch for a headstone, 1799; and an American memorial card order form, c.1890. The customer's order sheet is from an illustrated folder, which also prints a selection of 'poetry', to be ordered by number.

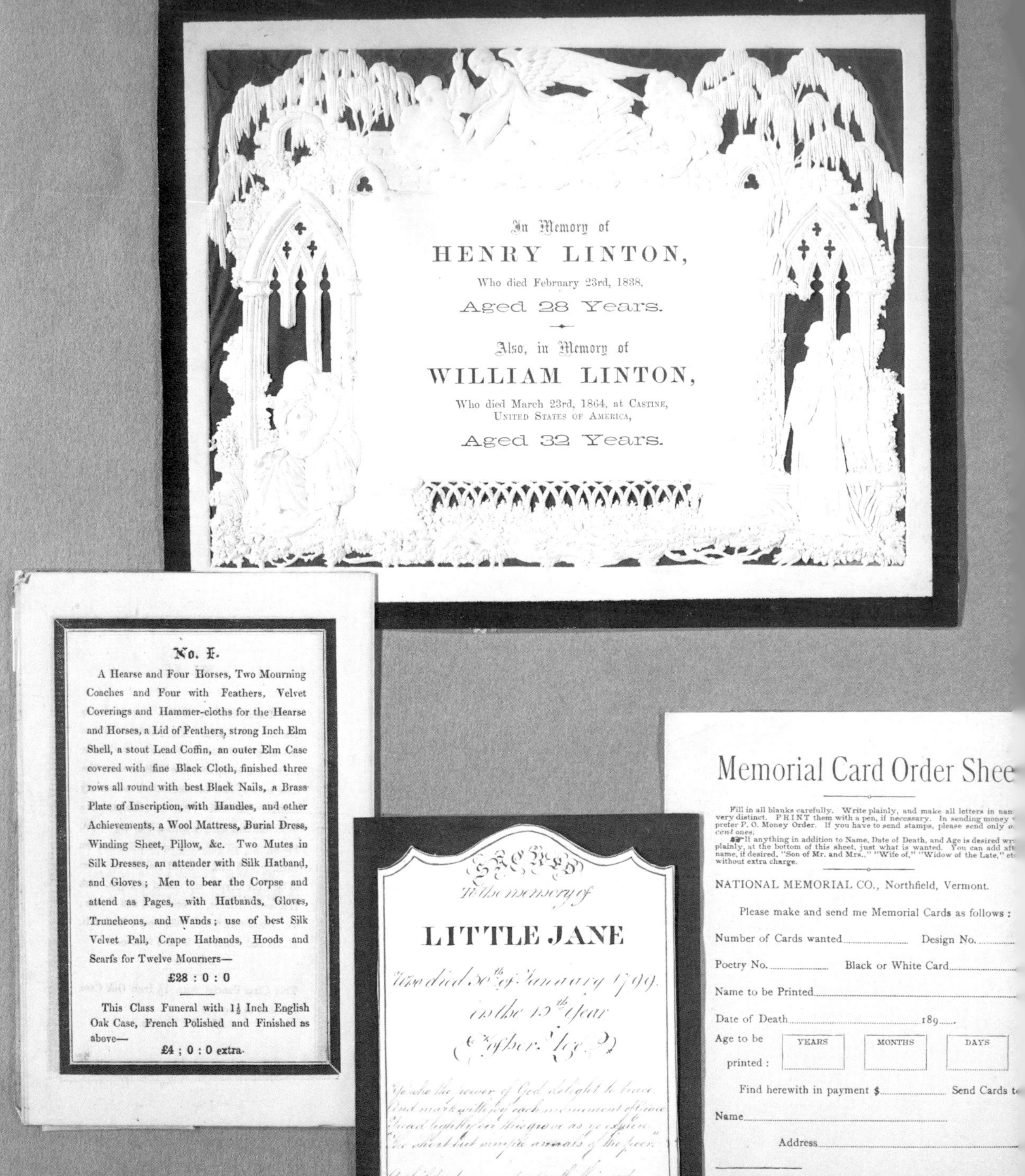

In Memory of
HENRY LINTON,
Who died February 23rd, 1838,
Aged 28 Years.
Also, in Memory of
WILLIAM LINTON,
Who died March 23rd, 1864, at Castine, United States of America,
Aged 32 Years.
No. I.
A Hearse and Four Horses, Two Mourning Coaches and Four with Feathers, Velvet Coverings and Hammer-cloths for the Hearse and Horses, a Lid of Feathers, strong Inch Elm Shell, a stout Lead Coffin, an outer Elm Case covered with fine Black Cloth, finished three rows all round with best Black Nails, a Brass Plate of Inscription, with Handles, and other Achievements, a Wool Mattress, Burial Dress, Winding Sheet, Pillow, &c. Two Mutes in Silk Dresses, an attender with Silk Hatband, and Gloves; Men to bear the Corpse and attend as Pages, with Hatbands, Gloves, Truncheons, and Wands; use of best Silk Velvet Pall, Crape Hatbands, Hoods and Scarfs for Twelve Mourners—
£28 : 0 : 0
This Class Funeral with 1½ Inch English Oak Case, French Polished and Finished as above—
£4 ; 0 : 0 extra.
To the memory of
LITTLE JANE
Who died 30th of January 1799.
THE YOUNG COTTAGER
Memorial Card Order Shee
Fill in all blanks carefully. Write plainly, and make all letters in nam very distinct. PRINT them with a pen, if necessary. In sending money prefer P. O. Money Order. If you have to send stamps, please send only o cent ones.
If anything in addition to Name, Date of Death, and Age is desired wr plainly, at the bottom of this sheet, just what is wanted. You can add aft name, if desired, "Son of Mr. and Mrs.," "Wife of," "Widow of the Late," et without extra charge.
NATIONAL MEMORIAL CO., Northfield, Vermont.
Please make and send me Memorial Cards as follows :
Number of Cards wanted
Design No.
Poetry No.
Black or White Card
Name to be Printed
Date of Death 189
Age to be printed :
YEARS
MONTHS
DAYS
Find herewith in payment $
Send Cards t
Name
Address
PRICES of Cards are as follows : 1 Card, 15c. ; 4 Cards, 50c. ; 8 Cards, 75c. 12 Cards, $1.00 ; 25 Cards, $1.75 ; 50 Cards, $3.00 ; 100 Cards, $5.00.—Larg Envelopes, for mailing cards, 2c. each ; 25 or over, 1c. each.

55%

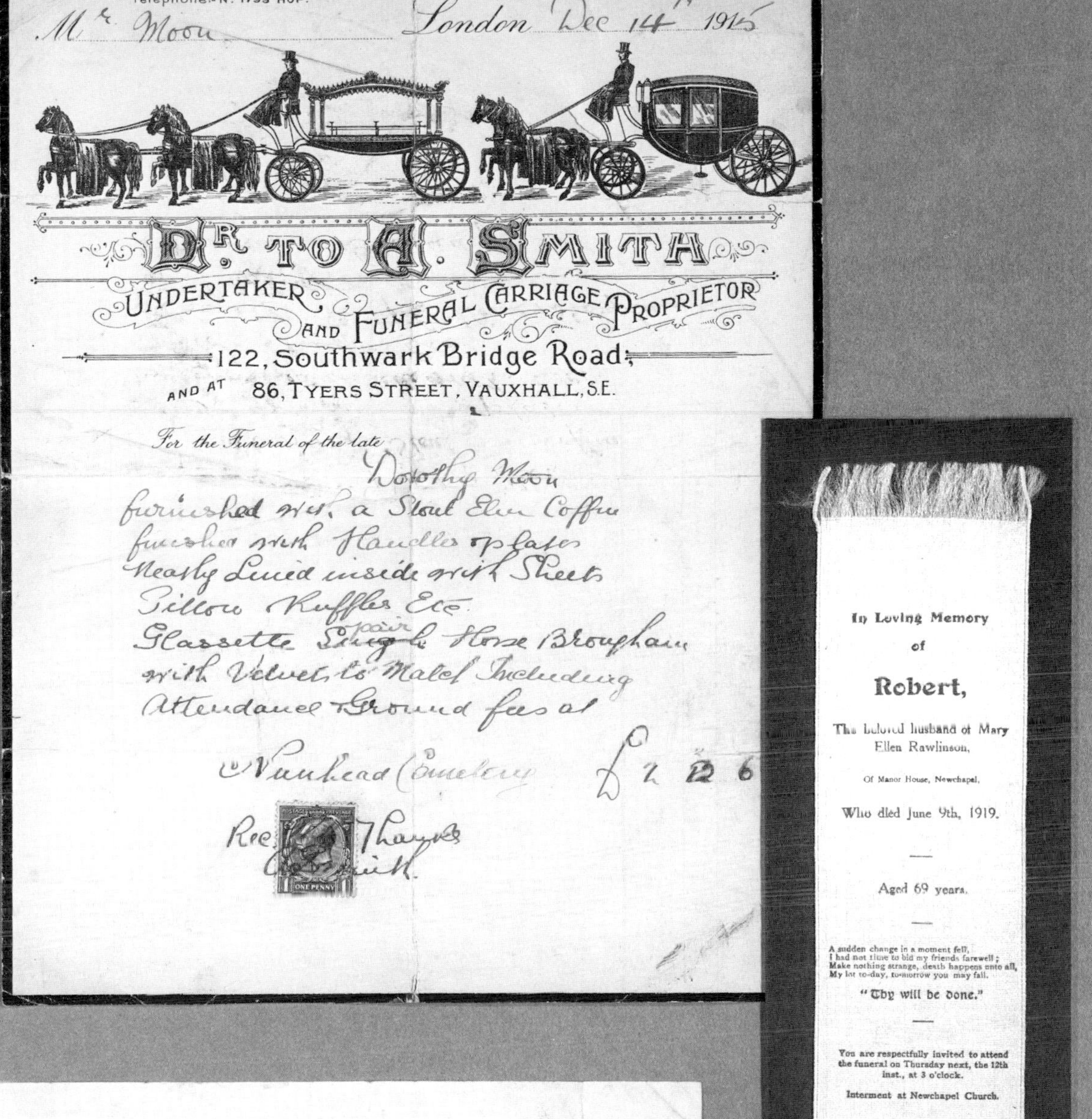

Telephone:- No 1799 HOP.

Mr Moon London Dec 14th 1915

Dr. TO A. SMITH

UNDERTAKER AND FUNERAL CARRIAGE PROPRIETOR

122, Southwark Bridge Road;

AND AT 86, TYERS STREET, VAUXHALL, S.E.

For the Funeral of the late

Dorothy Moon

furnished w.t. a Stout Elm Coffin furnished with Handles & plates Neatly Lined inside with Sheets Pillow Ruffles Etc. Glassette pair Horse Brougham with Velvet to Match Including Attendance & Ground fees at

Nunhead Cemetery £2 12 6

Rec Thanks A. Smith

ONE PENNY

In Loving Memory

of

Robert,

The beloved husband of Mary Ellen Rawlinson,

Of Manor House, Newchapel,

Who died June 9th, 1919.

Aged 69 years.

A sudden change in a moment fell,
I had not time to bid my friends farewell;
Make nothing strange, death happens unto all,
My lot to-day, to-morrow you may fall.

"Thy will be done."

You are respectfully invited to attend the funeral on Thursday next, the 12th inst., at 3 o'clock.

Interment at Newchapel Church.

FUNERAL NOTICE.

The funeral of the lamented **C. E. HUNTER, Esq.,** will be preached in the M. E. church in this place to-morrow at 1 o'clock P. M., by Rev. F. S. Cassady. The corpse will be deposited in the church until the service is over, and then be removed to the English burying-ground above town. His friends and the public are invited to attend.

As the 1915 billhead of A. Smith indicates, the showy funeral survived in Britain into the first half of the nineteenth century—though the 'mutes in silk dresses and attendants with silk hatbands and gloves' of the 1860s had begun to disappear.

The memorial silk 'In loving memory of Robert' did duty as funeral invitation and bookmark, an unusual form of memento from Newchapel, Wales, in 1919

The funeral notice for 'The lamented C. E. Hunter Esq.' appears to refer to a Methodist Episcopalian service in some foreign part, c.1850.

55%

Crime and punishment

What it may lack in visual appeal the ephemera of crime and punishment makes up in dramatic content. For the collector of this material the attraction lies not in its looks, but in the human interest of the facts and figures it conveys.

Much of it is concerned with the documentation of prison organization and methods—locking people up and letting them out again; feeding and clothing them; setting them to work. Another major section is enquiry and reward. Another is welfare—provision of such amenities as tobacco, recreation, libraries etc.—and after-care on release. Not least, though everywhere diminished in latter years, is the section on capital punishment.

Much of the material is part-printed, allowing individual details to be entered by hand. The record sheets on this page are typical. The full range includes committal and discharge papers; death warrants, reprieves and transportation orders; summonses and arrest warrants; visiting orders and intimations to relatives; receipts from suppliers, contractors, locksmith, hangmen and others. All of these are found as forms to be filled in.

Completed forms are on the whole more rewarding—as, for example the potato-stealer's record card from 1847 (top) showing a penalty of 14 days prison for a 12-year old, and the comment 'an idle boy'. But even unused forms ('Account of Lockings, male and female') may give fresh impact to facts already well understood.

In the field of reward notices text matter is distinctly more explicit, often graphically informative, sometimes surprising. The Fayville Store Robbery (opposite) with its haul of silks and shoes, strikes an unexpected note: did the American robber really go for silks and shoes in the 1860s?

No.	NAME.	PARISH.	AGE.
23	Joseph Lee	[illegible] Stratford	12

When Committed - - September 9th 1847
By whom Committed - Wm Ballantine
Offence & where Committed Stealing Potatoes
Sentence - - - - 14 days
Expiration of Sentence - Sep 22nd 1847
If before in Prison - - Yes
Remarks - - - - an Idle Boy

DERBY COUNTY GAOL.

Daily Account of Time and Materials used on the day of 18

Name of Person employed, and Trade.	Description of Workmen, and Time Employed.	Description of Work, and Materials Su

Derby Gaol

ACCOUNT OF LOCKINGS.
MALE AND FEMALE.

Unlocked in the Morning A Yard........
2 Do. ....
3 Do. ....
4 Do. ....
B 1 Do. ....
2 Do. ....
Out.......................... 3 Do. ....
4 Do. ....
C 1 Do. ....
2 Do. ....
3 Do. ....
In .... E 1 Do. ....
2 Do. ....
F 1 Do. ....
2 Do. ....
3 Do. ....
Infirmary ....
Reception Cells...
Solitary ....
Female ....
Total locked up ....
184

DERBY COUNTY GAOL.
DEPOSITED IN THE OFFICE,
To be delivered to
On Discharge from Prison:—
Pounds.
Shillings.
Pence.
This Ticket is of no use but to the Person whose Name is inserted thereon, and to him only while within the Gaol.
18

H.M. PRISONS ONLY
RIZLA • BRITISH MADE
H.M. PRISONS ONLY

59%

Local printers were often quick off the ark when it came to vard notices. It was uncommon for bills like this one to be sted on the morning the day following a obbery—sometimes en on the same day. he word 'Reward', and the printer's rint were often kept standing, ready for ant use. In this case eed of response had to a crucial error—'Detention' for 'Detection'.

200 DOLLARS REWARD!

The "FAYVILLE STORE," at SOUTHBORO', was entered on the night of 23d inst., and robbed of $20 to $30 in Change and Plain Black Silks and Shoes to the value of $200 to $300.

The above Reward will be paid by the Proprietor of the store for the recovery of the property and the detention of the Thief or Thieves, or one-half for either, upon application to

SYLVESTER C. FAY,
FAYVILLE,
AGENT FOR THE PROPRIETOR.

SEPT. 24, 1859.

Farmer, Printers, 18 Exchange St., Boston.

he Hired and Stolen m (1890) is a postal otice of reward, sent by sheriffs to police authorities at large. his too was quick off e mark. The theft is corded as happening on July 1; the card, and its postal frank, are dated July 3.

HIRED AND STOLEN

From the stable of FRANK STONE, OTTER RIVER, Templeton, Mass., July 1st, 1890, one red roan MARE, close built, carries low head; weight about 900 lbs.; starts out a little lame behind, but soon drives sound. One side-bar, Corning body, TOP CARRIAGE, painted black, gear striped green; one wheel lately repaired. One black trimmed breast collar HARNESS.

The man's name supposed to be LANE; medium height, hair cut close, dark mustache. When last seen had on dark suit of clothes, and was selling metal polish.

Arrest man, or any clue telegraph

W. H. RICHARDSON, *Deputy Sheriff*,
ASHBURNHAM, MASS.

JULY 3, 1890.

GRANBY, NEW-GATE PRISON, Feby 7th 1827

I certify that Parley Crosby has this day delivered Six bushels rye paid 85 cts per bushel $5-10

for which he has credit, and is charged with this certificate.

A Denison Prison Keeper.

To Martin Sheldon Agent.

Among the most notable of crime-and-punishment part-printed items is the gaol warrant entrusting the person named to the care of the keeper of the gaol—in this case London's famous Newgate.

Wholly handwritten, with its full complement of errors and oddities, is a discharge warrant from Greenwich, in the state of Connecticut, 1829: 'Mr Nathan Wilson [Junr?] if Mr Samuel Ney payes the cost in full and gives his Note for twenty Dollars payable in two years with intrust I will discharge him from gale on my part [.] Want you to take care of the [above?] Greenwich 6 May 1829 David Jeffry'.

28

To the Keeper *of* His Majesty's Gaol of Newgate, *or his Deputy.*

MIDDLESEX, (TO WIT.) } RECEIVE into your Custody the Body of George Swann herewith sent you, brought before me Sir William Parsons Knight one of His Majesty's Justices of the Peace in and for the said County, by William Mattingly Headborough and charged before me the said Justice , upon the Oath of John Howard, George Griffin and others on suspicion of having feloniously stolen fifty four pounds weight of Butter, a wicker Basket, and a Linen Cloth the Property of the said John Howard Against the Peace &c —

Him therefore safely keep in your said Custody or until he shall be discharged by due Course of Law; and for so doing this shall be your sufficient Warrant.

GIVEN under my Hand and Seal this Twenty third Day of July One Thousand Eight Hundred and fourteen.

W Parsons

PLEASE HELP THE

Police Court

and

Prison Gate Mission

in its warfare against Sin and Crime

In Liverpool and S.W. Lancs. nine MISSIONARIES are daily in the Police Courts, outside the Prison, and in the Homes of those who are in trouble. The MISSION has helped thousands of people since it began in 1879.

Secretary:
Miss K. M. HADCOCK
3, Tithebarn Street, Liverpool, 2

FIVE GUINEAS REWARD.

ESCAPED from RALPH DUXFIELD, Special Bailiff, appointed by the Sheriff of Newcastle upon Tyne, in a Warrant issued upon a Writ of *Pluries Capias*, JOHN BARBER, of Newcastle upon Tyne, Attorney at Law.

Whoever will give Information of him so as he may be apprehended, shall receive the above Reward, by applying to the said Ralph Duxfield.

Newcastle, 17th May, 1796.

Mr Nathan Wilson Junr if mr Samuel Ney payes the cost infull and gives his Note for twenty Dollars payable in two years with intrust I will ~~Discarg~~ ~~Dch~~ Discharge him from Gale on my part want you to take car of the above Greenwich 6 may 1829 David Jeffry

THE TRIALS OF

CHARLES SHAW, aged 16, for Murdering JOHN OLDCROFT, aged 9.

RICHARD TOMLINSON, for Murdering MARY EVANS, his Sweetheart.

MARY SMITH, for Drowning her Infant Child.

Who all Three received Sentence of Death, at the late Staffordshire Spring Assizes, and were Ordered for

EXECUTION

Last WEDNESDAY, MARCH 19, 1834.

"Thou shalt do no Murder!" Mathew, ch. xix. v. 18.

"Whoso sheddeth man's blood, by man shall his blood be shed." Genesis, ch. ix. v. 6.

THE trials took place on Monday, 17th March, 1834, at the Staffordshire Spring Assizes, before The Hon. Mr. Justice Patteson

Charles Shaw,

A well-looking lad of 16, was charged with the Wilful Murder of John Oldcroft, aged 9, by fixing a cord round his neck. The only assignable motive of the prisoner for the commission of the offence was the acquisition of 1s. 6d. which the deceased possessed. The prisoner and the deceased were both in the service of Mr. Hawley, a potter. Both had been paid their wages at about six o'clock, on the 3d of August last. The deceased had due to him 1s. 4½d.; but, as he was a good lad, his master made it up 1s. 6d. In a few minutes after they were paid, the deceased and prisoner went away together, they were seen by various persons going towards the Etruria race-course. On their way they passed a boy named Robinson, who was bathing in the canal. He saw the prisoner dangling a piece of cord, and when afterwards the prisoner was reminded by Robinson that such was the case, he denied that he had any cord at all. The prisoner and deceased, after some little rough play with Robinson, then went on in the direction of Maccaroni-bridge, and they were seen playing with copper-money on a bank. The deceased not returning, his parents went in search of him, and proceeded to the house at which the prisoner lived, and the account he gave was, that he had left the deceased with gamblers, at the race-course. The parents continued their search without success; but one of the peasantry having a wood-lark, which is a bird fond of some of the contents of a wasp's nest, he went in search of a wasp's nest, and found concealed under some willows the body of the deceased, with a cord round the neck, corresponding in appearance with that the prisoner carried. In consequence of suspicion the prisoner was taken up. There were several marks of blood on the prisoner's shirt, which had been covered with potter's clay, but it was found to be blood, he said his nose had bled, and he began rubbing his nose as if to make it bleed.

Witnesses were called to prove his insanity, and that the deceased died of drowning, and not of strangulation, the Jury however returned a verdict of Guilty, and he was sentenced to be hung on the next Wednesday.

COPY OF VERSES.

OH! listen to a tale of woe, I now to you unfold,
Of the Murder of John Oldcroft, a boy of nine years old;
His body was found all in a ditch, it's true what I do say,
With a rope tied round his neck, his life was taken away.
This poor boy worked at a pottery, his living for to seek.
And all the wages that he earn't, was eighteen pence per week.
When his week's work was done, upon each Saturday night,
His wages to his mother gave, which gave him great delight.
Charles Shaw was a wicked lad, and only fourteen years old,
That he robb'd and murder'd this poor boy, makes the blood run cold,
The poor mother is tearing of her hair, the father distracted wild,
Crying, oh dear! oh dear! we are undone, we've lost our dearest child.

Richard Tomlinson,

A rough-looking fellow, about 22 years old, was charged with the Wilful Murder of Mary Evans, at Ranton, on the 16th December last, by striking her on the head with a stone, and then throwing her into a ditch. The prisoner at first pleaded Guilty, but, on advice, pleaded Not Guilty. It appeared, by his own Confession, that he and the deceased had a quarrel relative to some property, he had previously given her, which she said he afterwards secretly took away again. At length it was agreed to go to a *Wise Man*, named Light, at High Ercall, to learn who really did take them. She, on going thither, still kept accusing him, when, he told her, if she said so again, he would knock her down. She dared him; when he struck her. He then left her, and went to a beer-shop, where he acknowledged the murder. At the trial, witnesses were called to prove his insanity, but the Jury returned a Verdict of Guilty; and he was ordered to be executed on the following Wednesday.

COPY OF VERSES.

Come Lovers all of every class, pray listen unto me,
While I unfold the sad details of this black tragedy.
These sweethearts a quarrel had, which rose to th' highest pitch,
When he struck her on the head, and threw her in a ditch.
So Young Men and Maidens all pray warning take in time,
By this misguided pair, who thus perish'd in their prime.
And all thro' their own folly, as plainly you can tell,
For, had they curb'd their passions, all would now have been well.

Mary Smith,

Was convicted at the last assizes, for the Wilful Murder of her infant child, only twelve days old, by throwing it in the canal near Bloxwich. She was sentenced to be executed on the same day as the above-named culprits.

COPY OF VERSES.

IT'S of a cruel mother's fate, I now to you unfold.
Who most cruelly slew her babe, when only twelve days old.
She drown'd her own dear offspring—oh, dreadful to relate!
But mark, good people, what miseries did her then await.
She was plac'd in a gloomy cell, all in a dismal jail,
Until her day of trial came, when her defence did fail.
The Judge then doom'd her, poor lost wretch! to die upon a tree,
A sad and deadful punishment, for this mother's cruelty.

G. Smeeton, Printer, 74, Tooley Street.

As in the public press of today, crime and punishment were major topics of nineteenth-century street literature. The 'execution broadside' was a more or less standard production, often purporting to record the behaviour and 'last dying words' of malefactors on the scaffold. This one professes only to report the trial, but as usual carries a picture of the scene at the hanging. The illustration is a stock woodcut, the centre portion is pierced to allow an appropriate number of figures to appear on the scaffold. One of the prisoners in this case being a woman, one figure has been cut off at the base, to suggest a skirt.

The broadsides—even those with prisoners' dying speeches, were on sale to the crowd from the very moment of the prisoners' despatch.

A DISTRIBUTION OF

SOUP

TO THE DESTITUTE

in the district extending from the

Paygate to Felbridge

WILL TAKE PLACE AT

Mr. George Lynn's,

on Thursday the 31st Instant,

and every TUESDAY and FRIDAY afterwards

at 3 o'Clock, till further notice.

Application for TICKETS to be made to the Committee, at

SACKVILLE COLLEGE,

at three o'Clock on Wednesday the 30th.

Smith, Printer, East Grinstead.

NO MAY-DAY SWEEPS.

CAUTION.

The Inhabitants of this Parish are most respectfully informed, that the UNITED SOCIETY OF MASTER CHIMNEY SWEEPERS intend giving their Apprentices a Dinner, at the Eyre Arms, St. John's Wood, on the 1st of May, instead of suffering them to collect money as heretofore; the public are therefore cautioned against encouraging in any way such collections, as they are too frequently obtained by persons of the worst description, or for the sinister purposes of their Employers,

N.B. The Procession will start from the Bedford Arms, Charlotte Street, Bedford Square, at Eleven o'Clock.

Printed by G. Taylor, 8, Lamb's Conduit Passage.

Charity

As a collecting and social studies field, charity has much to offer. Perhaps no other area provides so much evidence so simply and so accessibly. The material, not yet widely explored—or even much recognized as collectible—is still easily come by. It appears as a common ingredient among local government and ecclesiastical paperwork and crops up as strays in dealers' 'bargain boxes'.

Certainly no other form of ephemera reflects its subject matter more poignantly and with such economy of effort. 'Supply the bearer with a bag of coals', says an 1860s card, no bigger than a tram ticket, the epitome of Victorian social security. 'Please deliver to Sarah Duncalf meat to the value of five shillings', says St Thomas's vestry clerk at Christmas, 1875. These are small mementoes of serious matters; to the bearers they may well have seemed matters of life or death.

The full canon of charity ephemera embraces every aspect of human need. As well as tickets for soup, meat, suet, bread, coals, there are cards appealing for help for deserving cases; subscription lists, charity sermon hymn sheets, soup kitchen and general relief announcements, institutional charity appeals, workhouse and hostel tickets, donation receipts, and personal petitions from the sick, distressed and homeless.

There are also, on the other hand, items tending to discourage the giving of charity. Says the Kent Mendicity Society in its promotional leaflet, 'Those who are disposed to indiscriminate almsgiving should remember that the vast majority of tramps are proved to have adopted mendicity as a profession, and that such charity is year by year augmenting that number.' The society recommends the use of its own bread tickets. A similar view was expressed in 1831 by the United Society of Master Chimney Sweepers, who (left) caution the public against 'May-day sweeps' and their street collections. Then, as now, the charity scene was not without its snags.

Mayor's Relief Fund—Longton Section.

25 WARD.

Supply bearer with
One Quart of Soup.

JAMES H. BARLOW, Chairman of Committee.

Mr. Cuthbert 5/

Supply the Bearer with

A BAG OF COALS.

Jan., 1861. H. S. THOMPSON.

SKYNNER'S BREAD CHARITY.

ST. MATTHEW'S, IPSWICH.

This Ticket entitles the Bearer to Bread of the value of three-pence which may be obtained from any Baker in the Parish.

R. C. BROWN,
A. T. NIGHTINGALE, } Churchwardens.

The Trustees will give Cash for this Ticket on the first of the month.

No. 3

ST. THOMAS, SOUTHWARK.

Meat TICKET.

Mr. Alfred Wells
Borough

Please deliver to Sarah Duncalf
Meat to the value of Five shillings

Edward Clapton
CHURCHWARDEN.

F. W. ARKCOLL,
VESTRY CLERK.

December, 1875.

Hallowell, March 15th 1842

Gentlemen, Leonard Peters a reputed child of Hannah Dick & Benjamin Peters

An Inhabitant of your town has now become chargeable in this town as a Pauper. We conceive it necessary to give you this information, and to request that you order his removal, or otherwise provide for him as you may judge expedient. We have charged the expense of his support, which has already arisen, to your town, and shall continue so to do, so long as we are obliged to furnish him with supplies. Said Peters is a colour'd Person & sometimes known by the name of Leonard Dick

We are, Gentlemen, with respect, Per order
your obedient and humble servants, of the

Benj F. Melvin } Overseers of the Poor for Hallowell.

To the Overseers of the Poor of the town of Bristol }

George St Westminster

181

London.—RECEIVED of The Rt. Hon. Lord Glenbervie

the Sum of One Guinea, for One Year's Subscription to the Society for Maintaining and Educating Poor Orphans of Clergymen till of Age to be put Apprentice, due February, 1813.

£1 1 0 James Nash Treasurer.

A Donation of Twenty Guineas constitutes a Subscriber for Life.

Hayden, Printer, Brydges Street, Covent Garden.

St. Ann's Society Schools

LOUIS DAVID EDWARDS

Aged Nine Years,

Son of a Clergyman.

Mr. Edwards is, through mental derangement, in reduced circumstances and totally incapable of maintaining his Wife and 4 Children, who are wholly dependent on their mother's parents for support.

Recommended by the following Subscribers:

The Right Rev. the Lord Bishop of LLANDAFF,
The Right Hon. the Earl of DENBIGH,
E. COWCHER, Esq. 2, Spencer-place, Brixton-road, Surrey,
J. FARNELL, Esq. Isleworth, Middlesex,
The Rev. J. HUTCHINS, Weston-green, Ditton-common, Surrey.
HOPKIN PERKINS, Esq. Stowe-hill, Newport,
The Rev. C. WODSWORTH, Hardingstone, Northamptonshire.

The Honorary Chaplain, the Rev. D. LAING, 67, Great Portland-street, London, has kindly offered to receive any Subscriptions towards this peculiar and distressing case.

January, 1879.

SOUP TICKET,
1d.

In America, as in Britain, overseers of the poor were concerned to avoid responsibility for paupers coming in from neighbouring areas. In forms like the one shown here (Halliwell, Maine, 1842) they requested removal of these 'outsiders' at the same time stating that charges would be incurred in their maintenance, present and potential, in the 'host' area.

The soup, coal, bread or meat ticket epitomizes the nineteenth-century view of social welfare—intervention at arm's length—with the certainty that aid was not being spent on drink or gambling. Some cards had year-round validity, others only in exceptionally bad weather or in special emergencies.

The Louis David Edwards item represents another charity device, the orphan appeal for election to a place in an institution.

NOTICE.

A PUBLIC

MEETING

Will be held at the TOWN HALL, GLASTONBURY, on THURSDAY, 27th December instant, at half-past Eleven o'Clock in the Forenoon, to adopt means for affording some relief to the Poor during the present severe weather, at which the Inhabitants of Glastonbury are respectfully requested to attend.

J. J. ROCKE, MAYOR.

Dated Glastonbury, 24th December, 1860.

J. BROCK, Printer, Stationer, Binder, &c., Glastonbury.

No. 6 ***Watts's Charity.***

THIS WARRANT ADMITS THE BEARER,

CITY OF

ROCHESTER.

to the Traveller's Hall, on the right-hand side of the entrance, and is an order for a Night's Lodging, which with Fourpence, is conformable to the Will of the late Richard Watts, Esquire, bearing date August 22, 1579.

The additional comfort of fire and candle is given during the Winter months, i. e. from 18th October, until 10th March.

Nov. 29 1853

Provider.

The monks called merciful brethern pray very humbly to be favoured with a mild gift; for they take care gratis of every sick body without regarding the difference of nation, religion or illnes.

King. June 29. 1851

Mr Provider
Please to give these Three
Poor Travellers Four Pence
Each
1..0 J. A. Hulkes
42.

WINTER CLOTHING,

Adapted for Donations to the Poor,

SUPPLIED BY

T. TOMLINSON & Co.

No. 78, NEW BOND STREET.

Lancashire Flannel, the Piece, 46 yards	..	39s. 45s.
Real Welch ditto	per yard,	9d. to 12d.
Ditto, very soft and warm	..	1s. 1d. 1s. 2½d. 1s. 4d.
Linsey Woolsey, blue and striped Ditto, twilled	..	11½d. to 1s. 4d.
Coloured Bed Rugs	each,	2s. 4d. 3s. 2d. 4s. 9d.
Blankets	per pair,	5s. 6d. 7s. 8s. 6d. 10s.
Great Coats	each,	10s. 6d. 12s. 13s. 6d. 14s. 6d.
Cloaks	..	4s. 6d. 6s. 7s. 6d. 9s.
Blue and various-coloured Prints for Gowns	per yard,	7d. 8d. 9d.
Stout Calico	..	6d. 8d. 9d.
Ditto Linen Sheeting	..	10d. 1s. 1s. 2d.
Irish Linen	..	11d. to 1s. 2d.
Lamb's-Wool Comforters	per doz.	7s. 6d. 9s. 6d. 12s. 6d.
Men's Knit Shetland Hose	..	7s. 6d. 10s. 6d.
Ditto, large and good quality	..	12s. 6d. 15s. 6d.
Grey Lamb's-Wool Hose	..	14s. 6d. 16s. 6d.
Flannel Under Waistcoats	..	30s. 33s.
White and Spotted Knit ditto		20s. 28s. 31s.
Ditto, (large size)	..	34s. 6d. 36s.
Calico Shirts	each,	2s. 2d. 2s. 6d.
Ditto, very stout and strong	..	3s.
Linen and Suffolk Hemp ditto	..	4s. 6d. 5s. 6d.
Flannel Drawers	per doz.	28s. 31s.
Welch Wigs	..	7s. 9s. 6d
Scotch and Red Worsted Caps	..	6s. 6d. 9s. 0d. 15s.
Yarn Gloves	..	6s. 6d. 10s.
Children's Knit Shetland Hose **Youth's** ditto	..	6s. 6d. 8s. 9s. 6d. 11s. 6d.
Women's White Worsted and Lambs'-Wool Black and Slate-coloured Worsted	..	11s. 6d. 12s. 6d. 13s. 6d.
Strong Flannel Petticoats Linsey Woolsey ditto	each,	2s. 8d. 3s. 3s. 4d.
Calico Chemises	..	2s. 3s 6d.
Linen ditto	..	4s. 5s.
Woollen Gloves	per doz.	6s. 9s.

A Variety of other suitable Goods, are Sold on the same advantageous Terms.

Ladies' and Gentlemen's Angola and Spanish Wool Under-Clothing, of peculiar softness; very fine Welch Flannel; Gauze and Double Milled ditto; Welch Knit Stockings and Socks; Fleecy Goods of all Kinds; Dressing Gowns; Ready-made Linen; Wash-Leather Waistcoats and Drawers; and an extensive Stock of every Description of Gloves and Hosiery.

WOOD, Printer, Stationer, and Engraver, 17, Lad Lane, London.

Society's short-term concern for public welfare is reflected in town meetings, public announcements, hostel tickets and hospice appeals (opposite). Private-enterprise price lists (this page) declare the presence of a minor 'charity industry', in which manufacturers purveyed low-grade products for pauper relief.

The monk's hostel appeal on the facing page is from Linz, Austria. The two Watts's charity items, printed (1853) and hand-written (c.1790) are from Rochester, Kent. The printed version offers 'the additional comfort of fire and candles' during the winter months.

Both pages 68%

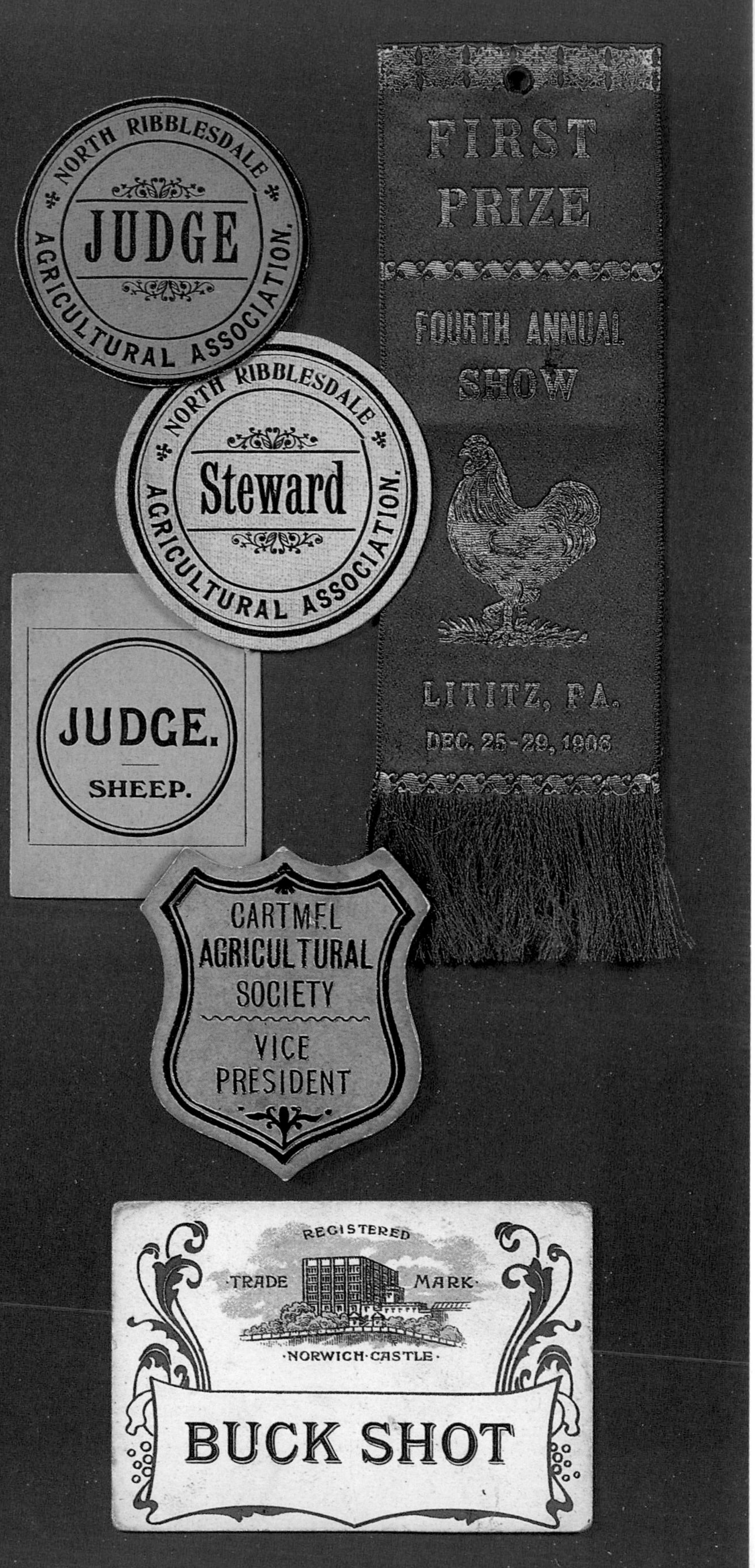

Rural life

For many today's nostalgia is not merely for the past as such, but for the apparent simplicity of pre-industrialized society. It is thus that the ephemera of the countryside now comes into its own. With its air of timeless tranquillity, uncomplicated, unpolluted, it conveys not only another age but another place. The certificates of agricultural societies, the cattle sale announcements, blacksmiths' bills, farm inventories, rent accounts, folk recipes, stewards' badges—these are mementoes, almost literally, of another country.

Reflected in the items is both the aspiration and the reality of rural life; on the one hand the prize tickets and awards, on the other the foot-rot liniment label; on the one hand the labourer's long-service certificate, on the other 'Directions for applying the horse-wart ointment'.

Timeless as it may have seemed, the nineteenth century nevertheless brought change. It saw the mechanization of farming, industrialized production of pesticides and veterinary products. In Britain it brought the trend to 'combination'—employers' associations and employees' trade unions. It also brought the battle of the Game Laws, the struggle of the landlord and the poacher for the wildlife within the landlord's fences.

Above all it brought developments in printing, an industry not only of record but of influence. Not least of the powers of the press was in the art and craft of advertising. Before the century was three-quarters through the farmer was a well-defined advertisers' market target, and by the end of the century even blacksmiths were known to print and publish their working rates.

On the whole, however, the rural scene preferred its well-established ways. Some conventions, rooted in the mid-nineteenth century, have survived into our own times.

Among the officials' badges on this page we note that of the Vice-President of the Cartmel Agricultural Society. This splendid item dates not from 1900 (as its design might suggest) but from the late 1980s.

THORLEY'S HORSE AND CATTLE SPICE

is now creating such a sensation throughout the World, that all practical Horse-keepers, Flock-masters and Cattle-feeders are pronouncing it the greatest discovery of the nineteenth century.

For your HORSE, mix a Packet at each time of Feeding, with the usual Corn and Chaff damped with water, and at three weeks hence the improvement will be so great that your neighbours will "get it up" you have been buying a Splendid New Animal.

For your COW, mix a Packet at each time of Feeding, with the usual Chaff and Meal, damped with water, and in a few days you will be agreeably surprised at the large increase in the quantity and superior quality of MILK and BUTTER.

For Dogs, Pheasants, Poultry, and Rabbits, a Tea-spoonful mixed up with Kitchen Stuff, or the usual Food, at each time of Feeding.

Sheep.—A Packet to every 4. The Corn and Chaff should be damped with water, so that the Condiment adheres to it, & then well mixed up.

For GEESE and DUCKS, mix a Table-spoonful with Barley Meal and Boiled Potatoes at each time of Feeding, and in a fort-night you will be astonished

For CALVES, One Packet mixed with Milk made into Gruel, will be found sufficient for four.

THORLEY'S
HORSE & CATTLE
SPICE
CAN ONLY BE HAD
IN
PENNY
PACKETS
THORLEY'S
FOOD FOR
CATTLE

For a BULLOCK, Mix same as mentioned for the COW, and you will produce Beef in half the usual time, and Two-pence per Pound superior in quality.

For a PIG, Mix a Packet in the usual Slop or Coarse Meat at each time of Feeding, and it will lay on Flesh rapidly, and "rest and be thankful."

ONE PENNY PER PACKET.

CASES CONTAINING 448 PENNY PACKETS, 34s.

SPICE MILLS AND OFFICES—THORNHILL BRIDGE, KING'S CROSS, LONDON.

NONE GENUINE WITHOUT THE INVENTOR'S SIGNATURE ON EACH PENNY PACKET. } *Joseph Thorley*

Joseph Thorley's Spice was rural Britain's big name of the nineteenth century. The aromatic condiment was good for livestock from ducks to bullocks, increasing milk in cows and ewes, fattening pigs in half the usual time, brightening the eye of horses and making them shine like velvet.

This colour handbill did for the farmyard what pink-pill advertising did for hypochondriacs. (All without a hint of the product's actual ingredients.) Dating from the latter part of the 1860s, the bill is ahead of its time in its use of colour and the all-embracing advertising claim.

'Buck Shot' (opposite) is the name given to the lead pellets used in shot-guns. The label-card may have been used in gunsmiths' window displays.

79%

Rural items on these pages include (top left) a hunting fixture card; (top right) a receipt for a stud (mating) service; and a typical 'game' preservation notice (opposite). Game notices in the 1830s and 40s were among the most common of items of rural ephemera—some of them threatening intruders with man-traps, or spring guns.

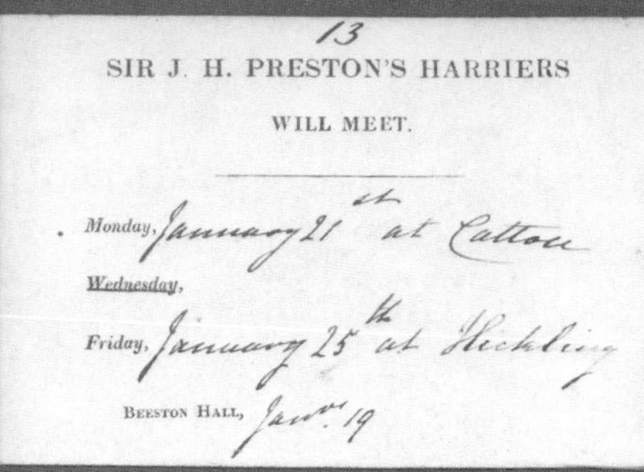

13

SIR J. H. PRESTON'S HARRIERS

WILL MEET.

Monday, January 21st at Cattow

Wednesday,

Friday, January 25th at Hickling

BEESTON HALL, Jan.y 19

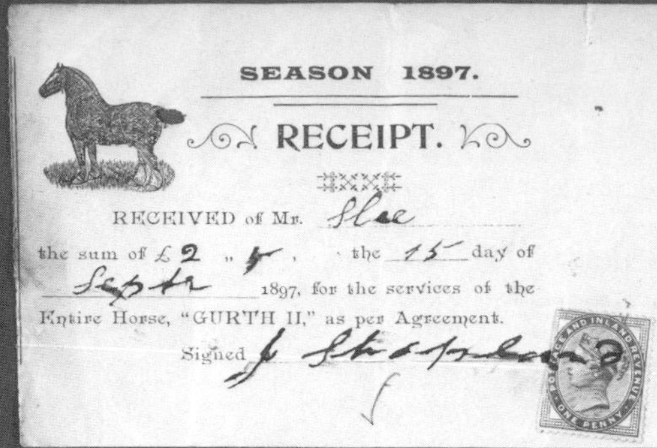

SEASON 1897.

RECEIPT.

RECEIVED of Mr. Slee

the sum of £2 „ 4 „ the 15 day of Septr 1897, for the services of the Entire Horse, "GURTH II," as per Agreement.

Signed J

SPACEY HOUSES

Auction Stock Sale.

985 Head of Cattle, &c.

CATALOGUE

OF

Beasts, Sheep, Pigs,

&c., to be

SOLD BY AUCTION,

WITHOUT RESERVE, BY

MR. R. BURTON,

On Monday, Jan. 8th,

at 9-15 a.m. prompt.

ALL STOCK TO BE IN THE YARD BY 9.

TERMS—CASH.

☞ All Bulls to be led into the Ring, and a man left in charge until delivered at station.

Future Postal Address:—
Spacey Houses, Pannal, via Leeds.

J. Hodgson, Machine Printer, Harrogate.

PETERBOROUGH BRANCH

OF THE (MASTERS)

Shoeing Smiths' Association.

In consequence of advances in Prices of Materials, on and after July 1st, 1900, and until further notice the following

Net Prices for Horse-Shoeing will be charged by all the Firms in the above District

Heavy Draught Horses	4/6	per Set and upwards.
Light Cart & Van Horses	3/6	,, ,,
Hunters and Carriage Horses	4/-	,, ,,
Cobs, Butchers & Bakers Horses	3/6	,, ,,
Ponies under 14 hands	3/-	,, ,,
Farm Horses shod for Farm purposes	3/-	,, ,,
Dealers' Heavy Horses	4/6	,, ,,

Welsh Ponies shod in Droves 6d. per shoe & upwards

Removing and Ruffin Half-price. Toe Piecing 1/- per set extra.

Punching Plug & screw holes in Shoes 1/- per set extra

Special Rates will be charged for Horses requiring extra attention on and after the above date. No special Contract below the above rates will be renewed.

The following Firms are Members of the above Association.

DAVIS & SONS, New Road, Peterborough.	C. WRIGHT, Broad Street, Peterborough.
W. PILLSWORTH, Lincoln Road, ,,	J. W. GRAHAM, Monument Street, ,,
C. H. HOWLETT, New Road, ,,	G. GREEN, Geneva Street, ,,
JOHN H. AYRE, King Street, ,,	J. W. ROWE, Millfield, ,,
E. SAYER, Narrow Street, ,,	W. JUDD, ,, ,,
PARKINSON & TODD, Cumbergate ,,	JOHN. NEWTON, Park Road, ,,
C. DAWSON, "Boy's Head" Woodstone	

D. M. BARRON, PRINTER, MIDGATE BUILDINGS, PETERBOROUGH.

53%

THE FARMERS & MECHANICS'

ASSOCIATION

OF THE TOWNS OF SULLIVAN, FENNER & LENOX,

Award this Diploma to Mrs Harriet Mead, for the best Ottomans, exhibited at their first Annual Fair, held at Perryville, on Thursday, October 1st, 1857.

ALVAN FAY, PRESIDENT.

IRA M. NICHOLS, SECY.

The Farmers and Mechanics Association diploma (1857) is for the best example of 'ottomans', (fabrics of silk, or silk and wool). The card itself is unusually elegant; the surface is in a 'porcelain' finish, and the wreath motif is heavily gold-embossed.

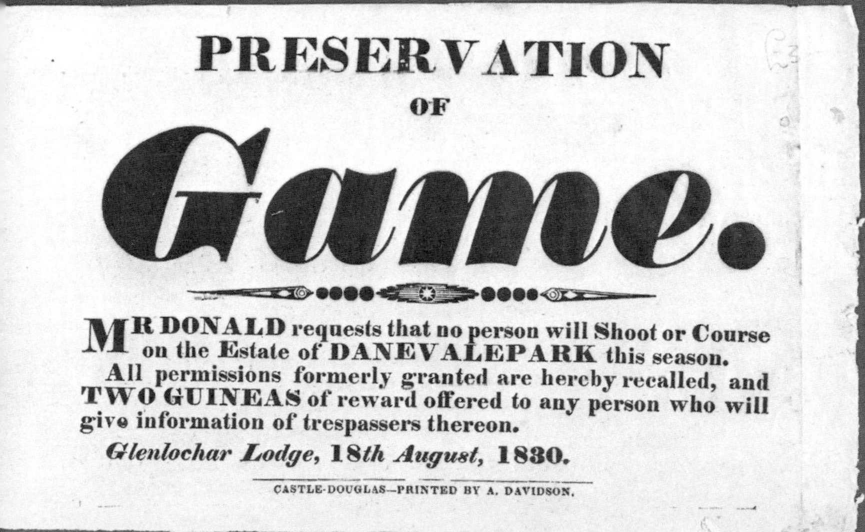

PRESERVATION OF

Game.

MR DONALD requests that no person will Shoot or Course on the Estate of DANEVALEPARK this season.

All permissions formerly granted are hereby recalled, and TWO GUINEAS of reward offered to any person who will give information of trespassers thereon.

Glenlochar Lodge, 18th August, 1830.

CASTLE-DOUGLAS—PRINTED BY A. DAVIDSON.

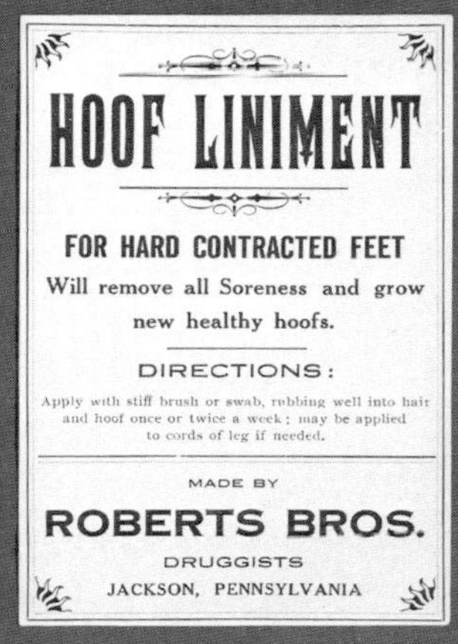

HOOF LINIMENT
FOR HARD CONTRACTED FEET
Will remove all Soreness and grow new healthy hoofs.
DIRECTIONS:
Apply with stiff brush or swab, rubbing well into hair and hoof once or twice a week; may be applied to cords of leg if needed.
MADE BY
ROBERTS BROS.
DRUGGISTS
JACKSON, PENNSYLVANIA

53%

Gebrüder Weigang, Bautzen.

Melina (Blattgold)

komplett RM 318.– für 1000 Stück 4teilig.

Deckelbild № 98391 RM 124.– Etikett № 98393 RM 63.–
Auflegerr " 98392 " 101.– Schluß " 98394 " 30.–
2. Aufleger № 62843 (280/180 mm, Blattgold) RM 84.–
Außendeckelbild № 98396 (Blattgold) RM 128.– extra.
Rücken-Etikett " 98395 " " 89.– "
Garantie-Etikett " 98254 " " 18.– "

Lager-Größe 280/180 mm.

Größere Formate bedingen entsprechende Preiserhöhung.

[Streifen № 2957 (geprägt) RM 35.– für 1000 Stück.]
Diese Packung ist auch in Neugold-Ausführung in gleicher Größe zu RM 233.– (4teilig) lieferbar.

Cigar packagin

The items on this and the facing page form complete 'label kit' for a cigar manufacture some time in the early 1900s.

The set, itemized in the German printer' price list (below, left) was designed not for special brand of cigars but for any manufacturer to use for his run-of-the-mill product, regardless of its quality, flavour or plantation origins.

Apart from a handful of 'pedigree' cigar companies the overwhelming majority of manufacturers built their trade on these off-the-peg identities, dressing their product in the finery of the label industry's ready-mad

The labels are printed in the main by the embossed chromolitho process, with embellishments in gold embossing; the treatment presents every mark of tradition, stability and authenticity. But a close look shows no true sign of provenance, no actual manufacturer's name and address, no authentic guarantee. The 'royal' coats of arr are fanciful, so are the factory and plantatio illustrations, and so are the 'prize' medals—all of which bear stars instead of inscription

Though spurious, these productions are splendid examples of the label-maker's art—feats of skill far beyond the capabilities of th commercial printer of today. They are collectors' items, not for their value in the history of individual elements in the cigar industry, but for their brazen virtuosity.

In one particular respect the extravagance of these labels is remarkable. In the *Melina* se shown here the same portrait appears on fou separate items, each produced by the classic stipple effect, hand-drawn on a series of lithographic stones (see page 90). Unlike today's approach to the matter, in which one original would be adapted photographically to the four applications, each of these chromolitho renderings was individually re-drawn, requiring its own complement of up to a dozen separate stones, each matching the other exactly. The skills involved—not to mention the man-hours—are by today's standards unimaginable.

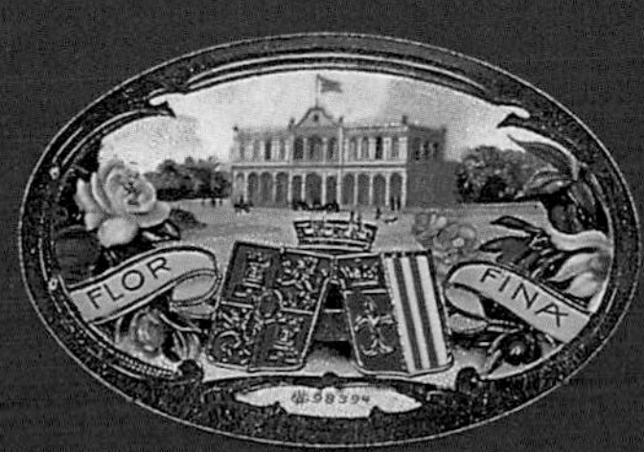

The Melina *set of labels included (facing page) a back label (top), and two end labels, one gold embossed, the other simulating the traditional impression of a brand-iron on wood. On this page are the inside lid label (top), the outer lid label (centre), the oval closure label (designed to seal the lid-pin); the guarantee label (imitating the Cuban Government's tax label), and the edging stamp. Most important of these from a sales point of view was the inner lid label, which served as an eye-catcher when the box was displayed, open, on a cigar-store counter. Other cigar-box trimmings, not in the* Melina *set, include (for the American market) the legal 'Caution Notice' warning against the re-use of boxes; 'flaps' (hinged papers lying over the cigars) and 'top sheets' (loose papers serving the same purpose).*

LAS FUMAS
DE PUERTO RICO

LA DOMINENCIA
CIGARS
LA PREFERENCIA
CHOICE CIGARS
ALMERIA
HENRY DEISEL & CO.
FERNANDEZ GARCIA Y CIA
SMART SET
HABANA
HOYO DE MONTERREY HABANA
JOSE
GENER
PRINCE BIBESCO
HABANA
HABANA

Merlindas
Cortina, Gómez y Ca.
REINA VICTORIA
EXTRA
MADRAZO Y CORRALES.
VERACRUZ.
Princesa Superfina
Queens
Regalia Chica
FLOR DE DINDIGUL
REINA VICTORIA

EXTRAFINA

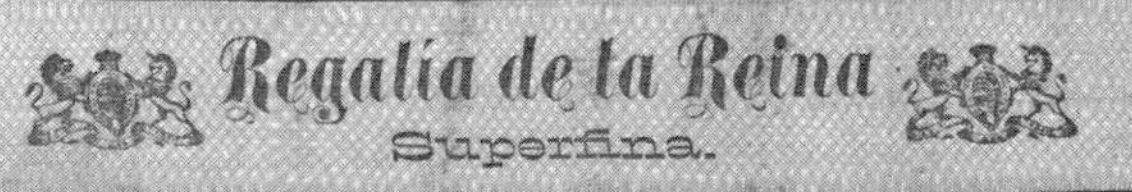
Regalía de la Reina
Superfina.
Regalia Bolsa

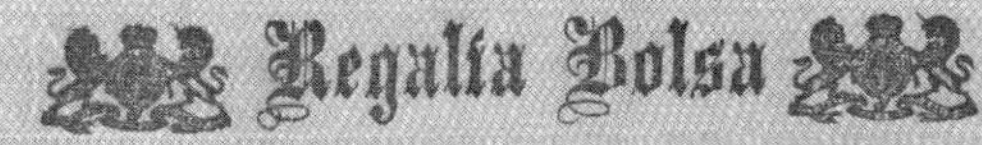
Royales.
"Flor de Tabacos"
Princesas

DU PONT
BRONZE
POWDER

Pale Gold 7205F

…chievement in the Development of the Bronze Powder Industry in Americ…
…brilliancy and covering qualities distinguish Du Pont Bronze Powder as a superior produc…
…red for use wherever the finest and most lasting effects in bronze are desired, either in…
…ossing, lithographing, engraving or flat printing.

…U PONT DE NEMOURS & COMPANY, Incorporated
…ARTMENT, CHEMICAL PRODUCTS DIVISION
WILMINGTON, DELAWARE

RUDOLPH
VALENTINO
Rudolph Valentino

PRIMEROS
SUPERIORES
AROMA DE CUBA
ESPECIAL
EXQUISITOS

In America the heyday of the cigar industry was the period 1870 to 1920. In the 1880s there were 1400 cigar manufacturers and a total of 20,000 brands. By the turn of the century some 30,000 brand names had been registered. As the cigar craze boomed the same product was continually named, re-named and re-styled as fashion dictated. The label industry excelled itself; no form of printing extravagance was neglected. The cigar band and the bundle band became a cult, with collectors competing for 'new issues'. The business of printing yellow bundle ribbons (to order or from stock) also expanded. The collecting craze, at its peak in the 1920s, still flourishes today.

Both pages 62%

Education

Among the earliest of educational ephemera was the 'battledore' (right), the ABC folder of the eighteenth- and nineteenth-century dame school. With its three-panel format and characteristic corner cuts, this famous teaching aid was everyone's introduction to literacy and general knowledge.

It is said to have been introduced by Benjamin Collins, a Salisbury printer, in the mid-1700s. In the period 1770–80, history has it, he sold over a hundred thousand of them.

The shape—and the name—derives from an earlier classroom aid, the 'hornbook'. This was not a book in the modern sense, but a small wooden panel bearing an alphabet, faced with a sheet of transparent horn. The panel had a handle to hold it by, and the bat-shaped ABC board was inevitably used in ball-games—in and out of the classroom. It came to be called a battledore (compare Spanish *batidor*: beater), and the name was transferred to the later cardboard version. The left hand panel, with its corners cut, is said to be a vestigial handle; the card was used, it seems, as its wooden predecessor.

The original hornbook, though for generations the most commonplace of all everyday objects, is today a rarity—so much so that reproductions are often sold at high prices as originals. But the cardboard battledore, produced in its time in millions, is less rare; large numbers survived into the twentieth century and examples were still turning up in country stationers' stores in the middle 1940s.

The hornbook and battledore appeared only in black and white. It was with the coming of colour that teaching aids came into their own.

Colour was at first applied laboriously by brush—free-hand or by stencil—but printing in colours began in earnest in the middle of the nineteenth century. All of the colour items shown here are hand-coloured, a class of ephemera much prized by the collector.

74%

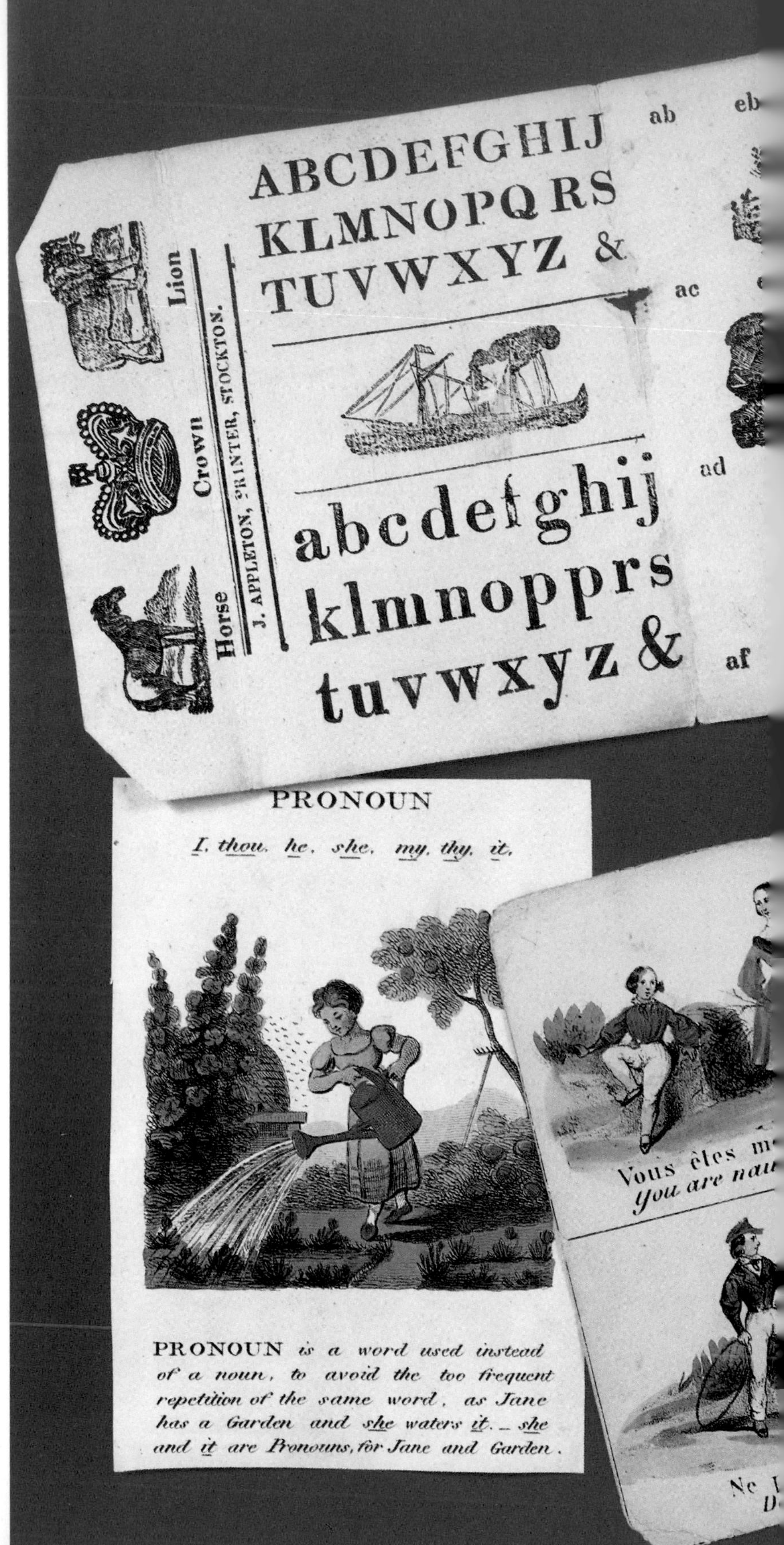

ub
oc
uc
od
ud
of
uf
K
k
K is the King, may he have a long Life!
Je serai bon.
I will be good.
J'ai faim
I am hungry.
Prenez - Garde.
Take care.
Entendez - vous.
Do you understand.
Allez a lecole.
Go to school.
Lisez votre livre.
Read your book.
A had an Apple, K had a Kite
Bat String Tail Loop Fly
G R
IV
A Trumpet
Spectacles
A Gridiron
An Air Balloon
A Sedan
A Coffee Pot

The authority of the black and white cardboard battledore was not above question. Concocted by local printers from stock blocks and random type, they sometimes erred, as in this example, in which the printer himself did not mind his Ps and Qs.

Hand colouring of black lithographed or engraved images brought a plethora of aids in spelling, grammar and foreign-language teaching. The cards shown here are selected from extensive sets; the 'parts of speech' card ('pronoun is a word used instead of a noun') is one of a set of twelve.

Other sets explained the elements of arithmetic—some by means of versified multiplication tables.

74%

The nineteenth-century private school prospectus may be seen as a collecting field in itself. Certainly school prospectuses spared no pains to convey the highest standards, notwithstanding occasional lapses of spelling (the word 'gauging' was a perennial source of trouble). The prospectus was commonly presented as a four-page folder. The blank back page was used for the address when, as often, it was folded for transmission by post.

Charles Dickens in Nicholas Nickleby did much to debunk these documents with the text of an advertisement for 'Mr Wackford Squeer's Academy . . . at the delightful village of Dotheboys'. Squeers's Academy . . . like Mr Thornton's and all such listings, also included the statutory nineteenth-century accomplishment, 'The use of the globes (Terrestrial and Celestial).'

AT

Mr. THORNTON'S

Establishment,

CHESHUNT, HERTS.

(Opposite the 12 Mile Stone,)

THIRTY YOUNG GENTLEMEN

ARE

BOARDED AND EDUCATED,

WITH THE GREATEST CARE AND EXPEDITION,

FOR

BUSINESS OR PROFESSION.

THE

ENGLISH, LATIN, GREEK & FRENCH LANGUAGES

TAUGHT, WITH THE STRICTEST ATTENTION TO

ORTHOGRAPHY, READING, PARSING, QUANTITY AND COMPOSITION.

WRITING; ARITHMETIC; AND ALGEBRA.

MENSURATION DEDUCED FROM CORRECT PRINCIPLES OF GEOMETRY;

GUAGING; TRIGONOMETRY; HISTORY; GEOGRAPHY; MAPPING;

AND THE

USE OF THE GLOBES.

Terms per Annum,

THIRTY GUINEAS, EXCLUSIVE OF THE CLASSICS AND MATHEMATICS.

TWO GUINEAS, WASHING.

Music, Dancing, Drawing and French, on the usual Terms,

BY THE MOST APPROVED MASTERS.

74%

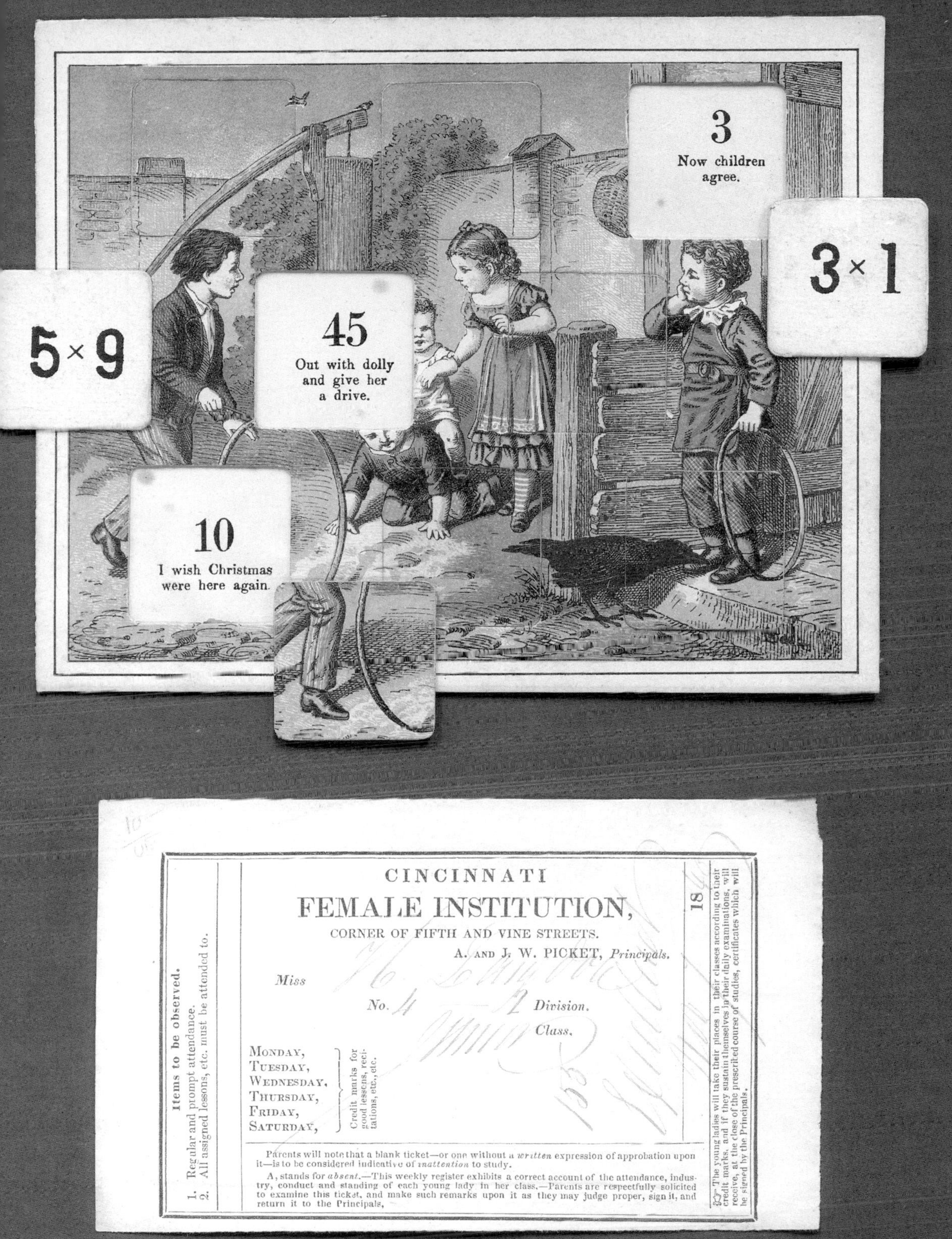
5×9
45
Out with dolly and give her a drive.
3
Now children agree.
3×1
10
I wish Christmas were here again.

CINCINNATI

FEMALE INSTITUTION,

CORNER OF FIFTH AND VINE STREETS.

A. AND J. W. PICKET, *Principals.*

18

Miss

No. *Division.*

Class.

MONDAY,
TUESDAY,
WEDNESDAY,
THURSDAY,
FRIDAY,
SATURDAY,

Credit marks for good lessons, recitations, etc., etc.

Items to be observed.

1. Regular and prompt attendance.
2. All assigned lessons, etc. must be attended to.

Parents will note that a blank ticket—or one without a *written* expression of approbation upon it—is to be considered indicative of *inattention* to study.

A, stands for *absent*.—This weekly register exhibits a correct account of the attendance, industry, conduct and standing of each young lady in her class.—Parents are respectfully solicited to examine this ticket, and make such remarks upon it as they may judge proper, sign it, and return it to the Principals,

☞ The young ladies will take their places in their classes according to their credit marks, and if they sustain themselves in their daily examinations, will receive, at the close of the prescribed course of studies, certificates which will be signed by the Principals.

Early teaching aids included games to play at home under the eye of a governess. This pictorial puzzle (c.1860) taught multiplication at three learning levels; using picture, number and rhyme. The number cards, bearing portions of the illustration on the back, slotted into their correct positions in the overall picture.

The school report, whether for the year, the term, the month or the week, served not only as a record of pupils' performance but as a link with parents, who were asked to return it, signed, with their comments to the school. The teacher's report on Miss H. Langden for the week of November 7, 1840 is 'Excellent'.

74%

Entertainment

The programme for the Palace Theatre of Varieties, 1894, marks a high-point in the ephemera of entertainment. With its chromolitho extravagance it brings showbiz out of the age of the throwaway handbill, into the dawn of the coming century.

The three-panel folder is printed on the other side with the programme for the performance in question (matinee, Saturday April 7, at 2.15), with a motley complement of advertising to go with it.

All the ingredients, the seductive colour work, the programme itself and the advertisements, speak unmistakably of the turn of the century. The acts include 'Prof Duncan's marvellous troupe of performing collies', 'An entirely new series of tableaux vivants' and 'Hill and Hull—original eccentric dwarf speciality'. Among the advertisements are an announcement of the service of Arthur Fownes, stage coach proprietor (who also gives lessons 'four in hand, tandem, pair etc'); and of Dr Soules, whose elixir 'positively cures diabetes, gout, rheumatism and kidney disorders (without change of diet)'.

Advertising in programmes became widespread in the 1880s and 90s—a revolutionary change from the programme of former times, when the 'bill of the play' had served as poster, handbill and auditorium programme all in one.

But the ephemera of entertainment reflects more than just the stage presentations of the theatre; attractions as diverse as fireworks, wax museums and magic lantern shows have their mementoes, and the collector has a huge range to choose from.

The theatre programme takes much of the collecting limelight, though it must be said that many hundreds of thousands have survived. The habitual playgoer tends to keep them as personal mementoes, and cupboards and boxes all over the world are full of them. In theatrical ephemera the rare 'collector's item' may lie in less crowded areas.

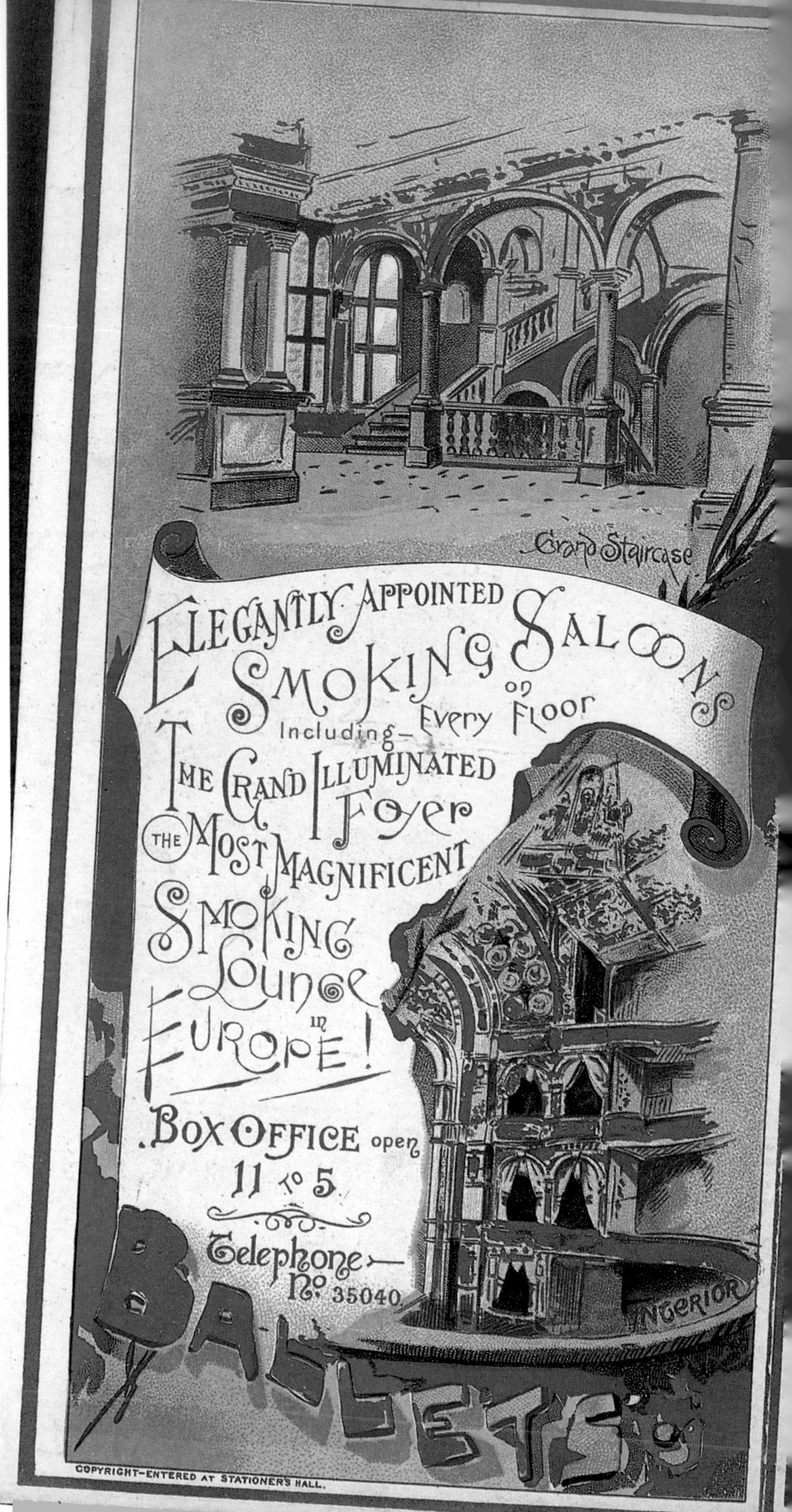

Both pages 80%

The Palace

Theatre of Varieties

The Handsomest Music Hall in Europe.

Varieties & Novelties

Open All the Year Round

ASTLEY'S

ROYAL AMPHITHEATRE OF ARTS.
Proprietor & Manager, Mr. WILLIAM BATTY, Bridge Road, Lambeth, Surrey
LICENSED BY THE LORD HIGH CHAMBERLAIN.

GRAND

SPECTACLE

EXTRAORDINARY!

CONTINUED SUCCESS OF MAZEPPA!

FOR SIX NIGHTS LONGER!

In compliance to the demand for places to witness MAZEPPA, and on account of the Extensive Preparations for the New Military Spectacle, Lord Byron's magnificent Drama of the **Wild Horse** will be **repeated for Six Nights longer!** when it must be positively withdrawn. On MONDAY next, Nov. 20th, First Night of a series of

National Military Equestrian Fetes!

Commencing with the Splendid French Spectacle of

THE WARS OF MURAT!

THE GENERAL, PRINCE, AND KING!

Produced on a scale of Splendour and extent surpassing even the productions of the "AFFGHANISTAN WAR," "ENGLAND's MONARCH," "CONQUEST OF GRANADA," &c.

MONDAY, NOVEMBER 13, 1843,

AND DURING THE WEEK,

The Curtain will rise at half-past 6, with **LORD BYRON's**

SPLENDID EQUESTRIAN & DRAMATIC SPECTACLE OF

MAZEPPA,

AND THE

WILD HORSE.

The Spectacle re-produced under the Direction of Mr. W. D. BROADFOOT.

POLES.—Castellan of Laurinski, Mr. CONRAD,
Count Premislaus.........(the Palatine)......Mr. G. ALMAR,
Olinski......(Daughter of the Castellan)....Mrs. COOKE,
Drolinski (Godson to the Chamberlain) Mr. T. BARRY,
Rudzoloff....(Chamberlain of the Castellan)....Mr. KEMP,
Zemila......(Orlinski's Maid)....Mrs. MONTGOMERY,
TARTARS.—Abderkhan.........................(King of the Tartars)..........................Mr. G. GRAY,
Mazeppa.....(his Son, assuming the name of Cassimer).........Mr. J. DANAVILLE,
Thamar and Zemba (Chieftains) Mess. HARWOOD and CROWTHER,
Kadac and Koscar.... Messrs. STEWARD & J. GEORGE
Oneiza..........................(a Shepherdess, betrothed to Koscar).....................Mrs. HARWOOD,

Astley's 'Royal Amphitheatre of Arts' was a cross between a theatre and a circus. In its central arena in front of the proscenium dramatic spectacles were presented. These featured horses, chariots and on occasions enactments of pitched battles. The 'Grand Spectacle Extraordinary' of Mazeppa and the Wild Horse *was based on Byron's poem celebrating the story of the Polish Cossack hero, punished by being lashed naked to a wild horse which was then turned loose. Some of the action took place on the stage; the wild horse part was in the arena.*

The poster, unusual in featuring an illustration, represents a halfway stage between the purely typographic playbill and the pictorial poster.

61%

AUXHALL.

POSITIVELY

ne Last 5 Nights

UNRIVALLED ATTRACTIONS

ONE-SHILLING

ssal Globe

. WYLD'S

LARGE

DEL OF THE EARTH

IN

Leicester Square,

Now Open

TO THE PUBLIC,

FROM NINE O'CLOCK IN THE MORNING

Admission,

ONE SHILLING

Printed by W. J. GOLBOURN, 6, Princes Street, Leicester Square

Theatre Royal, Bradford.

LICENSED ACCORDING TO ACT OF PARLIAMENT.

Mr. J. MOSLEY, Lessee and Manager of the West York Theatrical Circuit.

TICKET NIGHT

On TUESDAY EVENING, JANUARY 22nd, 1856,

The Entertainments will commence with Colman's Comedy of

JOHN BULL

OR, THE ENGLISHMAN'S FIRESIDE.

Pereqrine........................Mr LEANDER MELVILLE
Sir Simon........................Mr WATSON
Hon. Tom Shuffleton........................Mr HUNTLEY
Frank Rochdale........................Mr J. B. STEELE
Job Thornberry........................Mr MACKAY
Dennis Brulgruddery........................**Mr NUNN**
John Bur........................Mr ROBINSON
Dan........................Mr R. ROSS
Simon........................Mr ROUGHTON
Lady Caroline Braymore........................Miss ADELAIDE BOWERING
Mrs Brulgruddery........................Mrs JONES
Mary Thornberry........................Miss SELTON

LA PAS COMIQUE - - M. ALFREDE GLANVILLE
COMIC SONG - - - MR. R. ROSS
DANCING - by the MISSES MACGREGOR

To conclude with the interesting Drama, called

THE TOWER OF NESLE

OR, THE CHAMBER OF DEATH!

Buridan, a Captatn in the Italian Army........................Mr LEANDER MELVILLE
Philip D'Aulnay........................Mr J. B. STEELE
Gaulter D'Aulnay, of the Queen's Guards........................Mr G. W. STANLEY
Savoissy........................Mr R. ROSS
Enguerrand Marigny........................Mr JONES
Sieur Roual........................Mr ROBINSON
Orsini, Host of L'Agneu........................Mr MACKAY
Landri, a Ruffian Tapster........................Mr HUNTLEY
Richarde........................Mr WATSON
Jehan........................Mr ROUGHTON
Page........................Miss MACGREGOR
Marguerite de Bourgogne, Queen of France and Navarre........Miss A. BOWERING
Jeanette, the Veiled Woman........................Miss SELTON
Matilda........................Mrs STANLEY
Julia........................Miss M. MACGREGOR

DOORS OPEN AT AT HALF-PAST SIX, CURTAIN TO RISE AT SEVEN O'CLOCK.

PRICES OF ADMISSION:—Front Boxes, 2s.; Side Boxes, 1s. 6d.; Upper Boxes, 1s.; Gallery, 6d. Half-price at NINE o'clock, Boxes, 1s. No half-price to the Upper Boxes or Gallery.

NOTICE.—Pass-out Checks are not transferable—No money returned.

PRINTED FOR J. MOSLEY, AT THE THEATRE ROYAL PRESS.

Handbills for the last five nights of Vauxhall Gardens, 1861, and Mr Wyld's Colossal Globe, 1851, are rare survivors of nineteenth-century throwaway printing. The playbill for Bradford's Theatre Royal, 1856, is of a category much more readily found. Playbills in general, though they purvey detailed information as to plays, players, dates and places, have not attracted overmuch collecting attention; they survive in fairly large numbers.

The expression 'ticket night' was applied to performances at which the management made tickets available to minor members of the cast, for sale to friends for their own personal benefit.

61%

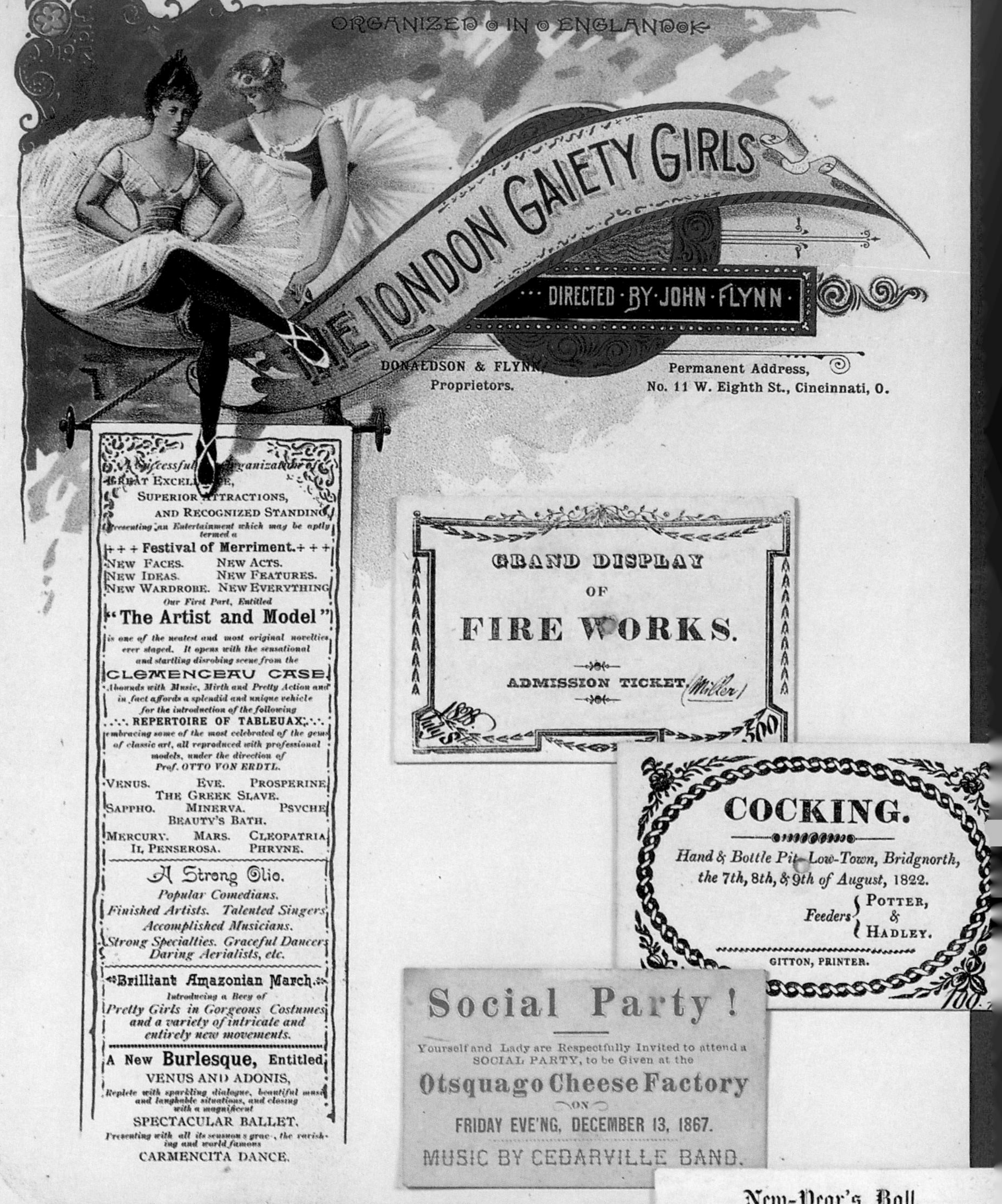

The items on this and the facing page convey something of the wide range of the ephemera of entertainment. Fireworks and magic lantern shows are among the more conventional attractions, but cockfighting (illegal in Britain since 1849) is an entertainment less often mentioned in ephemera.

The London Gaiety Girls letterhead enshrines a British export of the naughty nineties. 'Organised in England', and based in Cincinnati, the show boasted 'a startling disrobing scene' and 'pretty girls in gorgeous costumes and a variety of intricate and entirely new movements'. The girls were famed for their beauty and their capacity for marrying into the peerage.

67%

The Master of the Household
has received Her Majesty's command to invite
Lady Harriet Bligh
to a Dance to be given at Buckingham Palace
by The Queen and The Duke of Edinburgh
on Tuesday, 20th December, 1977 at 8.30 p.m.

Dress: Dinner Jacket
or
Lounge Suit

This card does not admit

FIRST
ANNUAL BALL.
Fort Stanwix Engine Co.
No. 3.
CARD OF INVITATION.

ADMIT TWO.

Madame Tussaud & Sons

MR. MAITLAND.
BOX.
THEATRE.

DEDICATION LEVEE.
The Company of [illegible] is solicited
— AT THE —
MOUNT HOPE HOUSE,
IN FALL RIVER,
ON TUESDAY EVENING, AUG. 27th, 1844.
IN BEHALF OF THE PROPRIETOR,
W. T. WOOD, ISRAEL BORDEN, — MANAGERS — B. W. WOODMAN, CHAS. A. GLAZIER.
An answer is solicited.

As with the firemen's ball item on page 148, the card of invitation of the Fort Stanwix Engine Company No 3 leaves no-one in doubt of the heroism of the hosts. But for all that the card shows a fitting elegance, as do the other items on this page. Mr Maitland's permanent pass to a theatre box is printed, like the firemen's card, on a gold-printed stock design—in Mr Maitland's case, in an edition of one. The levee invitation is also on a stock card, an early example of the embossed designs put out by Dickinsons, the Boston stationers and printers.

67%

The last days of the nineteenth century showed little hint of the electric world to come. The bill for McCarthy's benefit at the York music hall appeared in traditional guise and nothing in the Bush Street theatre programme, or that of Park Opera House suggested the end of an era. But within a decade the vitascope halls and picture palaces (with their 'blue velour plush tip-up chairs') had stolen the show. Handbills like that for Stamford's electric cinema appeared everywhere.

52%

KYRLE
PICTURE
PALACE,
ROSS.
SPECIAL ARTISTES
EACH WEEK.
MOVING PICTURES
SHEWN EACH DAY,
7,000 FEET IN LENGTH.
CHANGE OF PROGRAMME,
MONDAYS & THURSDAYS.
Pianist, Miss MAY WYATT, of Matlock.
Doors Open 7-30 Commence at 8
Matinees Thursdays & Saturdays, at 3.
Prices--1s., 6d. & 3d.
School Children, on Saturdays—1d. 2d. & 3d.
COME EARLY TO SECURE A SEAT.

EDISON'S
LATEST IMPROVED
PHONOGRAPH
ENTERTAINMENT.

AT 7:30 O'CLOCK.
50 FIRST-CLASS Selections,
Including Marches, Band Music, Songs, Hymns, Comic Pieces, Solos, Etc., Etc.
The following are a few of the many selections.

Little Boy In Blue.	
Safe In the Arms of Jesus.	Liberty Bell March.
Nearer My God To Thee.	Creole Belle March.
Uncle Josh and the Street Car.	Willow Grove March.
	22d Conn. Reg. March.
	Imitation of Chimes.

Uncle Josh's Trip To Boston, Etc.
and many other of the latest Songs, Marches etc.
ADMISSION, 10 CTS.
THOMAS W. CLOUGH.

COMING! COMING!
The Greatest Moving Picture and Stereopticon Exhibition
OF THE SEASON
Thrilling Dramas—Roaring Comedies—Scenes From All Over The World
The Very Latest Productions
nteresting and Instructive. Everyone
vill Enjoy this Superb Entertainment
COME—AND BRING THE CHILDREN
me
ce
MISSION: Adults
Children

SALON IDEAL
WEDNESDAY 26th December, 1917
LUCILLE & HUGO
The Purple Domino
What is The Purple Domino? THE PURPLE DOMINO is the grandest serial film in the world market.
Every episode is full emotion.
Over 6.000.000 spectators have admired this serial the Butterfly Cinema, of New-York.
This serial will commence o…

The moving picture show was, at first, merely a display of moving pictures—enough in themselves to cause excitement. But before long there were 'thrilling dramas, roaring comedies'. (The stereopticon exhibition showed only still pictures, projected from stereo pairs in red and green from two magic lanterns and viewed through red and green spectacles.) The movie serial—a money-spinning habit-former—came into vogue everywhere in the second decade of our century.

In a class by itself was the public phonograph entertainment, immortalized here in the handbill of Thomas Clough, itinerant purveyor of marches, hymns, comic pieces etc., at ten cents per person per evening.

52%

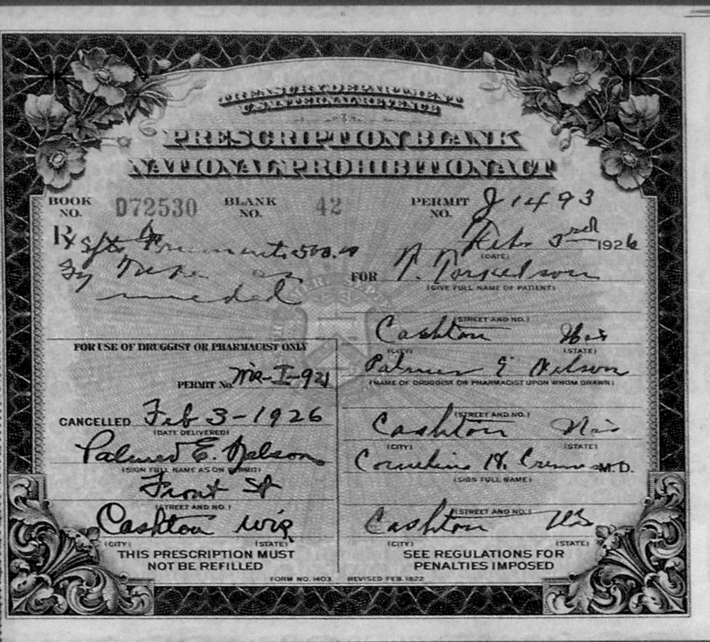
TREASURY DEPARTMENT
U.S. INTERNAL REVENUE
PRESCRIPTION BLANK
NATIONAL PROHIBITION ACT
BOOK NO. D72530 BLANK NO. 42 PERMIT NO. J 1493
℞
(DATE) Feb 3rd 1926
FOR (GIVE FULL NAME OF PATIENT)
Cashton
(STREET AND NO.)
(CITY) (STATE)
(NAME OF DRUGGIST OR PHARMACIST UPON WHOM DRAWN)
(STREET AND NO.)
Cashton
(CITY) (STATE)
(SIGN FULL NAME) M.D.
(STREET AND NO.)
Cashton
(CITY) (STATE)
SEE REGULATIONS FOR PENALTIES IMPOSED
FOR USE OF DRUGGIST OR PHARMACIST ONLY
PERMIT No.
CANCELLED Feb 3-1926
(DATE DELIVERED)
(SIGN FULL NAME AS ON PERMIT)
Front St
(STREET AND NO.)
Cashton
(CITY) (STATE)
THIS PRESCRIPTION MUST NOT BE REFILLED
FORM NO. 1403 REVISED FEB 1922

PRINTED BY
CHARLES WHITING
BEAUFORT HOUSE STRAND LONDON
FOR PROTECTION AGAINST
FORGERY

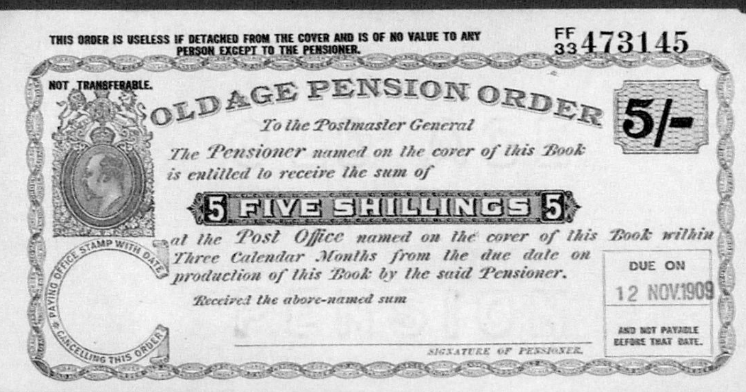
THIS ORDER IS USELESS IF DETACHED FROM THE COVER AND IS OF NO VALUE TO ANY PERSON EXCEPT TO THE PENSIONER.
FF 33 473145
NOT TRANSFERABLE.
OLD AGE PENSION ORDER
5/-
To the Postmaster General
The Pensioner named on the cover of this Book is entitled to receive the sum of
5 FIVE SHILLINGS 5
at the Post Office named on the cover of this Book within Three Calendar Months from the due date on production of this Book by the said Pensioner.
Received the above-named sum
SIGNATURE OF PENSIONER.
PAYING OFFICE STAMP WITH DATE & CANCELLING THIS ORDER
DUE ON
12 NOV.1909
AND NOT PAYABLE BEFORE THAT DATE.

Security printing

The term 'security printing' is applied to the production of every form of document in which the risk of forgery calls for special protective measures.

Broadly speaking, security printing calls for expertise not only beyond the capacity of the kitchen-table amateur, but also beyond that of the better-than-average quality printer. Essentially it requires resources—and efforts—of great complexity.

Its methods are used of course in the production of currency notes, share certificates, and revenue and postage stamps. But there is an ever-increasing secondary field, which includes passports, licences, permits, travel cheques, postal orders and national insurance stamps. Also within the field are such items as authorization cards, visitors' passes, season tickets and, by no means least, cash and credit cards.

Security devices include special papers (watermarks, metal threads, embedded lint etc.), soluble inks (to deter the tampering artist-craftsman) and printing methods. Among the earliest, dating from the early 1800s and still the most widely applied, is the complex pattern, produced as an engraved image by a geometric lathe. Also popular are the multiple micro-legend (an all-over pattern of tiny lettering) and colour merging.

Among the earliest of efforts to beat the forger was the invention in 1820 of compound-plate printing (this page, centre). In this an interlocking 'jig-saw', composed of two separate plates, separately inked, printed two colours at one impression. The accuracy of the fit (the 'register') of the finished image was unattainable by the ordinary printing technology of the day. So was the unbroken continuity of the white-line pattern as it traversed the colour changes.

More recent specimens of security printing are the alcohol prescription blank from the Prohibition era (1926) and Britain's Old Age Pension order (1909).

As with any other printing enterprise, banknote companies may produce their own promotional material to show off their special expertise. Shown here are twentieth-century examples from Bradbury Wilkinson and Waterlow's, two leading British companies. Designed without the restraints imposed by a specific customer's briefing, these 'promotional notes' present every trick of the security printer's trade—often, as in the variant versions of the Wren design, showing a choice of colour treatment.

The Thomas de la Rue 'No Value' items are produced for use as dummies in testing the company's electronic note-counting, sorting and verifying equipment.

59%

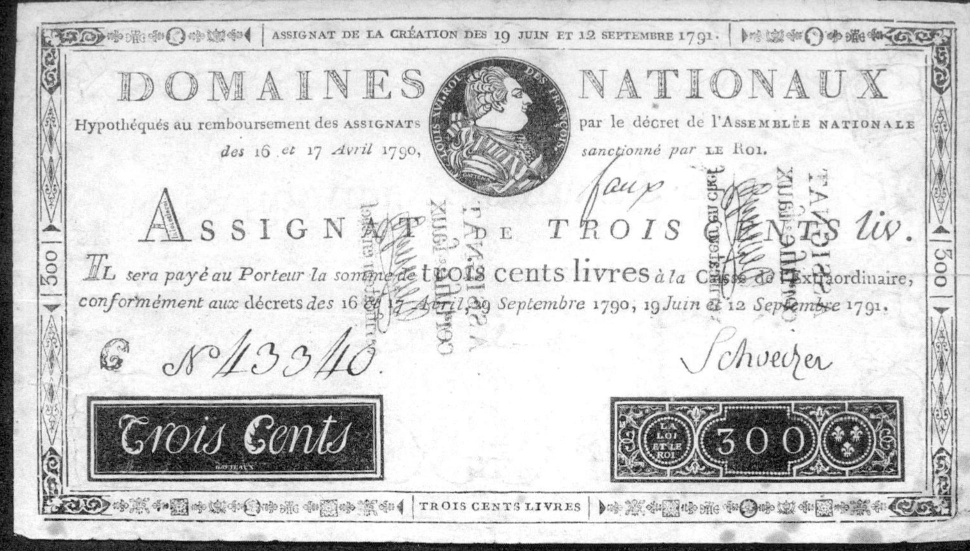

Forgery of currency notes ranges from the hand-drawn crudities of the amateur to the near-perfection of the professional. The examples on this page are the work of (top) the British Government, in a bid to destabilize the French currency after the introduction of the assignat *in the 1790s; (centre) the German Government attempting to do the same for the British 'fiver' in the 1940s, and (bottom) an unknown penman of the early years of the century.*

Forging of assignats *was so widespread as to induce the appointment of teams of official* verificateurs. *The* assignat *shown above is stamped on the back* 'certifié faux' *and signed by the Verifier in Chief.*

The forged fiver is distinguishable only by a slight inaccuracy in the lettering of the watermark.

64%

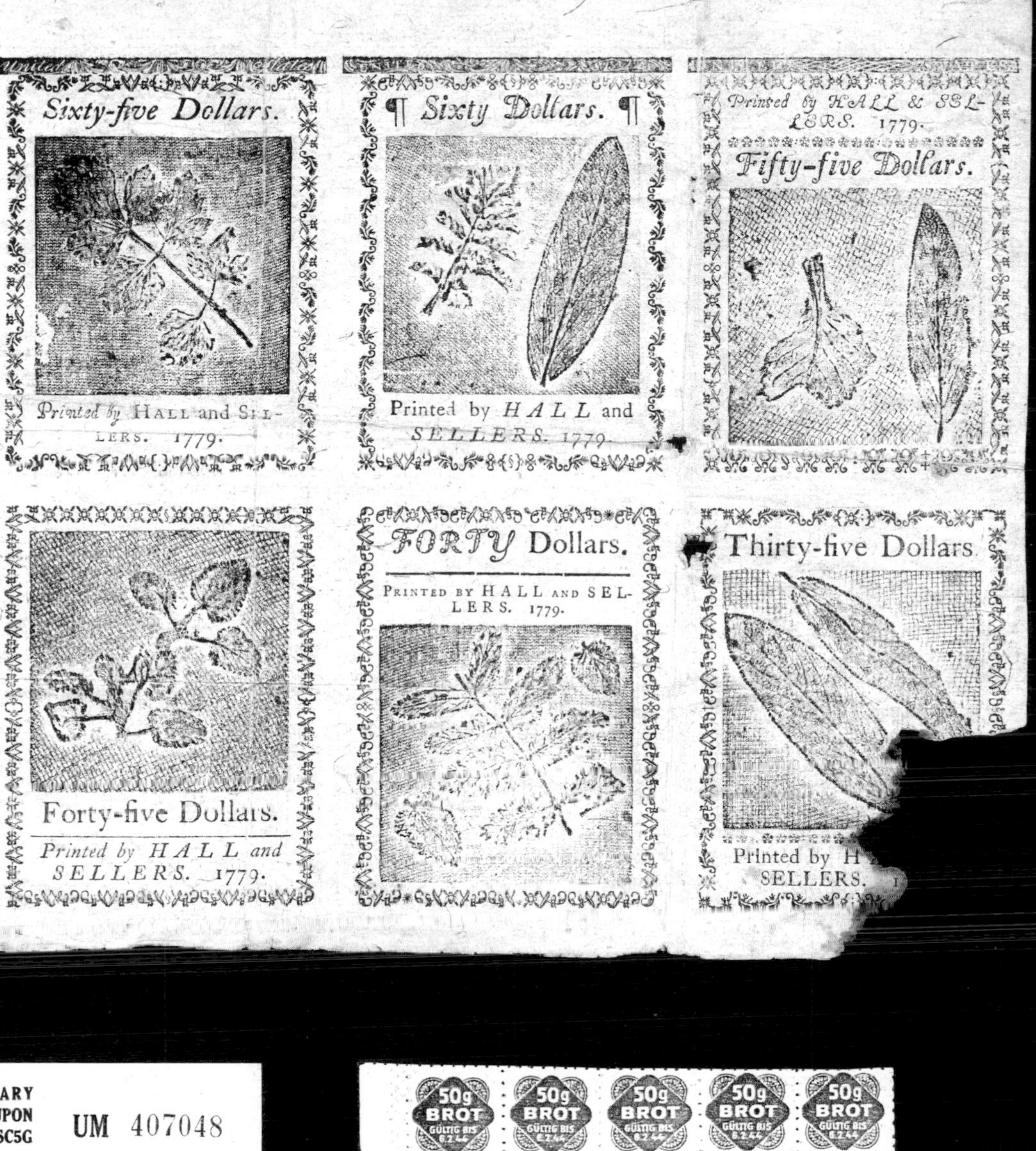

Early attempts to foil the forger included the use of the so-called 'nature process'. In this method, invented by Benjamin Franklin in the late eighteenth century, leaves and stretched cloths formed part of the original design, their delicacy being thought too fine to copy. In the Continental Currency composite sheet shown here, the nature process is reinforced by additional complexities in the printer's borders.

Currency notes are not the only target for forgery; ration coupons also call for security measures. The British wartime clothing coupons (bottom left) are printed on fibre-bearing paper similar to that used in American dollar bills.

German wartime bread coupons ('valid until 6.2.44') were printed by the British for use by agents and members of the Resistance.

SUPPLEMENTARY CLOTHING COUPON SHEET SC5G UM 407048

Name JAMES WILLIAM MORLEY (BLOCK LETTERS)
Address 84 HANSON LANE (BLOCK LETTERS)
(town) HALIFAX (county) YORKS.
Nat. Reg'n (Identity Card) No. KENZ 349/1

IMPORTANT.—These coupons may not be used unless the holder's name, full postal address, and National Registration (Identity Card) Number have been plainly written above IN INK.

CLOTHING COUPON

50g BROT GÜLTIG BIS 6.2.44

64%

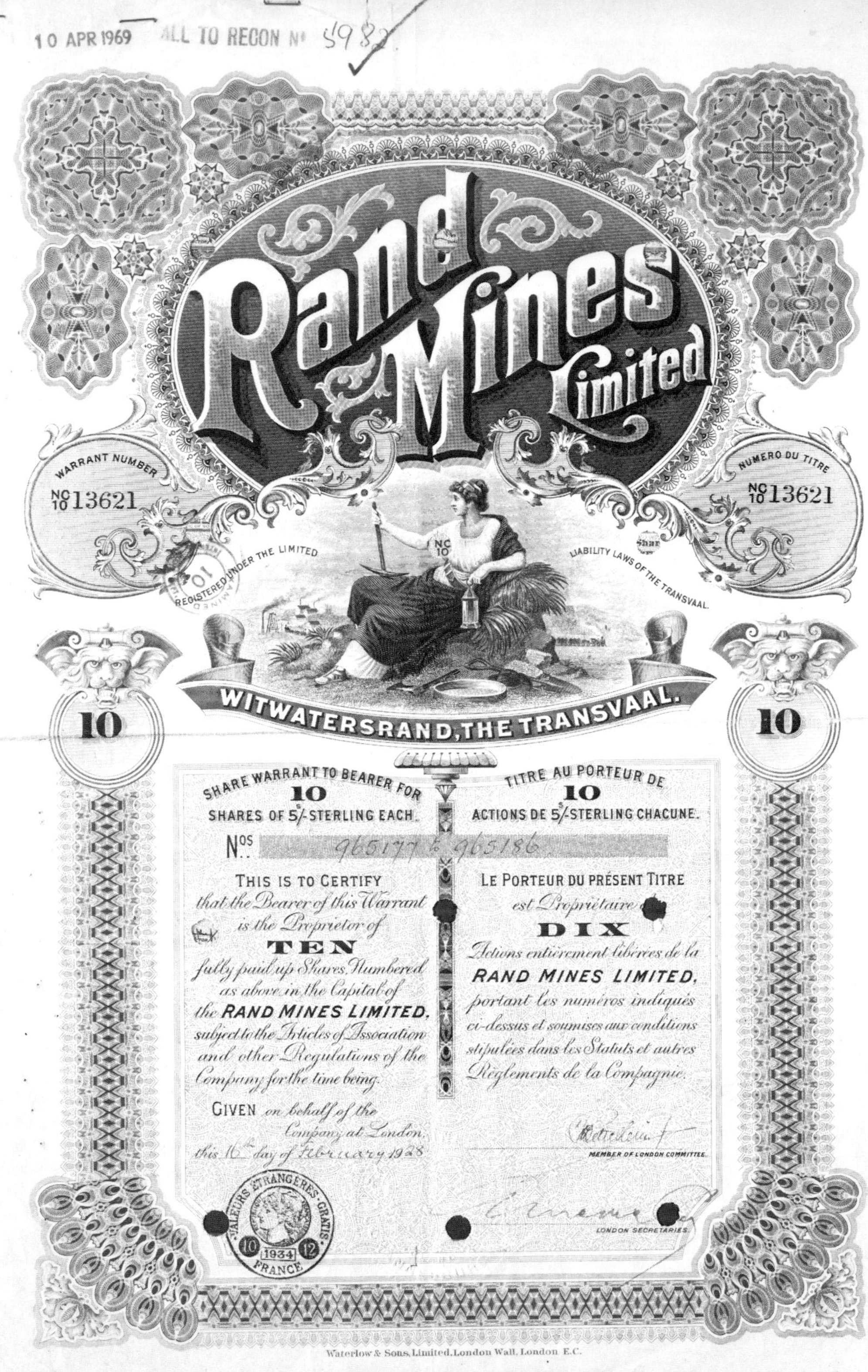

The share certificate, like the currency note, must combine complexity with an air of solid reliability. This Waterlow design for a Witwatersrand gold mine fulfills both requirements. The finely engraved centre-piece, with its classical figure and landscape, is typical of the romanticism normally associated with share certificates—even into the twentieth century Both the pictorial element and the company title were of course custom-designed, but the decorative framework was doubtless pieced together from existing designs.

Public interest in 'scripophily', the study of share certificates, has greatly increased in recent years. They are collected for their printing virtuosity, their historical interest and their decorative appeal.

55%

How To Recognize Japanese Yen Travellers Cheques

IN DENOMINATIONS OF: ¥5,000, ¥10,000, ¥20,000, AND ¥50,000

1. Logo and name of bank issuer (legal Obligor) will appear in this position. For names of Issuing Banks, see below.
2. A sharp and clearly defined printed reproduction of Mercury never blurred.
3. When the cheque is held up to the light, one star on the back will appear through the star-shaped opening in the orange oval.

¥10,000
JAPANESE YEN TRAVELLERS CHEQUE
¥10,000
CITICORP
SPECIMEN
J0123-456-789
ISSUING BANK'S NAME
SPECIMEN

4. Printing color changes from black to green to black across the face of the cheque.
5. Multi-shaded watermark of the head of Mercury appears when held up to the light.

What You
Japar

THE CITICORI
Yen Travellers Chequ
Citicorp Trademark and grap
on each cheque in the area
by the following banks (listed alpha
THE SANWA BANK LIMITED •

FOR YOUR PROTECTION
Examine each cheque for evidence of
detect any evidence of tampering (such a
discoloration), request another form of pa
It is strongly suggested that you ask yo
make each cheque payable to your order
endorse each cheque immediately to you
procedure, and a record of the cheque nu
you further protection in the event that th
have accepted are lost, stolen or destroy
receive value for them.

COLLECTION
These Yen Travellers Cheques can be pre
bank in the same manner as any cheque,
be processed through normal banking ch
have any questions, please write to the a
reverse side.

How to Recognise Thomas Cook Travellers Cheques

U.S. $20
united states dollar travelers cheque
U.S. $20
MB00-000-123
Twenty
U.S. Dollars
For Thomas Cook Inc New York
Thomas Cook

This cheque is the most recent design. Cheques of earlier design are still in circulation and share the features described below. They should be accepted without hesitation. *(Relate circled numbers to those below.)*

Thomas Cook Travellers Cheques have the following features:

1. The **portrait of Thomas Cook** on the right of the cheque
2. The **raised texture** of main text and cheque borders
3. **A watermark** showing the Thomas Cook portrait, clearly seen when the cheque is held up to the light.

• **A different colour** for each denomination.

Overprints
• Some cheques may show a Selling Agent's name or emblem immediately to the left of the Thomas Cook portrait, and cheques may also carry the MasterCard symbol. Such cheques should be accepted in the normal way.

Size
• Cheques of different currencies may vary in size.

How to Accept Thomas Cook Travellers Cheques

4. **WATCH** your customer countersign each cheque in top left-hand space and...
5. date each cheque in top right hand space.
6. **CHECK** that this countersignature is the same as the original signature in bottom left-hand space marked signature of holder.

If your customer has already countersigned the cheque, or if you doubt that the two signatures are the same, have the cheque countersigned again on the reverse **while you watch. Check** that this signature is the same as the original in the bottom left hand space on the front.

If the **countersignature** is the same as the original signature you may accept the cheque.

Cheques showing evidence of mutilation or alteration should not be accepted.

Reimbursement
Having accepted the cheques, immediately stamp or write your company name on the front of each one, taking care not to obscure the line of numbering across the bottom of the cheque. Then simply pay the cheques into your bank in the normal way.

All Thomas Cook Travellers Cheques will be honoured on presentation, provided they have been accepted in accordance with the procedures described in this leaflet.

As a secondary form of currency—and one designed to be especially safe—the traveller's cheque and its use must be closely monitored. Explanatory leaflets, with annotated specimens attached, show counter clerks the points to watch.

Printed by banknote companies, the cheques convey their origins, not only in their specific security devices but in their general design. In the Japanese yen cheque a classical figure echoes the note and share certificate; the Thomas Cook design makes much of intricate patternwork.

1984
DEMOCRA
NATIONAL
CONVENTION
MOSCONE CENTER, SAN FRANCISCO
JULY 16-19, 1984
CHARLES T. MANATT, CHAIRMAN
PERIMETER
5718
THURSDAY JULY 19, 1984
THURSDAY JULY 19, 1984
5718

5¢
CASH BONUS
5¢
CANADIAN TIRE
CORPORATION LIMITED
REDEEMABLE IN MERCHANDISE—REMBOURSABLE EN MARCHANDISE
AT CANADIAN TIRE STORE OR GAS BAR
AU MAGASIN OU BAR D'ESSENCE CANADIAN TIRE
TREASURER
PRESIDENT
5¢
BON D'ACHAT
5¢

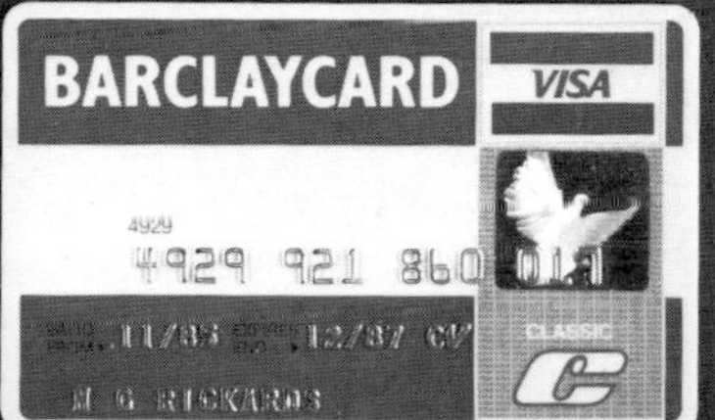

BARCLAYCARD
VISA
4929 921 860 011
11/85
12/87
CLASSIC

Both the Democratic Convention ticket and the Canadian tire token adopt the 'security' look; both are printed by banknote companies. The American item also uses a hologram (not apparent in this reproduction), as does the cash/credit card. Some cash cards claim as many as a dozen security features.

55%

Today's ephemera

Today's ephemera is no less significant—and for many connoisseurs, no less collectable—than that of yesterday.

Certainly the trickle of the past has today become a raging torrent. As the human race becomes more numerous, our affairs more complex, and our future less certain, the ephemera record expands.

Not least of the reasons for its growth is the spread of 'instant' printing. With photo-composition, transfer lettering and in-house or round-the-corner printing, the process of image reproduction is within the reach of the world at large. If only with the typewriter and an office copier, we all have the ability to print and publish.

With such proliferation, and so many concerns to register, it is not surprising that today's ephemera is sometimes overlooked. Somehow these familiar fragments—stickers, handbills, folders, cards and notices—are too commonplace and too transient to preserve. It is this very disposability that may make them rarities; as the ephemerist's maxim has it, 'Today's throwaway is tomorrow's museum piece'. In a few year's time, all the items shown here will be gone for good.

But it may be objected that output is too great for even a portion to be preserved. How do we choose—even a tiny portion? The truth is that some will choose itself; it will survive by the same accident that preserved the nineteenth-century turnpike ticket and the watchpaper. Other items, like those on these pages, will be consciously selected to reflect the spirit of our time. As the eye roves from one item to the next we see a general picture: fear-of-flying treatment ... 'Squatting is Still Legal' ... 'Nuclear power? No thanks' ... 'No Barefeet Allowed' ... it takes the ephemerist's special instinct to separate the throwaways from the throwaways to keep.

WARNING

LOST OR CANCELLED CARD NOTICE

The 'Blue White and Gold' credit card *described overleaf* is no longer valid. If this card is presented, *retain both the card and the goods* and telephone Barclaycard Authorisation (see over).

Any transaction involving this card could result in the AMOUNT being CHARGED BACK to your Company.

£25 Barclaycard will pay **£25 REWARD** for the return of this 'Blue White & Gold' Credit Card-whatever its condition. **£25**

CC42UK 6/75 BARCLAYS BANK LIMITED Reg. in London, England Reg. No. 48839 Reg. Office 54 Lombard Street, London, E.C.3

Both pages 61%

Service with a smile.

DOG OWNERS
PLEASE DO NOT ALLOW YOUR
DOG TO FOUL THE PILLAR BOX

THAIRAPY
FEAR OF FLYING TREATMENT
Glen H. Arnold, LCSW
Licensed Counselor • Commercial Pilot
4500 Campus Drive • Suite 348 • Newport Beach, CA 92660
(714) 546-3629 ext. 4102 • (714) 962-0870

THAMES FLOODING

Don't wait until it happens.

If you live, work
or travel in London
you should learn your
Thames flood drill now.

GLC
Working for London

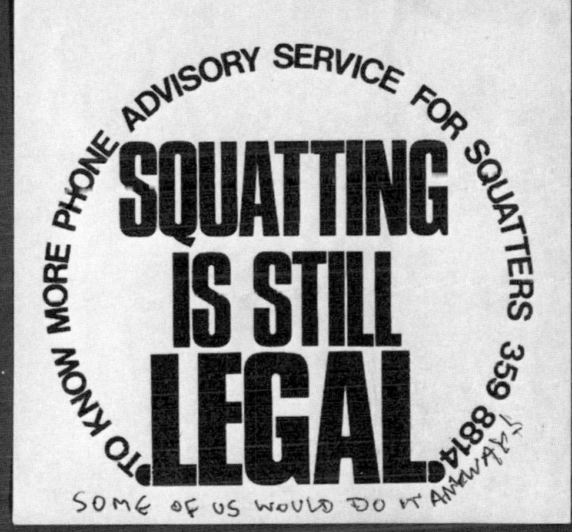

SQUATTING IS STILL LEGAL.
ADVISORY SERVICE FOR SQUATTERS
TO KNOW MORE PHONE 359 8814
SOME OF US WOULD DO IT ANYWAY!

Alive and well!

But does your family know?

Missing people can record
a message for their family

Phone: (01-)567 5339

No Barefeet
ALLOWED

Management

WOULD THE LAST BUSINESSMAN
LEAVING THE COUNTRY
KINDLY SWITCH OFF THE LIGHTS

SPECIAL NOTICE

THE DISTRICT POSTMASTER REGRETS THAT DUE TO RECENT BOMB INCIDENTS, POSTING BOXES IN THE W1 DISTRICT WILL REMAIN CLOSED UNTIL FURTHER NOTICE.

BRANCH POST OFFICE COUNTERS IN W1 WILL ACCEPT MAIL UP TO NORMAL CLOSING TIMES 5.30/6.00 PM. POSTING BOX FACILITIES MAY BE AVAILABLE IN OTHER DISTRICTS.

WESTERN DISTRICT OFFICE
26 NOVEMBER 1974

WARNING

MAILING marijuana, cocaine, heroin, PCP, LSD or other illegal drugs is a crime.

OFFENDERS are subject to prosecution.

CONVICTION can result in imprisonment up to 15 years and fines up to $25,000 under federal law. 21 U.S.C. 801, 841(a)(1); 18 U.S.C. 1716.

AND, you may also be subject to prosecution, fine, and imprisonment under state law.

Bomb attacks, drug laws, tax avoidance, sex movies, the Denver boot, cat protection—here are some of the talking points in this latter part of our century. Like the items on the previous pages, this selection presents a view from one man's waste-bin. It may not be everyone's image; as in any collection a prime component is the collector's personal approach. Only time will evaluate one as against another. In the meantime, ephemerists take their pick. Most of it is significant of its time; all of it, unlike collectors' items in general, is quite free of charge.

CAN YOU HELP CATS IN THIS AREA?

WE ARE DESPERATE FOR HELP WITH FEEDING

COLONIES OF FERAL (SEMI-WILD CATS)

AT BOTH ENDS OF TOTTENHAM COURT ROAD

PARTICULARLY DURING THE WINTER.

IF YOU LIVE NEARBY OR WORK AROUND THIS AREA

AND CARE ABOUT CATS

THESE CATS COME TO SEE YOU WHEN YOU CALL THEM,
BUT ARE TOO WILD TO HANDLE
(THEY HAVE ALL BEEN NEUTERED)

COULD YOU POSSIBLY THINK ABOUT FEEDING THESE CATS PERHAPS ONCE A WEEK

PLEASE CALL ME (TEL. 01-363-9125)

(MONEY WOULD BE PROVIDED IF NECESSARY)

GIVE UP SMOKING ONE DAY AT A TIME

WEDNESDAY 12 MARCH

CHALLENGE FOR NATIONAL NO SMOKING DAY 1986

CONTRACT AND SPONSORSHIP FORM

Tax Avoidance and Evasion

One Day Conference
(CPE Accredited 5 hours)

at

Café Royal
Regent Street London W1

on

Wednesday 4th February 1981

It's easy to get clamped.
Now it's just as easy to get unclamped!

HAVE YOU SEEN OUR EXCITING MOVIES?

ASK MANAGER

IN CASE OF TROUBLE – VIOLENCE

THIS BUSINESS OPERATES AN EARLY WARNING SYSTEM IN CO-OPERATION WITH THE POLICE AND PROSECUTION WILL ENSUE

ISSUED BY YORK & DISTRICT L.V.A. & N.A.L.H.M.

31%

Information

GLOSSARY

ASSIGNATS Notes representing crown and church lands assigned to the bearer by the revolutionary French government. They were devised as a substitute for a metallic currency in the financial emergency of the period 1789–96. They were seen as bonds entitling the holder to buy Crown and Church lands which the State had confiscated as public property. The notes could also be used as a form of currency. The scheme was a disaster. Many millions were circulated, reducing their value to virtually nothing. To swell the tide of inflation, neighbouring countries—among them Britain—injected large numbers of counterfeits.

BASSO RELIEVO Italian: low relief (basso rellee-ayvo).

BROADSHEET/BROADSIDE Often used interchangeably, these terms have distinct meanings. Both refer to large sheets of printed paper: a broadsheet is printed on both sides; a broadside, commonly intended for pasting on a wall, is printed on one side only.

CHAPBOOK Cheap printed booklets formerly sold, together with trinkets and other easily portable items, by itinerant pedlars. The word is derived from *chapman*—merchant, trader, dealer. *Chap* as a general term is a remnant of the same concept.

CLIPPER CARD Sailing announcement cards were distributed to boost the clipper-ship traffic out of New York and Boston in the second half of the nineteenth century. Brightly coloured, and with a graphic style of their own, the clipper cards were distributed some weeks in advance, drumming up loads for uncertain departure dates. The cards have become coveted collector's items.

DECKLE-EDGE In hand paper-making, the deckle is the rectangular meshed frame fitting closely over the mould in which the liquid pulp is placed. The edges of the sheet thus produced are irregular—deckle-edged. The effect is the hallmark of quality hand-made paper, though it also occurs at the edges of paper made in a continuous roll, the pulp being retained between flexible bands.

DIE-CUT A shaped paper item stamped out with a metal cutting die, notably as in the chromolitho 'scraps' of the Victorian era. The term die is used to refer to virtually any form of stamping tool.

ENDPAPERS Papers, plain or decorated, pasted to the inside covers of a book and forming flyleaves, front and back.

FORMAT In a general sense, the shape, size, bulk, style and form in which a printed item is produced. More often, the dimensions of a printed sheet.

FRONTISPIECE The illustration in a book facing the title page. The term was earlier applied to an illustrated title page.

GUARDBOOK A book designed to contain pasted-in items, in which the added bulk is provided for by the use of page-length strips bound between the leaves. The strips, known as guards, may be used for edge pasting of double-sided items.

INDULGENCE Strictly, the formal remission by the Church of the penalty due to forgiven sin. The term is also loosely applied to the document certifying such remission. In the twelfth century the practice of granting indulgences became common, notably for participation in the Crusades. At some periods indulgences, and the documents themselves, were the subject of sale by professional 'pardoners', whose activities were finally prohibited in 1567.

INTAGLIO The printing method in which the image is incised into the surface of the plate instead of being raised above it as in the letterpress method. The word is Italian, from *tagliare*, to cut. (Pronounced in Italian intahl-ye-oh; in English intag-lee-oh.)

KEEPSAKE Apart from its normally accepted sense of sentimental memento and its early nineteenth-century use for literary annuals, the term has a specific reference in printing tradition. It was a long-standing custom, in honour of a distinguished visitor to the workshop, to set up the guest's name in type, printing it and presenting it as a decorative souvenir of the occasion. Keepsakes were also printed at special events, celebrations and fairs, sometimes on printing presses mounted on procession wagons.

LOTTERY PUFF The word 'puff' was formerly used for any extravagant promotional device, often with reference to spurious plaudits in newspaper reviews and advertisements disguised as news. The term was extended in the lottery era to apply to the mass of small handbills put out by lottery promoters.

MACHINAGRAPHIC A term coined by Ebenezer Bacon and Company to describe the engraved pattern-work of their geometric lathe. They called themselves 'Machinagraphists, Etc', but the designation did not catch on.

POUNCE A fine powder, used before the introduction of blotting paper, to dry ink. It was prepared from pulverized cuttle shell. It was also used to prevent the ink from spreading over an erasure, or on unsized paper, and was applied to the surface of parchment and vellum to facilitate writing.

SOLANDER BOX Daniel Charles Solander, the eighteenth-century Norwegian botanist, gave his name to the bookform box widely used in libraries and museums. He originally devised it for the storage of his own notes and specimens, but the idea was taken up generally.

WAYBILL A part-printed document used in many forms of common-carrier transportation, setting out the route of the vehicle, details of goods or passengers, and revenues received.

PAPER

In the course of a long history, paper has been manufactured from a wide variety of materials. It can in fact be prepared from almost any substance capable of being mashed into a porridge-like pulp. The fluid is held as a thin deposit on a supporting mesh, drained and dried. As it dries, the fibres of the mix interlace, producing an integral sheet.

Among the substances used, the record shows sea-weed, straw, potatoes, leather shreds, sails and old rope. In general however, basic ingredients have been rags and wood pulp. Rags are still used for expensive hand-made papers, but in the course of the nineteenth century a mass market brought the need for a cheaper material. The use of wood, mixed with various chemicals and additives, became general.

For the ephemerist—as for librarians and archivists—this change-over represents a watershed. Rag paper is robust and durable. Wood-pulp paper is not. The effect is seen dramatically in newspapers, where issues prior to the change survive in some numbers, while those from the late nineteenth century (and the twentieth) discolour and disintegrate.

An important feature is the watermark. Where this appears it may help to identify the item's origins, and of course a date mark is a bonus. For most ephemerists, inspection for watermarks is an almost instinctive part of the process of assessment (so much so, there is an impulse to hold even vellum and parchment—animal skins—to the light).

Specialists have written of the identifying value of the watermark, but for the general collector only the date and manufacturer's name are much to the point. For the rest, over the centuries and from one country to another, there is a plethora of symbols—flowers, lions, post-horns and so on—distinguishable in detail only by the expert.

The watermark is produced by a shaped wire, attached to the mesh on which the paper is made, producing a thinning of the paper where it impinges on the wet surface. The most common form of mark is the 'tram-line' effect produced by the parallel wires used in the manufacture of 'laid' paper. Paper without these lines is described as 'wove'.

Paper is made in a wide range of weights, thicknesses and textures. Additives and after-treatments affect its characteristics. An important ingredient is size (earlier, parchment parings), which governs the paper's absorbency. Papers designed for writing with pen and ink are highly sized, obviating spread and splutter at the point of the pen. Wholly devoid of size are blotting papers, designed for absorbency.

An incidental effect of sizing is its capacity to impart to paper its characteristic 'crackle', a feature normally absent in blotting papers.

Other additives affect 'body', surface, colour and translucency, and after-treatments include pressure-rolling to produce embossed textures, and 'calendering', in which pressure rolling imparts a highly polished surface.

Paper dimensions, often quoted in such terms as 'foolscap', 'demy' and so on, are not much to be relied on. Early usage was inconsistent, printers, publishers, stationers and papermakers using their own terms as the mood and tradition took them. Not until the advent of the European DIN sizes in the 1920s was a start made on a rationalized principle. The system was adopted by the International Standards Organization in 1968 under the title ISO and has become virtually universal in Europe. American sizes still remain outside the system.

CONSERVATION MATERIALS

Conservation, repair and storage supplies are available from numerous sources, chief among which are the British company Ademco, whose products are marketed under the name Archival Aids, and the American company University Products Inc. The Archival Aids range is available in the United Kingdom through the Ademco Company's head office at Coronation Road, Cressex Estate, High Wycombe, Bucks, HP12 3QU, England, and in the United States through University Products Inc, PO Box 101, Holyoke, Massachusetts, 01041, USA.

Super-quality polyester film, suitable for use in archival storage is manufactured in Britain under the trade name Melinex, and in America by the Dupont Company as Mylar. Information is available from Imperial Chemical Industries, Petrochemicals and Plastics Division, Welwyn Garden City, Herts, AL7 1HD, and from the Dupont Company, Wilmington, Delaware, USA.

Archival storage boxes are produced by a number of firms, including, notably, the University Products company. In Britain a major specialist, supplier of solander boxes to many national museums and libraries, is G. Ryder Ltd, Denbigh Road, Bletchley, Milton Keynes, MK1 1DG, England.

The kneadable eraser, listed below, is available from Picreator, Park View Gardens, Hendon, London NW4 2PN, England.

In the listing below products are keyed to show sources (A: Ademco; U: University Products; P: Picreator).

Repair tape (A) A thin acid-free pressure-sensitive tape, non-yellowing and barely detectable in use. May easily be removed with industrial spirit. Has passed tear and fold tests and artificial aging up to 176 years. May be used for light items in 'stamp-hinge' mounting.

Framing tape (A) White acid-free paper lick-tape, may be used in stamp-hinge mounting of heavier items. Also suitable for some forms of repair, and widely used in hinging window mounts. Also used to seal the backs of picture frames. Removable with water.

Cleaning powder (A) Used for dry cleaning less fragile documents and ephemera, a non-abrasive powdered rubber is gently rotated over the surface with the finger tips.

Deacidifier spray (A) Aerosol treatment for ephemera, documents and bound volumes. Adjustable spray-head allows treatment of more fragile or larger materials.

Lamination tissue (A) Used in conjunction with heated presses or hot tacking irons, the tissue provides a barely detectable protective covering for fragile items.

Acid-free blotter (A/U) High-quality white acid-free blotting paper, soft textured, super-absorbent, for use in wet conservation and repair procedures.

Archival cloth (A) For use as backing for maps and charts, the material is impregnated with fungicide, bactericide and mothproofer. Also used for hinging window mounts and for reinforcing bindings and storage-box hinges.

Acidity detector (U) Used like a pen in conjunction with distilled water, the detector will determine levels of acidity or alkalinity in paper in 15 seconds.

Kneadable eraser (P) Processed natural rubber, permanently tacky and shaped as desired, merely requires dabbing lightly on specimen to lift off dirt. Non-abrasive, non-staining.

Encapsulation unit (U) Encloses specimens between two sheets of Mylar or Melinex, a pre-taped pressure-sensitive edging forms an instant seal.

Neutral adhesive (U) Fast setting, light in colour and reversible, this modified dextrine adhesive is used in a wide variety of conservation applications.

BIBLIOGRAPHY

ABBINK, A. L.and TE MEIJ W. E. L., *Menus Historiques*. Osmar B. V. The Hague, 1982

ALLEN, ALISTAIR, *The History of Printed Scraps*. New Cavendish Books, London, 1983

ANDERSON, JANICE and SWINGLEHURST, EDMUND, *Ephemera of Travel & Transport*. New Cavendish, London, 1981

BEAVER, PATRICK, *The Match Makers: The Story of Bryant and May*. Henry Melland, London, 1981

BERESINER, YASHA, *Paper Money*. Andre Deutsch, London, 1977

BIERBRIER, M. L. (Ed), *Papyrus: Structure and Usage*. British Museum, London, 1986

BLADES, WILLIAM, *The Enemies of Books*. Elliot Stock, London, 1888

BLAIR, ARTHUR, *Christmas Cards for the Collector*. Batsford, London, 1986

BOWMAN, ALAN K., *The Roman Writing Tablets from Vindolanda*. British Museum, London, 1983

BRIGHAM, CLARENCE S., *Fifty Years of Collecting Americana 1908–1958*. Worcester, Massachusetts, 1958

BURDICK, J. R., *The American Card Catalog*. Burdick, East Stroudsburg, PA. 1960

CALVERT, H. R., *Scientific Trade Cards*. Her Majesty's Stationery Office, London, 1971

COYSH, A. W., *Collecting Bookmarkers*. David & Charles, Newton Abbot/W. Vancouver BC, 1974

DAVIS, ALEC, *Package and Print*. Faber and Faber, London, 1967

DOGGETT, FRANK, *Cigarette Cards and Novelties*. Michael Joseph, London, 1981

DYSON, ANTHONY, *Pictures to Print: The Nineteenth Century Engraving Trade*. Farrand Press, London, 1984

FAIRCHILD, GORDON and WOOTTON, PETER, *Railway & Tramway Tickets*. Ian Allen, Shepperton, 1987

FRIEDMAN, TERRY, *Engrav'd Cards of Trades-men in the County of Yorkshire*. Lund Humphries, Bradford, 1976

GASCOIGNE, BAMBER, *How to Identify Prints*. Thames and Hudson, London, 1986

GIFFORD, DENIS, *The Complete Catalogue of British Comics*. Webb & Bower, Exeter, 1985

HARRIS, ELIZABETH, *The Fat and the Lean: American Wood Type in the 19th Cent*. Smithsonian Institution, Washington DC, 1983

HEAL, AMBROSE, *London Tradesmen's Cards of the XVIII Century*. Dover, New York (Reprint), 1972

HORNUNG, CLARENCE P. and JOHNSON, FRIDOF, *200 Years of American Graphic Art*. George Braziller, New York, 1976

HUNTER, DARD, *Papermaking*. Dover, New York (Republished), 1978

HYMAN, TONY, *Handbook of American Cigar Boxes*. Arnot Art Museum, Elmira, NY, 1979

JAMES, LOUIS, *Print and the People*. Penguin, Harmondsworth, 1976

KANDAOUROFF, DIMITRY, *Collecting Postal History*. Peter Lowe, London, 1973

LEE, BRIAN NORTH, *British Bookplates*. David & Charles, Newton Abbot, 1978

LEE, BRIAN NORTH, *Early Printed Book Labels*. Private Libraries Association, London, 1976

LEE, RUTH WEBB, *The History of Valentines*. Lee Publications, Wellesley Hills, Mass. 1952. Batsford, London, 1953

LEVY, LESTER S., *Picture the Songs*. (Sheet Music) Johns Hopkins University Press, Baltimore MD, 1976

LEWIS, JOHN, *Printed Ephemera*. W. S. Cowell, Ipswich, 1962. Antique Collectors Club, 1988

MARZIO, PETER C., *The Democratic Art*. Godine, Boston, 1979

MCCULLOCH, LOU W., *Paper Americana*. A. S. Barnes, New York/London, 1980

NEUBURG, VICTOR E., *Popular Literature*. Penguin, London, 1977

NEWMAN, ERIC. P., *The Early Paper Money of America*. Western Publishing, Racine WI, 1976

OPIE, ROBERT, *The Art of the Label*. Simon Schuster, London, 1987

OSBORNE, KEITH and PIPE, BRIAN, *Beer Labels, Mats and Coasters*. Hamlyn, London, 1979

PALMER, ROY, *A Ballad History of England*. Batsford, London, 1979

PEARSALL, ROWLAND, *Victorian Sheet Music Covers*. David & Charles, Newton Abbot, 1972

PIESKE, CHRISTA, *Das ABC des Luxuspapiers*. Museum für Deutsche Volkskunde, Berlin, 1983

RICKARDS, MAURICE, *The Public Notice*. David & Charles, Newton Abbot, 1973

RICKARDS, MAURICE and MOODY, MICHAEL, *The First World War: Ephemera, Mementoes, Documents*. Jupiter Books, 1975

SHEPARD, LESLIE, *The Broadside Ballad*. EP Publishers (UK), 1962; Legacy Books (US), 1978

STAFF, FRANK, *The Valentine & Its Origins*. Lutterworth, London, 1969

THOMAS, ISAIAH, *The History of Printing in America*. Weathervane Books, New York (Reprint), 1970

TURNER, MICHAEL, *The John Johnson Collection*. Bodleian Library, Oxford, 1971

TURNER, MICHAEL and VAISEY, DAVID, *Oxford Shops and Shopping*. Oxford Illustrated Press, Oxford, 1972

TWYMAN, MICHAEL, *Printing 1770–1970*. Eyre & Spottiswoode, London, 1970

TWYMAN, MICHAEL, *John Soulby, Printer, Ulverston*. University of Reading, 1966

VICINUS, MARTHA, *Broadsides of the Industrial North*. Frank Graham, Newcastle upon Tyne, 1975

WOOD, ROBERT, *Victorian Delights*. Evans Brothers, London, 1967

SOCIETIES AND COLLECTIONS

The Ephemera Society
12 Fitzroy Square, London W1P 5HQ, England

The Ephemera Society of America Inc
PO Box 10, Scoharie, NY 12157, USA

The Ephemera Society of Australia
345 Highett Street, Richmond Victoria, Australia 3121

The Ephemera Society of Canada
36 Macauley Drive, Thornhill, Ontario, Canada L3T 5S5

Transport Ticket Society
42 Hillview Road, Orpington, Kent BR6 0SF, England

American Transit Collectors' Association
8304 16th Street, Silver Spring, Maryland 20910, USA

Australian Ticket Collectors' Association
PO Box 292, Hamilton, NSW, Australia 2303

International Playing Card Society
188 Sheen Lane, East Sheen, London SW14 8LF, England

Cheque-Collectors Round Table
Box 125, Milford, New Hampshire 03055, USA

Bond and Share Society
Hobsley House, Frodesley, Dorrington, Shrewsbury SY5 7HD, England

Bond and Share Society
24 Broadway, New York, NY 10004, USA

Bookplate Society
20A Delorme Street, London W6 8DT

American Society of Bookplate Collectors and Designers
Apt F, 605 N Stoneman Avenue, Alhambra, CA 91801, USA

Writing Equipment Society
4 Greystones Grange Crescent, Sheffield, S Yorkshire S11 7JL, England

The Poster Society Inc
138 West 18 Street, New York, New York 10011, USA

Labologists Society of England
211 Pinewood Park, Cove, Farnborough, Hampshire, England

South Hurstville Coaster Collectors Club
Connells Point Road, South Hurstville, New South Wales, Australia

American Printing History Association
PO Box 4922, Grand Central Station, New York, NY 10163, USA

Printing Historical Society
St Bride Institute, Bride Lane, London EC4, England

Philatelic History Society
Hunter's Lodge, Cottesmoor Road, Ashwell, Oakham, Leicestershire LE15 7LJ, England

International Map Collectors' Society
1A Camden Walk, London N1 8DY, England

The Postal History Society
Lower Street Farmhouse, Hildenborough, Tonbridge, Kent TN11 8PT, England

Postal History Society Inc
19 Fox Hunt Lane, Great Neck, NY 11020, USA

Association of Comics Enthusiasts
80 Silverdale, Sydenham, London SE26 4SJ, England

International Bank Note Society
PO Box 1222, Racine, Wisconsin 53405, USA

International Banknote Society
22 Papyrus Way, Sawtry, Cambridgeshire PE17 5TY, England

British Matchbox and Booklet Society
3 Langton Close, West Earlham, Norwich, Norfolk, England

Rathkamp Matchcover Society
1359 Surrey Court, Vandalia, Ohio 45377, USA

COLLECTIONS

John Johnson Collection, Bodleian Library, Oxford, England; American Antiquarian Society, Worcester, Massachusetts 01609, USA; Guildhall Library, Aldermanbury, London EC2P 2EJ, England; National Library of Scotland, Edinburgh, Scotland; New-York Historical Society, 170 Central Park West, New York, NY 10024, USA; British Library, Great Russell Street, London WC1B 3DG, England; Library of Congress, Washington DC, USA; Smithsonian Institution, Washington DC, USA; King's Lynn Museum, King's Lynn, Norfolk, England.

INDEX

ACKNOWLEDGEMENTS

The Author and publishers wish to acknowledge the kindness of the many individuals who have contributed guidance, information, and in numerous cases items of ephemera, in the course of the preparation of this book. Prominent among them are the following:

Gordon Fairchild; Tony Ambrose; Anne Cowan; Marcus Samuel; Calvin Otto; Laura Seddon; William Helfand; Cathy Terry; Dennis Dunkley; Henry Bristow; Ben Swanson; Lindsay Fulcher; Sam Murray; Albert Shaw; Ralph Hyde; Barbara Muir; William Mobley; Trevor Russell-Cobb; Henry Middleton; Maureen Greenland; Frank Staff; Linda Hannas; John Scott; Denis Gifford; Peter Jackson; Michael Legg; Cowan Smail; Asa Briggs; Peter Sindell; Alfred Malpa; Gerald Davis; Kenneth Greenland; Robert Opie; Lilian Thrussell; Valerie Harris; Michael Twyman; Martin Willcocks; Edmund Swinglehurst; Barrie Evans; Julie Anne Wilson; Patrick Robertson; Tim Nicholson; Derek Barlow; Helen Wilkins; Robin Alston; Glynne Williams; Derek White; Sally de Beaumont; Neil Johannesen; Frank Teagle; Edgar Lewy; Godfrey Omer-Parsons; Edward Sanderson; Jilliana Ranicar-Breese; Victor Short; Ken Schultz; Jeremy Winkworth; Bill Wright; Philip Poole; Jacqueline Norman; Elizabeth Greig; Robin Hunt; Kay Robertson; David L'Affineur; Desmond Lewis; Bryan Lyons; Undine Concannon; Dennis Morris; Wendy Shadwell; Anne Flavell; Brian Love; Maureen Staniforth; Brian Webb; Jill Trenholme; John Spake; Elizabeth-Anne Colville; Julian Royle; Peter Stockham; Elizabeth Lewis; Douglas Nethercleft; James Mosley; Lester Smith; Eric McKercher; Graham Page; Ken Sequin; David van der Plank; Mike Veissid; Joyce Tinker; Pierre Patau; David Miles; Stanley Shoop; Bryan Woodriff; Mario Aleppo; Yasha Beresiner; David Ellen; David Webb; Jill Forsyth; Jeanette White; Ronald Mansbridge; Amoret Tanner; Harriet Bligh; David Penney; Elizabeth Greig; Doris Jones; Tom Pattie; Graham Hudson; John Martin; Robert Latham; Marcus McCorison; Geoffrey Grant; Maria Hubert von Staufer; Jocelyn Mullinger; Richard Perfitt; Christa Pieske; Hedda Meyer; Helena Wright; Honor Godfrey; Howard Rosewell; Edith Parsons; Anthony Heal; Graeme Clipston; Johanna Harrison; Walter Kahn; Colin Cohen; Stanley Friedman; Robson Lowe; John Martin; Robert Ireland; John Fisher; Jeremy Smith; Michael Farr.

Also gratefully acknowledged is the kind cooperation of the following:

Egypt Exploration Society; British Records Association; New-York Historical Society; Vindolanda Trust; American Antiquarian Society; British Library; Bodleian Library; National Library of Scotland; Ritz Hotel, London; Public Record Office.